ALSO BY HUGH KENNER

The Mechanic Muse 1987

A Colder Eye 1983

Ulysses 1982

Joyce's Voices 1978

Geodesic Math and How to Use It 1976

A Homemade World: The American Modernist Writers 1975

The Stoic Comedians: Flaubert, Joyce and Beckett 1975

A Reader's Guide to Samuel Beckett 1973

Bucky: A Guided Tour of Buckminster Fuller 1973

The Pound Era 1971

The Invisible Poet: T. S. Eliot 1959, 1969

The Counterfeiters: An Historical Comedy 1968

Studies in Change: A Book of the Short Story (EDITOR) 1965

Samuel Beckett: A Critical Study 1965

Seventeenth Century Poetry: The Schools of Donne and Jonson (EDITOR) 1965

The Art of Poetry 1959

Gnomon: Essays in Contemporary Literature 1958

Dublin's Joyce 1956

Wyndham Lewis 1954

The Poetry of Ezra Pound 1951

Paradox in Chesterton 1948

A Sinking Island

A SINKING ISLAND

The Modern English Writers

by HUGH KENNER

BARRIE & JENKINS
LONDON

First published in Great Britain in 1988 by
Barrie & Jenkins Ltd
289 Westbourne Grove, London W11 2QA

This edition published by arrangement with Alfred Knopf Inc

Grateful acknowledgment is made to the following for permission to reprint
previously published material:

Alfred A. Knopf, Inc.: Excerpt from *Parade's End* by Ford Madox Ford. Copyright 1924 by
Janice Ford Biala. Reprinted by permission of Alfred A. Knopf, Inc.
Black Sparrow Press: "Chaos of Enoch Ardens" and "Bless All Ports" by Wyndham Lewis.
Copyright © 1981 by the Estate of Mrs. G. A. Wyndham Lewis. Reprinted by permission of
the Wyndham Lewis Memorial Trust. Reprinted from *Blast 1* with the permission of Black
Sparrow Press.
Cambridge University Press: Excerpt from *The Letters of D. H. Lawrence*, Vol. 3: October
1916–July 1919, edited by James Boulton and Andrew Robertson. Copyright © 1985 by
Cambridge University Press. Reprinted by permission.
Dodd, Mead & Company, Inc.: Excerpt from "Tiare Tahiti" from *The Collected Poems of Rupert
Brooke*, by Rupert Brooke. Reprinted by permission of Dodd, Mead & Company, Inc.
Faber and Faber Limited: Excerpts from Poem XX from *The North Ship* and an excerpt from
"The Whitsun Wedding" from *The Whitsun Wedding* by Philip Larkin. Reprinted by permis-
sion of Faber and Faber Limited.
Farrar, Straus and Giroux, Inc.: Excerpts from "Going, Going" and "This Be the Verse" from
High Windows by Philip Larkin. Copyright © 1974 by Philip Larkin. Reprinted by permis-
sion of Farrar, Straus and Giroux, Inc. World English-language rights excluding the United
States administered by Faber and Faber Limited, London.
Harcourt Brace Jovanovich, Inc.: Excerpts from "Preludes" and "The Waste Land," from *Col-
lected Poems, 1909–1962* by T. S. Eliot. Copyright 1936 by Harcourt Brace Jovanovich, Inc.
Copyright renewed 1963, 1964 by T. S. Eliot. Reprinted by permission of the publisher.

*Owing to limitations of space, all other acknowledgments of permission to reprint
previously published material will be found following the index.*

British Library Cataloguing in Publication Data

Kenner, Hugh, *1923–*
A sinking island: the modern English writers.
1. English literature. English writers,
1900–1985. Critical studies
I. Title
820.9'00912

ISBN 0-7126-2197-0

Printed and bound in Great Britain by
Butler & Tanner Ltd, Frome and London

IN MEMORIAM

BASIL BUNTING

1900–1985

"With never a crabbed turn or congested cadence,
Never a boast or a see-here."

Books, of any solidity, are almost gone by.

JOHN STUART MILL, 1836

You strange, astonished-looking, angle-faced
    Dreary-mouthed, gaping wretches of the sea,
Gulping salt water everlastingly . . .

LEIGH HUNT, 1836

I feel like Robinson Crusoe in this dreadful London.

W. B. YEATS, 1888

I rose from humble origins to complete disaster.

SAUL BELLOW

CONTENTS

A Sinking Island

A FIRST SCAN

"English," formerly "Anglisc," was the tongue of the Teuton "Angles" who invaded and then settled Northumbria and Mercia amid cries that the savages had come. Until recently it implied the culture of an island called England, a culture present or former colonies emulated. England was and is the nurturing-place of "English." From the seventh century clear to the twentieth—from the Venerable Bede to Basil Bunting—its idioms have been inextricable from the fortunes of men on that island: from their climate, their customs, their history, their shifting rituals of self-esteem. A word like "hearth" accretes warmth from the island's damp cold nights. Likewise, "oak" takes sanction from pride in England's history, "ale" from immemorial English custom, "lad" from peculiarly English imprecisions of fellow-feeling.

For centuries too, English literature was what some denizens of England wrote for others to read, the way Dutch literature is meant for reading in Holland. If some of it chanced to get written elsewhere— e.g., in America, a former possession—it was still made *literature* by English approbation; Walt Whitman was a real poet only after 1868, when William Michael Rossetti hailed his accord with Pre-Raphaelite revolutionary sentiment, and Americans felt duly flattered.*

That is no longer true. There is now a literature written out of English dictionaries that England either can't claim or doesn't know if it wants to. English by about 1930 had ceased to be simply the language they speak in England. It had been split four ways. It was (1) the language of International Modernism, having displaced French in that role. And it was (2) the literary language of Ireland, and

---

* The Rossettis, of course, were migrants, who'd (unlike Walt's Whitmans) had the sense to settle in England.

(3) of America, and yes, (4) of England, countries which International Modernism bids us think of as the Three Provinces.

International Modernism is a name for the durable writing no national tradition can plausibly claim. The prime example is *Ulysses*: part of no native Irish tradition but not part of England's Great Tradition either: about that F. R. Leavis was firm. Its text has lately been rectified on Munich computers by a German who learned his craft in Virginia. Doubtless in heaven Leavis, when that was announced, indulged an ironic sniff, though it typifies inevitabilities one could explain. Also James Joyce's life, and Irish politics, help explain how *Ulysses* came to be written in "English." That was really what needed explaining in its years of scandal. Allowances could have been made for the avant-garde had it only stayed continental. And anyone in 1895 who'd foreguessed a book so transcendently innovative would have expected its dictionary to be French.

Distressingly too, though a common auxiliary language is still called a *lingua franca*, the *lingua franca* of commerce is "English" now. "Mr. Eugenides, the Smyrna merchant," no longer makes his propositions in "demotic French." *Plakarten* in Frankfurt hawk "striptease"; Parisian *feuilletons* coo of "cover-girls." As a 747 gropes toward earth in Taipei, pilot and tower exchange a quasi-English jargon. (Why? Because the plane was manufactured in Seattle; because commercial aviation throve on North American enterprise; because a war scattered American air bases worldwide.) Rock-and-roll worldwide mouths an English dialect too, something it's less plausible to blame on America, though in the homeland of the Beatles they try.

So it has been easy for tight little islanders to dismiss the new literatures as analogous barbarisms: as the Babu-work, often plausibly syntactic, of people who lack an organic feel for idiom. But that parallel is empty. A plurality of idioms, notably the synthetic idiom of high modernism, has been drawing on a common word-stock, the existence of each idiom modifying all the others.

Ulysses (1922), and its companions, *The Waste Land* and the early *Cantos*, helped establish a potential independence of literary "English" from any nation. Thereafter, in the Three Provinces, things could never go on as before. Writers went on supplying what they'd always supplied, psychic and cultural insight for local use. But they did it, if they were at all responsible, in awareness that the resources of "English" had been expanded forever.

So in the Three Provinces, though least so in England, the poetry and prose they write for native consumption has been strongly marked by the International phenomenon. Mrs. Woolf, an English novelist doing the English novelist's traditional business—elucidating for her readers the manners and mores of England—knew about *Ulysses* and despised it, or said she did, but her *Mrs. Dalloway* is unthinkable without it. Faulkner wrote *The Sound and the Fury* on a tide of post-Ulyssean enthusiasm, dealing though he did with New York publishers and intending an American readership. As for William Carlos Williams, whose American readers were few, all his long life he hardly envisaged any other kind, and sixty years after *Spring and All*, few English ears detect any poetry in its verse.

Yet, if this late in the century it is in America that a great part of the tongue's vital writing gets done, America has its provinciality too. Linguistically or poetically considered, it is a very *large* province, where poets conduct conspiracies in public and nobody listens to anybody else. Coherence is perhaps for a critic to discern. And two of the best critics of William Carlos Williams, two sure guides to his saliences, are Mike Weaver and Charles Tomlinson, both Englishmen. Weaver's book (*William Carlos Williams: The American Background*) best explains the complex fate with which America confronted Williams; Tomlinson's choice of a *Selected Poems* has defined a Williams canon. That's different from the service Rossetti did for Whitman, entailing as it does a recognition of intractable otherness.

Not, though, that England has stayed a sure citadel of judgment. Tomlinson's own first major collection of poems, *Seeing Is Believing*, had to be published in New York: "a national disgrace," as his fellow Englishman Donald Davie said. Davie has also adduced "the silent conspiracy which now unites all the English poets from Robert Graves down to Philip Larkin, and all the critics, editors and publishers too, the conspiracy to pretend that Pound and Eliot never happened." Indeed, any reminder that they happened at all can suffice to touch off a tantrum. As late as 1986, in the *Times Literary Supplement*, Auberon Waugh spoke for an "intelligent reading public," consisting of people like himself, "fed to the teeth with the Modern Movement and everything it has produced." He attributed the repute of outrages like *Ulysses* to "fashionable fly-by-night magazines." Then in 1987, in the *New Republic*, there was Davie himself trashing Williams! It's fair to say, despite scintillant exceptions, that a half-century's literary goings-on in the Third Province have given new meaning to the word "provincial." How that came about—how the mother-country of

"English" became a headquarters for articulate Philistia—is one theme this book addresses.

International Modernism I've described in *The Pound Era*, the modern American adventure in *A Homemade World*, the Irish in *A Colder Eye*. This English case is altogether trickier. If England was the command post of the language, it was also, as the first to be industrialized, the country that, ahead of all the world, saw reading publics fragmented and reading become a drug. England has had long experience with the principle that whole classes can be marked by what they consume—sugar, tobacco, tea. Likewise, what did you read?—by that you were known; so whoever had the power to enforce a literary "value" defined major social norms. Such power is still the prize of relentless struggle. So *A Sinking Island* has more to say than did its sibling books about milieux and contexts.

Also, it has had to take note of personalities; nothing is more English than the English skill at exorcising danger by making it look like someone's eccentric behavior. When an age of sentiment felt threatened by Sam Johnson's shade, it got rid of him by dwelling on the queer man in the book by Boswell. Likewise, common sense dealt deftly with the challenge of Blake by bidding us imagine a mad poet and his wife sitting (as was said to be their custom) stark naked in their garden. Any such monster having been dismembered, editing, a gentleman's skill, could always reassemble the limbs if they were wanted; Sir Geoffrey Keynes performed that service for Blake, though Johnson has been left to the Americans at Yale.

To cope with the multiple shocks of modernism, this personalizing faculty had to be put into high gear, with such success that James, Ford, Yeats, Lawrence, Pound, Wells, Woolf—the list goes on—now hardly seem to be characters in the same story, but simply occupants of more or less adjacent cells in a well-regulated Bedlam. Ford was a bounder, a liar. Yeats conjured spooks. Mrs. Woolf was found in the Ouse, three weeks dead, and what about that? Poor Lawrence, he was sex-mad. Pound—so American he was ineducable ("hare-brained," says a recent book). And Eliot: was he not really, ah, hiding something? His sexual orientation, perhaps? That allegation won't be let die. On an occasion so deceptively neutral, not to say pedantic, as the appearance of the *Waste Land* drafts in expensive facsimile, it broke out anew in the *Times Literary Supplement* and raged on for weeks.

More recently, he has been guyed in a play about his first marriage. It was called *Tom and Viv*, and to gauge how odd that is we have only to weigh the unlikelihood of a play about the estranged Shakespeares, *Bill and Anne*. Yes, Eliot lives as a danger to be regulated. But Will of Stratford, Sweet Will, it's rightly judged, has no longer a presence sufficient to threaten anything.

Nor do well-credentialed masterpieces threaten either: the leaden *Music of Time*, the dim *Forsyte Saga*. For nobody reads them. Have no fear, they will not detain us. So intricate is our story that narration must be highly selective, enough so sometimes to produce what Leavis once called "effects that might be found ironical." Many good writers who simply did their job—Ivy Compton-Burnett comes to mind—are left unmentioned. Nor need mention imply what I'd deem a balanced treatment; if it's only as critics that Davie and Empson appear, that is not because I think their poetry unrewarding. And if Bunting is quoted copiously, that's to throw light on mid-century norms that couldn't accommodate him. I'd have copied out less of *Villon* and *Briggflatts* if I could assume readers familiar with them; but the dearth of such readers is precisely my point.

Be assured that the book contains no ironies where none are intended. It commences with the view from 1895, a year distinguished by nothing in particular except its plenitude of happenings.

1 : THE BEST OF TIMES

It was the best of times, the best of times. In 1895 the atlas colors that mattered were blue and red. Red, British red, asserted one island's suzerainty over more than a full quarter of Earth's land, and the blue seas were British too *de facto*. On them the fleet plied, and the merchantmen, coasters, lighters, colliers, tramp steamers. At any moment, day or night on every ocean, proud British flags were defying the salt spray. Waves plunged and broke, masts hummed and engines shuddered. Knitted together by the shipping lanes, an empire beyond the dreams of Alexander or Augustus was about its patient business.

One by one, all over the world, for two centuries and more, lands with exotic and barbaric names had been coming (never mind how) beneath the flag: . . . Sarawak, 1842; Saskatchewan, 1876; Savo Island, 1893; Selangor, 1874; the Seychelles, 1794; Sierra Leone, 1788; Sikkim, 1816; Sind, 1843; Singapore, 1819. . . .Whole peoples came with these places, and though many were of the higher races some were not. Sinhalese and Tamils; Malays, Bushmen, Hottentots; Bantus and pre-Dravidian aborigines; Fijians and cannibal Papuans; the Canadian Indians whose forefathers had tortured French Jesuits; the French-Canadians even: all these were British. So too were Irishmen, many of whom now spoke English of a sort.

God Save the Queen!—76 now, a little dumpy Queen in perpetual mourning. Her memorial to the prince she mourned was a large eclectic masterpiece, guarded by stone lions and bedecked with proud standing-marble denizens of Empire, the whole especially intimidating when it loomed through a morning fog. The book its stone prince held was not the Bible casual viewers took it for, but the Catalogue of the Exhibition of 1851.

Her cousins occupied the thrones of Europe. Her subjects ruled

Commerce, Manufacture, and The Arts. They were respecters of the Bible, an English book that dated from 1611. Moreover, they heeded what it was said to say, and it was not true either that they ignored its Word whenever money jingled. Otherwise would they have put Mr. Wilde in gaol, who'd had three plays running all at one time in London? But that was what they had resolutely done, though his crime was so much subtler than honest theft as not to be describable.

Since 1215, Magna Carta, a date every child had by heart, they had been, as everyone knew, the people who most of all people in the world respected individual liberties. Contrary to foreign usage, criminals were innocent until proved guilty. Fugitives from the political police of every country in Europe consequently settled in England. That made London picturesque, though many Londoners would rather read about Soho than walk in it. In particular, the city was full of Russian anarchists. Everyone who could read knew that.

Britons, co-linguists of Shakespeare, had long been a literate people. In 1895 they read newspapers. They read *Tit-Bits* and *The Strand Magazine*. They read romances and histories. They read Dickens, and thruppenny pamphlets of excerpts from Dickens: "Joe the Fat Boy"; "The Artful Dodger." They read themselves to sleep. Never in human history had there been so much to read. The *British Museum Catalogue* alone listed unthinkably many items, and there were more, it seemed, every time you opened your eyes.

"Penny Stories for the People" were read. *Through Weal and Woe, The Rightful Heir, Thrown to the Lions, The Smuggler's Doom*—these and their like got gobbled up (18,250,000 copies in five years! Had Horace known such a readership? Goethe? Even Wordsworth?). As for quarter-million-word novels, you could get thirty-thousand-word versions for just a penny; and who would pretend that every little word a novelist might have set down deserved attention? (Every other word? Every eighth word? One-in-eight was a commercial abridger's frequent ratio.)

Yes, there were commercial abridgers; there had to be, if you thought of it. Labor divided itself, to a point of minimal but finite returns. There were also commercial copiers, proofreaders, indexers, scribblers. Scribblers worked into the night by candlelight, in gloves and overcoat if it was winter. This most advanced of civilizations was built upon coal, the cost of which per peck (and of paper per quire, ink per ounce, soup per bowl) found equilibrium with the selling price of words per thousand in equations balanced by the Invisible Hand.

Despite marginal attrition (consumption, suicide) the great web of interdependency hung together, that men and women might eat and be clothed, and read.

Dead writers simplified this algebra by not exacting fees; hence, for instance, Dent's Temple Shakespeare, a shilling a play. People bought a quarter-million of them a year: over £12,000 per annum, willingly parted with. And for Shakespeare! That proved—did it not?—that literacy need not debauch.

As late as mid-century, nervousness about literacy had kept a penny tax on the daily papers. The tax would have doubled the cost of a penny sheet, a good thing if it was true that cheaper papers than the fivepenny *Times* were sure to be "radical." One argument against the tax had been that if a worker could read in the cheap local paper about somebody's rick burning down, he'd not visit the public house for that intelligence, and might thus stay sober. Keeping workers off the drink was a public duty. There had been other powerful arguments, and now the tax was forty years gone. Penny dailies proliferated, and *The Times* itself was down to thruppence. In twenty years more it would be a penny and well worth it.

Nothing else, probably not even the pin, was being mass-produced on such a scale as reading-matter. That was because readers needed something *new* to read, every week, every day even. "Literature" had nothing to do with this. The concept of Literature rests on the assumption that canonical texts exist to be read and read again. In the ages before printing, what was prized was copied by hand. Conversely, it was copied because it was prized. All that we have from the ancients is the little that copyists salvaged. Aeschylus wrote some eighty-three plays they didn't salvage, besides the seven they did. And copies perished as surely as May blossoms. What was not recopied before fire or thumbing claimed papyrus was gone forever, and parchment, though it might last a thousand years, was expensive and apt to be scraped clean for reuse. Homer and Virgil abide, but Sappho crumbled or got scraped.

An unbroken chain of generations having been wise enough to recopy Homer and Virgil, Literature became, in T. S. Eliot's famous metaphor, the "ideal order" of prizeworthy "monuments," an order that can be altered only rarely, when "the really new" makes good its claim to inclusion. The printing-press did not invalidate that metaphor at first, and Eliot in 1919 could talk as though printing had changed nothing fundamental. But that was never true.

Gutenberg may have supposed that his invention would simply mechanize the scribal process, but the very first printers soon found out differently. They were *in business* as scribes had never been: vulnerable to strikes, a-worry about idle machinery, forever anxious to "recoup initial investments, pay off creditors, use up reams of paper, and keep pressmen employed." They needed a steady flow of new stuff to print, and books were soon getting written that, save for the press, would not have been written at all. So when by 1704 the industry we call Publishing is fully established, lo, Swift in *A Tale of a Tub* is railing against Grub Street garrets, whence there poured down upon London a noxious verbal deluge, contracted for by the page from hacks with nothing to say but great skill at saying it verbosely. The new economics of scale was conjuring up copious nullity. Its pressure was, as we say now, "supply-side."

Supply-side pressure, as it proved, blew off much vapor to scant effect. Despite Swift's apprehension and Pope's, the hacks did no appreciable harm. The sheets of unbought hackwork were twisted to light ale-house fires, and the writers who were valued then are the ones we value now. Dr. Johnson had no qualms in concurring with the common reader, and it remains commonplace that Shakespeare was popular in his day, Dickens in his. We've heard it argued on that dangerous analogy that the Beatles were our time's collective Mozart, and forgotten that the analogy wasn't always dangerous. "Down to and including George Eliot," the social historian R. C. K. Ensor reminds us, "all the great English novelists had been best-sellers." That means the common reader had spotted them quickly.

But by about 1870 something had changed: major novelists—Meredith, James, Hardy—were coming onto the scene and enjoying some vogue but by no means best-sellerdom; meanwhile best-seller after best-seller was bursting and sparkling through the gray British sky en route not to classic status but to a graveyard. Who hears of Mrs. Henry Wood now? She wrote *East Lynne*, which sold half a million copies; her twenty-odd books had a total sale five times that.

And it's perfectly clear that by 1895 such bilge as Swift had excoriated was being pumped forth solely *because millions wanted it*. Publishing's new economics was demand-side.

* * *

Or, rather, not such bilge as Swift had excoriated: a new class of bilge, of which he could have formed no conception. Marie Corelli (1854–1924) was the 1895 best-seller (*The Sorrows of Satan*), and other books in other years kept her a best-seller for two decades. No novel had ever sold like *The Sorrows of Satan*: thirty-two printings in its first twelve months. True, few novels before it had cost a mere 6s. The long day of the three-decker—10s. 6d. per volume, a guinea and a half per novel, mostly not bought therefore but rented from libraries—had only just ended. But Marie Corelli! You have to sample her prose to believe a pen could have written it:

> . . . and then, with an indescribable slide forward and an impudent bracing of the arms, they started the *"can-can"*—which though immodest, vile, vulgar and licentious, has perhaps more power to inflame the passions of a Paris mob than the chanting of the "Marseillaise." . . . Danced by women with lithe, strong, sinuous limbs—with arms that twist like the bodies of snakes,—with bosoms that seem to heave with suppressed rage and ferocity,—with eyes that flash hell-fire through the black eye-holes of a conspirator-like mask,—and with utter, reckless, audacious disregard of all pretence at modesty,—its effect is terrible, enraging!—inciting to deeds of rapine, pillage and slaughter! . . . With all our culture we are removed only half a step away from absolute barbarism! . . . and I howled, stamped, shrieked and applauded as furiously as the rest of the onlookers.*

This told an English reader something she was always happy to believe, what awful people the French were, and it let her indulge the can-can in delicious revulsion with no risk of having her bottom pinched at a *café chantant*. As to what awful people the French were, Marie Corelli is explicit in an Introductory Note: "If a crime of more than usual cold-blooded atrocity is committed, it generally dates from Paris or near it;—if a book or a picture is produced that is confessedly obscene, the author or artist is, in nine cases out of ten, discovered to be a Frenchman." And as to indulging the can-can, what you've just read was cut by more than half. Marie Corelli's way was the pornographer's: spin out, spin out, find empty emphatic words, but keep it up. Her predilection for the dash may signal that there's no particular

---

* Whatever the last sentence seems to say, Marie Corelli never saw a can-can—gracious, no. Nor, she assures us, did she ever wish to. But on the steamer from Thun to Interlaken she overheard an Englishman's eulogy of it, "and I took calm note thereof, for literary use hereafter."

structure to her effects. The idea is to dwell, linger, urge, restimulate.

Do not be deceived, "Marie Corelli" was plain Mary Mackay, born (1855) in Bayswater. Yet she aspired to style, even thought herself "the prose Shakespeare," and when she had the cash she settled in his Stratford. ("From the way she writes," said Oscar Wilde in Reading Gaol, "*she ought to be here.*") She had her rewards, costly summers on Lac Leman and a friend from whom, like Gertrude Stein, she was never parted. She attended garden parties Henry James also attended, and lived till 1924, which was long enough to have seen *The Sorrows of Satan* pass its sixty-third printing (1918).

Reading her, if you were her fit reader, you could kill time and not know that was what you were doing, so wrought up could she make you feel with moral fervor. The admirers of her fervor included Gladstone. And killing time had become the new function of reading.

That began, possibly, in the 1840's, with the yellow-back novels they sold in railway stations because more and more people were spending more and more time confined for an hour or so to railway carriages. By 1863 the *Quarterly* was indignant about a new genre, "The Sensation Novel":

> The exigencies of railway travelling do not allow much time for examining the merits of a book before purchasing it; and keepers of bookstalls . . . find an advantage in offering their customers something hot and strong. . . .

The years passed, and paper, untaxed, got cheaper; the effects of that, remarked Prime Minister Gladstone, "will not be fully apparent until we of the nineteenth century are gone." It was cheap enough soon to be gobbled up by the roll instead of the sheet. Reading-matter, more knowingly contrived, got less demanding; steam, the century's bottled genie, learned to drive presses; new machines acquired steel fingers and learned to set type. Every sort of publication seemed to contain a weekly or monthly story. Even agricultural journals used stories to keep the advertisements for milk pumps from jostling: it was as though we expected a story in each month's *Popular Mechanics*. And novels got routinely published with advertising supplements fore and aft, even with advertisements printed on their hardcovers. More than anything else, patent medicines got advertised, since it's when you sit and read that you feel aware of your headaches, constipation, dizzy spells.

And by the mid-nineties, as Richard Altick writes,

> Reading had become a popular addiction. . . .Women wore out their eyes following the scandalous doings of fictional lords and ladies, or the spicy peccadilloes of real ones. Men and boys in the factories devoured tons of hack-written adventure stories. . . .The cook in the kitchen let the joint burn as she pored over the *Family Herald*, the millhand sat on his doorstep of a Sunday morning, smoking his pipe and reviewing the week's outrages in the *Illustrated Police News*. . . .

The word "literature" itself was sliding toward the *Oxford English Dictionary*'s sense 3c, "Printed matter of any kind," not excluding handbills and jokes printed on matchbox covers. The first instance of that usage it records is dated, by coincidence, 1895.

Gillott's improved steel pen of 1831 had helped make it all possible, there not being before long the geese in industrial Britain to give quills for so much scratching. Little thought was spared for the fingers that cramped round the pen-shafts, so anonymous were most of them, so interchangeable. Arnold Bennett recalled the London of about 1893 as "chiefly populated by grey-haired men who for twenty years have been about to become journalists and authors": one more indication of a demand for "copy" so indiscriminate that whoever could spell might dream of that line of work. "How to train a Cook," "How to keep parsley fresh," "How to bath the baby (Part One)": such paragraphs did not write themselves, and neither did all that fiction. But cheap papers and cheap books meant cheap authorship; George Gissing's *New Grub Street* (1891) portrays a gray, foggy milieu with the stale scent of failure everywhere: watches and coats pawned, meals made of old bread, eyes aching from pointless "research"; while Jasper Milvain, a cynical opportunist though not a bad fellow really, tests winds that blow toward success—i.e., a good income. There was such a thing as success: witness Miss Corelli. And somehow, in 1895, Joseph Conrad published *Almayer's Folly* and survived to publish further books. After eight hundred copies had covered the cost of production, a writer might commence to count incoming pennies.

*   *   *

The events of that year might have been synchronized for our convenience. Not only did Conrad make his debut in 1895; the harbinger of another future did too, H. G. Wells, with *The Time Machine*. Oscar Wilde climaxed his theatrical career with *An Ideal Husband* and *The Importance of Being Earnest*; he also stood trial, thrice, and went to jail. That event not only ended Oscar's career, and Aubrey Beardsley's connection with *The Yellow Book*; it ended too, in Richard Garnett's judgment, any prospect for innovative writing in England for . . . well, his guess was fifty years.

There were other endings. On 5 January the debacle of *Guy Domville* ended the dramatic hopes of Henry James, who turned resolutely to the fiction of his last phase. Thomas Hardy published *Jude the Obscure*, his last novel; thereafter he would devote himself to verse. George Meredith published his last novel too. And the early career of William Butler Yeats was terminated and enshrined with the 1895 *Poems*, which for decades would be synonymous with his name. Though long outgrown it couldn't just be abandoned, and by its last reissue in 1929 he'd reworked some of it nearly past recognition.

The year's huge sellers were *Trilby* and *The Sorrows of Satan*. Their noise helped obscure three events of greater portent: Roentgen's isolating of rays that slipped through solidity, Marconi's success at telegraphy without wires, the Lumières' demonstration that pictures on a screen could seem to move. The very next year an Animatographe would be drawing crowds in London, a special treat for privileged children like 14-year-old Virginia Stephen, later Woolf, and by the time they were grown the flickering shadows would be displacing print itself as the time-killer of choice.

Yet another time-killer was portended in 1895: self-propelled vehicles became legal on public roads, even when not preceded by a runner with a red flag.

On June 5, his twelfth birthday, Maynard Keynes received a safety bicycle that could free-wheel. Such a gear had been invented only months before. Now even a boy could go anywhere, fast and free; forget the horses man was so long tethered to. (Maynard promptly slammed it into a hansom cab, damaging his little finger.)

And King C. Gillette patented his safety razor. That would change the face of England. By the time 10-year-olds like D. H. Lawrence or Ezra Pound were grown a beard would mark you out. The Duke of York, 30, one day to be George V, could sleep immune to such thoughts; his beard was *royal*. (But imagine T. S. Eliot with a beard.)

And off in Dublin, on the lawn of Trinity College, top-hatted George Francis Fitzgerald, Fellow of the Royal Society, was making repeated attempts to get aloft on man-made wings, a queer sight for little boys jammed against the railings. Next year slim Jimmy Joyce, 14, would be reading in his schoolroom Ovid about Dedalus and Icarus. But that was in another country, one notably barbarous though as long as six centuries ago brought under the flag.

2 : THREE PUBLICS

1 : Tit-Bits

To read Marie Corelli, you had to be able to follow several hundred printed words at a time, and there were myriads in England who were up to it. Thus her publishers didn't release *The Master Christian* before they had seventy thousand copies ready. Literacy, though, could be seen to be expanding rather faster than the sale of even her books. The Education Act of 1870 should have been good for the trade—it *required* you to go to school, moreover till you were 14—but many of the first generation it benefited were tending to get lost after a sentence or two. It was for them that George Newnes in 1881 invented *Tit-Bits*, a weekly paper about half of which did not require concentration in more than thirty-second bursts.

What Newnes had discovered was the paragraph as unit of attention, and a "par" could be extremely short. His inspiration was a paragraph about a runaway train, in the *Manchester Evening News*: eight carriages had "travelled 14 miles in 17 minutes without the aid of an engine," and five children had escaped being hurt. You could make a paper, he thought, out of items like that. He did; it sold five thousand copies in its first two hours, and George Newnes duly became Sir George. One of his contributors, Alfred Harmsworth, would later raise daily journalism to the same principle, and himself be translated to the peerage as Lord Northcliffe. It was he who made the *Times* a penny paper, and his sister-in-law financed T. S. Eliot's *Criterion*.

An admiring biographer of Northcliffe's compared him to "a quick-witted child," a phrase that also fits the ideal reader of Newnes's *Tit-Bits*. Alert with an ideal insomnia, he'd first marvel at the banner atop

the first page, "ONE GUINEA PER COLUMN IS PAID FOR ORIGINAL CON-
TRIBUTIONS TO THIS PAPER." That opened casements on a world of
dreams; fees reckoned in guineas would put you in the class of phy-
sicians, barristers, other men with top hats. Next he'd grin at two
dozen three-line jokes ("Waitress, bring me one of your dog-biscuits."
"Yes sir, if you'll promise to eat it on the mat"). He'd take note of
longer items ("Fortunes in Postage Stamps"; "What a Pet-Poisoner
Said"*), perhaps linger, or perhaps not, on "Men and Women of Today" (LXXI—Sir Frank Lockwood, Q.C., M.P.), then settle in for a
delicious read on page 6, the *Tit-Bits* "Inquiry Column": answers to
questions which, as a quick-witted child might guess, no one would
have thought to ask save the office help who had the answers ready.

They were numbered sequentially, and as the years passed the *Tit-
Bits* Knowledge Engine processed unthinkable thousands. *7096 Has
any man lived long after being deprived of both arms and legs?* (Mrs.
Elizabeth Robertson, for fifteen years. "She maintained herself by
crochet-work, at which she became very expert.") *7100 Has a duel
on bicycles ever taken place?* (Not long ago, in Spain, between Señores
Moreno and Perez; "and it ended fatally for the latter." The weapons
were knives.) *7165 What is the horse-power of a 100-ton gun?* (Seventeen million; but that energy would just suffice to run thirty-one
incandescent lamps for a single day.) Any item is as substantial as any
other, and the paper's voice is implacable in its knowingness. One
reader who took note of such paragraphs was James Joyce, as students
of the "Ithaca" section of *Ulysses* may judge.

Elsewhere *Tit-Bits* offered knowledge ungarnished: that the tallest
British officer, Capt. Oswald Ames, stood "well over" six feet eight
inches, or that President McKinley's Saint Bernard, "Washington,"
got a daily mug of beer. And let us not omit "ARE ALL WHITE CATS
DEAF?—NO, by the owner of three."

Much more, including "Answers to Legal Questions" and even an
installment of a novel. Then lo, about page 13, the *pièce de résistance*:
the "Prize Tit-Bit," an original story, paid for, at a guinea the column,
to someone identified by name and address. Three guineas! Four!
What dreams of school pocket-money! Or of landladies placated! Of
champagne and oysters, even! Amateurs might dream; but what these

---

* "I poison a great number of cats, dogs, guinea-pigs, and other pets at 1s. each. . . ." *Tit-Bits*
tended to mention the going price of anything.

tales bespeak is a dreary professionalism, not least in the skill with which something too long for three columns is made to run just to the bottom of a fourth.

Though craft of perhaps a low order, *Tit-Bits* fiction did take craft. Unsurprisingly, winners' names recur: hacks, very likely, moonlighting. London teemed with hacks, doing work that is not for dabblers. One time a submission came in from Joseph Conrad, a penniless certified mariner; another time from James Joyce, a cheeky schoolboy. But neither displayed *Tit-Bits* skills, nor did the prepubescent Virginia Stephen, who tried too. She and her sister, Vanessa, were faithful readers; certainly *Tit-Bits* was more informative than *The Times*, which told you nothing otological about white cats. And by no means were all beginners rejected; Arnold Bennett first got published in its pages, age 24 (a contest winner, 20 guineas), and so did Aubrey Beardsley, age 17 (a column and a half, £1. 10s. 0d.).

And now it is time to savor in its entirety a piece of this engine-turned magazine fiction. The following comes unaltered from *Tit-Bits* for 1 May 1897. Its author? "Payment at the rate of one guinea per column has been sent to . . . Mr. Philip Beaufoy, Playgoers Club, Strand, W.C." Sing, larks, at those syllables: "Philip Beaufoy"! His most celebrated story, "Matcham's Masterstroke," has disappeared rather more completely than the canon of Sappho—the last known copy, as we learn from *Ulysses*, vanished into a Dublin jakes in mid-1904—but Mr. Beaufoy, or someone using his name, was prolific enough not to care. Every so often, from that rakish, unlikely address, he was back with another tale. Yes, Beaufoy, whoever you were,* you knew your métier. Gentle reader, suspend doubt now, and irony, and settle back for such a read as thousands relished a century ago.

FOR VERA'S SAKE

"Ivan, ask me no more. I have told you that I do not love you; that you can never be more to me than what you have always been—a good and sincere friend. Cease, then, to beset me with

---

* "Beaufoy" stories can differ so in style you wonder whether, like "Homer," the name covers multitudes. Henceforth I'll use "Philip Beaufoy" to designate simply the author of "For Vera's Sake."

your entreaties, and leave me as you found me—your well-wisher, now and always."

A fiery light illumined Ivan Turgoff's eyes for a moment.

"You love another," he said fiercely. "That cur of a Slavinski has won your heart, as I suspected all along. Can you deny it?"

The girl spoke no word, but a deep colour mounted to her cheek. Ivan went on, his tones growing louder as he continued:—

"I cannot understand women's ways. You turn from me who am willing to give you a life's devotion and who am an honest man, and you give your love to one who is not worthy to kiss the hem of your garment—Slavinski. He is known to all of us as a spy and a poltroon—an enemy of our Order and an agent of the Russian police. The very dogs would turn from such as he; and yet—yet, you can tolerate him, nay, can even love him."

Vera drew herself up proudly as she replied, in a firm tone, "Yes, I do love him, and without shame I confess it. Who can control love? It gives itself sometimes to the least worthy—it pardons all faults—it even loves such faults because they are part of the beloved. I love Slavinski, and it shall be my life's task to seek to reclaim him—aye, and at the eleventh hour, perchance, a woman's love may save him ere it is too late."

There was a pause.

"Have you thought," asked Ivan, after a few moments—"have you thought of what you are doing in allying your life with this man's life? Not one hour's peace will be yours, for at any time a message from the head-quarters of our Order may find him out— and then let him say his prayers, for his journey on this side of the dark river will be over for ever." She shuddered.

"You mean," she said, piteously, "that they would kill him?"

"That is my meaning. More than that I may not say, for my lips are sealed. So far, naught has been proved against this cur; but, sooner or later, something will be discovered, and then his days will be numbered. And this is the man whom you would call husband!"

"Yes," she returned, proudly, "that is the man whom I would call husband. Since danger is in his path, let me be at his side, to share it with him, so that, if death claims him, it may claim me as well."

"Death is a sad wedding guest," remarked the other, ironically, "and surely it were hard for one so young and fair as yourself to surrender thus soon. Think again. Think many times before you join yourself to this man, whose very presence is contamination—whose very breath is a lie."

He turned on his heel with a bitter laugh, and quitted the apartment.

His way led him through winding courts and vile slums until he reached a squalid house in the neighbourhood of Soho. There he muttered a password at the door, and passing rapidly up the stairs, entered a gloomy-looking room lit with a couple of candles, and presenting a thoroughly forbidding aspect. Half-a-dozen men were scattered about the room smoking and talking; but though all of them had much to say, not one of them raised his voice, but carried on his conversation in muffled tones. For spies were every-where, and prudence had to be observed.

Ivan took a chair near the window, and having lit a cigarette, conversed with his neighbour on the right. After some common-place remarks, the latter, a dark, beetle-browed man, said in a whisper:—

"Have you heard the latest report, my friend?"

"What report do you mean?" asked Ivan, carelessly.

"Dolt," said the other, "why affect ignorance thus? I mean the report of the committee appointed to inquire into the case of poor Michael Lestroff, who is now on his way to the mines. You re-member that we had some difficulty in discovering his betrayer."

"Perfectly."

"We have found him at last. His name is known to the broth-erhood."

"What is the name of this traitor?" asked Ivan. The other man looked up cautiously, and then, setting his lips near his compan-ion's ear, he whispered: "Petroff Slavinski."

A strange shiver ran through Turgoff's blood when he heard that name pronounced. For one moment a mighty feeling of joy welled up in his heart, for he knew that his rival would soon cease to be a rival more. Surely Fate was on his side, he reasoned. The man of all others whom he hated with a fierce hate was to be swept out of his path—the way would be left open to him to Vera and Vera's love. Glorious dreams of bliss floated through his brain, and he told himself that he had found happiness at last.

The room slowly filled, and at length silence was demanded,

and a thin, white-bearded old man took his seat at the head of the long, narrow table. This was the President of the Court of Secret Condemnation. An instant hush fell over the assembled throng as the President rose to his feet and opened a scroll, from which he proceeded to read.

The document set forth that, after much research, the Brotherhood of the Black Seal had discovered the individual by whose information the arrest and sentence of Michael Lestroff had been brought about, and that the individual in question was no other than Petroff Slavinski.

A murmur of execration ran through the room as the President paused. After a moment, he resumed: "Comrades, it is now our duty to resolve this meeting into a court to try this man for the foul treachery of which he has been accused. Call the witnesses."

One by one the witnesses told what they had to report, and as the words were uttered, faces round the table grew blacker, whilst stifled curses rose thickly on the air. When all the testimony was concluded, the President caused slips of paper to be passed round the board, on which each man was required to write his verdict. A great hush fell over the group, as the President, having opened the slips, began to read out the verdict. In every case the word written was "Guilty."

Then the President rose to pronounce sentence: "The sentence of this Court, composed of the English section of the Brotherhood of the Black Seal, is that Petroff Slavinski, spy and traitor, be executed. The executioner will be chosen by the drawing of lots, as is our custom."

Turgoff listened, whilst his heart beat fiercely. Suppose he should draw the fatal lot, and be appointed to slay the man who was his rival! Ah, no—he did not wish for that. Much as he hated Slavinski—who, in addition to having won Vera's love, had, in years gone by, done him a foul injury—much as he hated him, yet he would not be his murderer. A prayer went up in his heart that anyone save him might be chosen by the fatal lottery.

Five minutes later, he breathed a deep sigh of relief, for the awful task had fallen to another. His hands were not to be stained with his rival's blood, after all. Nihilists, when engaged on the work of vengeance, act swiftly. The man who had drawn the fatal lot was to seek Slavinski out that very night and put an end to his treacherous career with one fatal stroke.

The strangest thing in human nature is inconsistency. Men will often do the very things to-day which yesterday seemed to them thoroughly opposed to their natures and inclinations, and it would seem as though logic were the last thing thought of in the daily course of human actions. Inconsistency now entered Ivan Turgoff's heart, and he began to think.

A few hours before he had hated Slavinski and longed for his death, for then Vera might still become his wife. But now that the loathed rival lay under sentence of execution, a strange feeling of pity entered his heart—pity connected not with the spy, but with Vera.

He pitied her face when she received the news that the man she loved lay dead. He fancied he could hear her convulsive sobs, he believed he could see the anguish in her eyes when the terrible truth was known. Perhaps the shock might kill her—for women of Vera's stamp did not love lightly—and the ordeal would be overwhelming. Could he, loving her as he loved her, suffer her to pass through this bitterness?

He tried to stifle his better feelings, but the essence of this man's nature was good, and the better feelings prevailed; Vera's lover should be saved if he could save him. It was for her sake, and what would he not do for so sweet a sake as that? Yes, he would save Slavinski if he could.

He knew that Loris Manskoff, the conspirator appointed to carry out the sentence of the court, would not attempt his fell purpose until after midnight, and now it was wanting half an hour to that time. Slavinski's house was in Bayswater—there was yet time if he hastened. He hailed a hansom, and was quickly driven in the direction of the house he was seeking. Arrived there, he found all the lights extinguished, and it was evident that Slavinski had retired.

To rouse the household and to warn the spy of the impending danger would be madness, for would it not involve the arrest of Manskoff on his arrival, and the betrayal of the cause which he still clung to, heart and soul? No, he must find a better way than that. By some fortunate chance a ladder, left by workmen who had been painting the house, was resting against one of the windows. Glancing round hastily to see that he was unobserved, the intrepid fellow mounted the steps, and after wrestling with the window fastenings with his knife, gained admission to the house.

Was it fate which had led him to this room first of all, for there, stretched on the bed, sleeping as peacefully as a child, was Petroff Slavinski! A night-light burned on the table beside the bed, and on that table lay a photograph of one whom Turgoff knew. It was Vera's portrait, and she had sent it to her lover the day before.

Seeing the picture, there came of a sudden to him who gazed on it a violent return of the old jealousy, and for an instant he wavered in his good resolve. But it was only for an instant, and then the better purpose triumphed. He leaned over the sleeper and touched him gently on the brow. Slavinski awoke with a slight cry.

"Who are you?" he said, hoarsely, his words almost incoherent through fear, and then, looking keenly at his visitor, he recognised the man whom he had cruelly wronged in the days gone by. White as death, he gasped out:—

"Ivan—Turgoff! Heavens above!—so you have found me out at last? You have come—you have come to kill me——"

"I have come to save you. But hasten, for the time is short."

"What do you mean?" asked the other, as he gazed wildly about him. "What brings you here, and at this hour?"

In a low, hurried voice Turgoff replied:—

"Your death has been decreed this night by the Brotherhood of the Black Seal which you have so foully betrayed. Already the executioner is on his way—perhaps he is even now at your door. I have come to warn you and to save you if I can."

Slavinski, scarce knowing what he did, hurried on his garments, and then turned towards the door.

"Where are you going?" asked Turgoff. "Have you a place of safety to fly to?"

"I will go to my nephew's house," replied the other. "He will give me shelter for the night, and in the morning I will leave for the Continent. There I shall be safe, thanks to your timely warning. Merciful heavens, if you had come too late!"

"I would not have come at all," returned Ivan Turgoff, sternly, "but for one thing, all-powerful—all-compelling."

"And that is——?"

"The woman whom you see in this photograph," replied Turgoff, as he placed his hand on the portrait. "To-night I learned for the first time that she loved you and that you loved her. And now listen: I have saved your miserable life for her sake, and for her sake alone. Had you not been the possessor of her love, you might have died like the dog that you are. And now go."

But Slavinski, traitor and poltroon as he was, was nevertheless not altogether lost to some sense of gratitude. He took Turgoff's hand and raised it to his lips.

"May the Holy Father reward you as you deserve," he said, huskily, as he quitted the room, and a moment later the house door closed on his retreating form.

Turgoff breathed a sigh of relief. "He is safe at last," he said to himself, "and Vera's tears will not be shed after all."

His work being now done, the brave fellow turned to make good his exit, but even as he did so, he heard a trampling on the garden path below, and a moment afterwards, a man's face appeared at the window. He had mounted by the same ladder as Turgoff himself had used. It was Loris Manskoff.

The two men faced each other by the light of the flickering flame. Manskoff was the first to speak:

"You here, Turgoff," he said, fiercely. "What is your business here?"

But before the other could reply, Manskoff's eye fell on the bed, and the disarranged clothing told its own tale. In one instant the truth flashed upon him.

"Traitor and coward," he hissed. "It is you then who have warned him and helped him to escape. Perchance it was you too who aided him in the capture of poor Lestroff. Traitor—traitor—traitor!"

Very calm was the bearing of Ivan Turgoff, as he replied, quietly:—

"I admit that I have helped this man to escape. But in the capture of Lestroff I had no part—nor am I false to the brotherhood. I aided the escape of this dog of a spy because, cur and coward as he was, his life was dear to one whom I love more than life, and so I saved him. Aye, and if it all were to come over again, I would play the same part, and be proud to play it."

"Liar," cried Manskoff; "do not seek to cloak your infamy thus. This is a pretty story; but do not think that I am a child, that I should believe it."

"Very well then," replied Turgoff, steadily, "I have no further answer to give."

"But I have," cried the Nihilist. "I have one answer for traitors, and here it is."

A knife glistened in the air, and a second later Ivan Turgoff fell to the floor, mortally stabbed.

One fierce look of hate his assassin threw at him, and then quitted the room as he had entered it.

He who had struggled so faithfully for the woman he loved lay dying, the life-blood slowly ebbing from his side, every moment bringing him nearer to the great change.

Moving with difficulty, he reached the table where Vera's photograph rested, and he clasped the portrait to his breast.

"Vera," he whispered, speaking to the face in the picture; "Vera, it is sweet to die in your service since it is not permitted to me to live therein. Darling, as I lie here near the end, there rises in my heart a hope that perhaps after all we may be suffered to come together in the life hereafter to be bound in everlasting bonds. Vera, may that hope remain?"

The eyes of the photograph seemed to say, "That hope may remain."

His voice was very weak now.

"Vera—beloved of my heart, good-bye for ever on earth. Tell me, oh tell me, that in the other world you will come to me."

The lips of the photograph seemed to whisper: "I will come to you."

He lay back satisfied, his eyes fixed on the portrait till the last.

—And was that really so unfamiliar? The conversation with the portrait: imagine high violins and a slow dissolve to Vera's living face. Or the scene in the anarchists' den, accented voices rasping out of sinister shadows. It's a 1930's "B" movie we've been attending. Beaufoy was a hack for that decade, ahead of his time. The Playgoers Club could have been the Beverly Hills Hotel. Had TV been his era's technology, would he have had a feel for the half-hour script? Few movie hacks made that transition. Perhaps "For Vera's Sake"—we'd retitle it now—would pass, if certainly not for a gem of the genre, at least for a serviceable instance. It meets the first criterion of mass entertainment: conventions of motivation so sturdy that people anxious to get on with the tale won't question an implausibly handy ladder.

Nor does character solicit questions, or even exist. How bad, at heart, is Slavinski? No one asks. Who cares about the unspeakable Slavinski, once he has walked offstage toward his nephew's? Who even believes in Vera, or Turgoff? Nonsense. They are names attached to the postures adverbs can specify, as when they speak "fiercely," "proudly," "piteously," "ironically," "carelessly," "hoarsely," "sternly," "huskily," "quietly," and "steadily." The curve of the story's passion rises and falls through points plotted by those adverbs. Thus a sequence of quickly sketched postures can make a story, the elements of which lie ready for arousal in the trained reader's mind. This reader also welcomes any glimpse of unspeakable goings-on in the great drab city.

Russian nihilists were a formula for the unspeakable; in the dens they frequented, "stifled curses" always rose "thickly on the air." The tale James Joyce sent to *Tit-Bits* pertained, so his brother remembered, to Russian nihilists in London. It portrayed them as dashing thugs, and if it was prompted by "For Vera's Sake" its rejection would explain the cloacal fate Joyce famously accorded Beaufoy. Later, in *The Secret Agent* (1907), Joseph Conrad would reimagine the nihilist ambience. But in Russian nihilists as in all else, the public had its standards, and Conrad's presentation of seedy indolents was not approved of. "Indecent," said *Country Life*, and the *Edinburgh Review* detected neither "art" nor "service to society." Alfred Hitchcock's film version (*Sabotage*, 1936) was better liked; by Hitler's decade mass taste had come to agree with Graham Greene that espionage was grubby.

One more excerpt:

> "Baffled! baffled!" hissed Madame, when she had read the note; "God deliver me from my friends!" She paced up and down the room several times, and at last began to mutter to herself, as people often do in moments of strong emotion: "Bah! but he'll never get up by daybreak. He'll oversleep himself, especially after tonight's supper. The other will be before him. . . . Oh, my poor head, you've suffered too much to fail in the end!"

Philip Beaufoy again? No, Henry James, aged 21, in his first published story. That may suggest how far you can come from bad beginnings. Or it may hint that the beginnings weren't so bad. Whatever models young James was imitating in 1864, they pointed him to devices he'd quickly refine: firm scenes, pregnant utterances; and show, don't tell. Three decades later Beaufoy knew no more than that, but that much he did know. For the origins of such knowledge look to the stage, where they can say nearly anything if it's emphatic enough. "Playgoers Club": that address may serve as an emblem. Though he wrote with less conviction than Marie Corelli, Playgoer Beaufoy wrote better.

His clichés? Yes, we can't help noticing those, though we tend not to notice the clichés of our visual media. "The man whom he had cruelly wronged in the days gone by": that phrasing does stand out. In *Tit-Bits* it explains unforgiving rancor, much as "women of Vera's stamp did not love lightly" suffices to justify an admirer's chivalry. Not that either required much explaining, since even the simplest readers cooperated. They could understand that if Turgoff were not devoted beyond question to Vera, and did not also amply hate the man he was saving, there'd be little story. Add that only cooperative readers mattered, to Philip Beaufoy. When it's your time that is being agreeably killed, you'll always cooperate. For it is *your* time.

2 : *Everyman*

But we've mentioned the Temple Shakespeare, which sold so well, and the buyers of that would soon be buying the same publisher's Everyman's Library. He projected a thousand volumes, and began by issuing them in lots of fifty. Like the Shakespeare, they were decent texts printed decently, and sold at just a shilling in their gilded hard-covers: the price of four days of *The Times*. When the first fifty went on sale in February 1906, anyone with £2. 10s. to spend and four feet of shelving to spare could think about acquiring every one of them. Though their story postdates '95 by more than a decade, it belongs here because the public it characterizes dated far, far back.

Everyman's Library was a heroic conception, nothing less than World Literature Since Homer, not omitting the *Kalevala*, arranged into thirteen categories. A pair of "bookmen," the choleric unschooled publisher J. M. Dent and one underpaid editor, Ernest Rhys, whose credentials were those of a mining engineer, improvised lists in a frenzy of day-long meetings (bread, cheese, apples) between trips to the British Museum and glances at copyright status; no editorial boards, no supervising committees. They got all sorts of undocumented help; when they issued *Everyman and Other Interludes*, with the old play that had given the Library its name, an acknowledgment mentioned Mr. Ezra Pound, then a 24-year-old newcomer to London.

What they arrived at has proved less than perfect. Their knowledge had limitations, like their judgment, and simple availability posed other problems. The English for the Iliad wasn't Chapman's or Pope's but Lord Derby's; the Plato wasn't Jowett's; the poetry section sported Adelaide A. Proctor's *Legends and Lyrics** long before it admitted Dryden or Donne; Bulwer-Lytton, remembered for the deathless sentence "It was a dark and stormy night," got accorded one volume more than William Shakespeare. But, foibles and vagaries aside, what they did include! For fifty years Everyman's was the student's resource; the reading-list of many a decent curriculum had seldom to reach beyond it. Moreover, the books stayed in print, decade after decade. A generation whose experience of reprints is that they get snatched away with last month's magazines can hardly imagine stability of that order. It helped imply that the titles themselves were immortal.

The first title of such an enterprise arrests like an opening chord. Thirty years later Allen Lane would inaugurate Pelican Books with Shaw's *Intelligent Woman's Guide to Socialism and Capitalism*, and you knew you were deep in the decade of the Left Book Club. Dent's choice, in a gentler time, was less polemic. Volumes 1 and 2 of Everyman's Library contained Boswell's *Life of Johnson*, 1,264 unabridged pages, put on sale, as the preface remarked, at just one-thirtieth the price the great Croker edition had exacted in 1831.

Nostalgia had been his guide. In 1864 Joseph Mallaby Dent, aged 15, had "got up from that book feeling that there was nothing worth living for so much as literature," and in 1906 he had not forgotten its glow. Dent never came to care for Johnson himself, "a ponderous clumsy dirty old man."† What impressed him, boy and man, was the way sheer literary accomplishment could command the adulation of men more dazzling, Burke and Reynolds and Goldsmith. *That* was what literature meant: "otherwise how could this uncouth man rule over such a company?" In lordship over golden words lay secular

---

* "Spontaneous productions of a sweet wholesome nature, designed solely to brighten the lives of ordinary people." —Cooper & McVety, *Dictionary Catalogue of the First 505 Volumes of Everyman's Library*, 1911, 147.

† The only Johnson he would ever publish was *Rasselas*, chaperoned in *Shorter Novels, Vol. III* by *Vathek* and *The Castle of Otranto*. It's orienting to remember that Johnson had been dead only sixty-five years when J. M. Dent was born.

power, to override even origins, class, or accent. In that guise had destiny beckoned J. M. Dent toward the kingdom of books, and without ever learning to spell he became an influential bookman. He was small, lame, tight-fisted, and apt to weep under pressure, a performance that could disconcert authors and employees. When his temper had risen like a flame he'd scream; the scream, one employee recalled, was what broke men's spirits. His paroxysms were famous; a Swedish specialist thought of prescribing a pail of cold water for Dent to plunge his head into. For editing the Library he paid Rhys three guineas a volume—what senior office-boys might earn in two weeks. Dent's ungovernable passion was for bringing Books to the People. He remembered when he'd longed to buy books he couldn't afford. Yes, you could make the world better. He even thought enough cheap books might prevent wars.

Were there many stories like Dent's? Many fictions resemble his story, a long life's quiet triumph of purpose and virtual self-education. His father, a house-painter, taught music on the side and sold musical instruments, including pianos. The dictionary in the modest house was a reprint of Johnson's of 1755. In the nondescript stock of the little shop were some volumes of Scott's novels. "Having heard my schoolmaster speak of them," recalled J.M., "I began to read and did not leave off until I had devoured every book. . . . What a whirl of romance it was and what a high joy!" He was 10 or 11 years old.

What brought him to Boswell four or five years later was his little town's Mutual Improvement Society, where fervent young men "studied one book a week and the alternate week listened to and criticised a paper prepared by one of them." Their book-list included Paley's *Evidences of Christianity*. Dent somehow let himself promise a paper on Johnson, of whom he knew nothing, and Boswell was "hard work at first." Later, like Johnson, he would seek his fortune in London, where he lodged with a Mrs. Pook, set up as bookbinder, and made his way through selling books into publishing. He was quick to see the virtue of republishing works that were out of copyright, hence royalty-free, but packaging them nicely and keeping them in print. Several less ambitious series—the Shakespeare, and notably the bilingual Temple Dante—preceded his announcement of Everyman's Library.

The first years of the new century were auspicious for such a venture. "The copyrights of nearly all the great Victorians were falling in, such as Tennyson, Browning, Carlyle, Dickens, Huxley, Tyndall, and a host of others." That was because the Copyright Act of 1842 was still in force, and it released rights forty-two years after publication or when the author was seven years dead, whichever came later. So by 1906 a reprint house had access to anything anyone dead before 1900 had published prior to 1865. That explains much about the first list, including Adelaide Proctor, whose poems dated from 1858.

Books out of copyright were cheap to issue. Dent judged, moreover, that they were apt to be *good* books. This in turn augured a large potential sale: so reliable, he thought, was the magnetism of quality. His assessment of his public is fascinating: Everyman's Library was to appeal to "every kind of reader: the worker, the student, the cultured man, the child, the man, the woman." Impossible idealism! Yet he prospered, if not as Newnes or Northcliffe prospered. He seems un-alarmed by Philip Beaufoy and the *Tit-Bits* readership; betrays no sign, even, of awareness that they exist.

Everyman's first three batches of fifty titles were scheduled for its first twelve months; by then the series had all of Scott in print, by a year or so later almost all of Dickens. Nor were celebrated poets omitted: for its first year the Library announced one Tennyson volume, 1830–56, and two Brownings, one volume of the early work, one spanning 1844–64. The Copyright Act can be discerned behind these cutoff dates. After 1864, Browning's next publication had been *The Ring and the Book* (1868), and that would be available in 1910. Then in 1911 most of the *Idylls of the King* would enter the public domain, and a second Tennyson volume would be feasible. So Dent could plan his library's future, watching copyright after copyright duly expire and his Victorian list grow accordingly. He already had all of George Eliot's novels save two; in 1914 he could expect to add *Middle-march*. . . .

To understand the role of the great Victorians in J. M. Dent's marketing plans, we need only apply the old Copyright Act's arith-metic to our own immediate heritage. If we do that, we find to our astonishment that the whole of T. S. Eliot's poetry turns up in the public domain, for any reprinter to deal with as he pleases, as well as all the fiction of James Joyce, D. H. Lawrence, and Virginia Woolf. Imagine the buoyancy such names would lend a cheap series! Names like Tennyson's and George Eliot's had that power once. *Middlemarch* in the early years of Everyman's Library was a much more recent (and less daunting) novel than *Ulysses* is today.

For a while things went on schedule. In 1910 *The Ring and the*

Book joined Dent's earlier Brownings; next the second Tennyson volume, 1857–70, was duly published. And then, for a very long time, so far as Everyman was concerned, the canon of these poets was mysteriously fixed. So, for that matter, was George Eliot's; her greatest novel would not become a possession of Everyman till 1930, by which time her popular vogue had faded wholly.

What had happened was something beyond the scope of editorial policy. In 1911 the Copyright Act got rewritten, and the date of first publication became irrelevant. After 1 July 1912, the reprinter's magic year would be the year the author had been dead fifty years. That meant 1930 for George Eliot, 1939 for Browning, 1942 for Tennyson. Decades away! In effect, a mere Act of Parliament had rendered the stride of the series impossible to maintain. So the Second World War was being fought by the time Everyman's could issue a selection from the later Browning, and by then Browning was a period piece. Also, by then a long generation of readers had been picking up the two-volume sets of 1906, under the vague impression that they were as complete as made no difference: as though there'd been no "Balaustion's Adventure," no "Red Cotton Nightcap Country," no "Asolando." Thus reprint publishers inadvertently skewed perception of two major poets for half a century. As late as 1943 (the date of my copy) an Oxford Tennyson was offering quaint illustrations by Millais et al. but no poetry later than 1870.

And the effects of the new Copyright Act were to range still further. By inhibiting cheap reprints of everything published after 1870,* the Act helped reinforce a genteel impression that English literature itself had somehow stopped about that date: in fact, at about the time many of Everyman's first buyers were born. Had not all thereafter been transient novelty?

And the reader whose tastes were guided by the Everyman list, or by such rival series as the World's Classics (founded, 1901, by Grant Richards; acquired, 1905, by Oxford University Press, no less) was led insensibly to a new self-understanding. He was a proper bookman, impervious to novelty. That could even be made explicit. Ernest Rhys, Everyman's editor, in an essay many times replicated—he appended versions for years to every copy of every volume of the Library— encouraged Everyman to know himself as follows: "Everyman is dis-

---

* Inhibition, of course, did not prohibit; arrangements with an author's estate could always be made, and Everyman's acquired *Lord Jim* when Conrad had been dead much less than half the prescribed fifty years. That Dent had published it in the first place didn't hurt.

tinctly proverbial in his tastes. He likes best of all an old author who has worn well, or a comparatively new author who has gained something like newspaper notoriety." Rhys comes near to affirming that comparatively new authors are unlikely to outlast the attention of the *Daily Express*.

That being the case, you'd read them if you liked them, making no real claims for them save that they diverted you. We may be near an answer to a dark question: who were all those buyers, at 6s., of Marie Corelli? Not *Tit-Bits* browsers; her demands on sheer attention are too sustained. No, it seems likely that she found her six-shilling public among folk who spent many a dutiful shilling too on the Everyman Dickens, the Everyman Bulwer-Lytton, even the Everyman Homer.

Woman, I too take thought for this; but then I bethink me . . .

—so a line of Homer as rendered by Matthew Arnold, enshrined in Everyman's Library, No. 115, p. 271. If you could accept that as English—as sanctioned English—you might think Miss Corelli positively idiomatic.

In the 1930's, writers for the magazine *Scrutiny* enjoyed disclosing what it was dons really liked to read, by contrast with what they professed at the podium. P. G. Wodehouse was by then a donnish favorite, and in 1939 Oxford conferred on Psmith's creator the honorary doctorate it'd not have dreamed of offering Leopold Bloom's. *The best-seller public was the Everyman's public on holiday:* that seems, in the absence of statistics, a not unreasonable guess. What they read from outside the canon they read "for enjoyment," brooking no damned pretensions like interior monologue. That was for people who affected superiority; that was for highbrows.*

"For enjoyment" implies, of course, that you needn't expect to *enjoy* the canonical works, and it's true that you can't abandon your mind to *Rasselas*, not the way you might abandon it to *The Sorrows of Satan* or *The Green Hat* or *The Nine Tailors*. Abandoning your mind, that was what book-time enjoyment was coming to mean.

Meanwhile, the Ideal Order of the Classics abides, and such a series as Everyman's incarnates it. No wonder that by 1919 an ironical

---

* "Always with derisive implication," says the *OED Supplement*, which first spotted the word "highbrow" in 1911. By the 1920's it was code. "There was the theatre (so much better than the highbrows asserted)"—Hugh Walpole, 1921. "The programs are too highbrow"—*Punch*, 1925. "Stuff that, while good of its kind, is not suspect of highbrow-ism"—*Observer*, 1930.

T. S. Eliot would be referring to "monuments." When Eliot himself received the Everyman's imprint in 1931, it was not as the most influential poet of his time but as leaden introducer of the *Pensées* of Pascal.

So by the turn of the century two reading publics at least were discernible, that of Everyman, that of *Tit-Bits*. The former thought the latter vulgar when they thought of them at all, and were themselves thought stuffy. And neither of them was the right public for Henry James or Joseph Conrad—or James Joyce, for that matter. The public for what Eliot was to call "the really new"—for the innovative work with authority to claim entrance into the Ideal Order—would remain, through the mid-century and beyond, a shifting and beleaguered "highbrow" public apt to group itself into coteries or find itself being hectored from two sides, by C. S. Lewis for discriminating at all, by F. R. Leavis for not discriminating enough. That was unhealthy, and still is.

3 : Art

This third public was never well enough defined to support a stable organ such as *Tit-Bits*. An entrepreneur might have told you that it didn't know who it was or what it wanted, except that it kept wanting something *new*, which could mean something just a little dangerous. Well, "artists" and their lives were enticingly dangerous; one champion seller of 1895–96 was George du Maurier's *Trilby*, about informal goings-on in Paris that included smockless models, the can-can even (though when danced by Trilby O'Ferrall it was "funny without being vulgar"), above all the horrible Svengali, who "was not a nice man." Leslie Stephen, editor of the *Dictionary of National Biography*, didn't think a girl of 15 (his daughter Virginia) should read it. Svengali turned the tone-deaf Trilby into the most wonderful singer in the world and finally summoned her to join him beyond the grave, and he did it all with his hypnotic powers. *Trilby* would have been preposterous save for hypnotism's repute, which helped a book-reading middle class accept what Grandfather had called demonic possession.*

To read *Trilby* it helped if you could make out bits of French, but

---

* Incidentally, some talents run in families. George du Maurier's granddaughter Daphne wrote *Rebecca*.

it wasn't on the whole a book meant for literati. Yet those were fascinated by "artists" too, and for their benefit John Lane and Elkin Mathews had planned a quarterly, *The Yellow Book*. It was Yellow, to flaunt the flaring "aesthetic" color, which was also the color of French novels. It was a Book, in hardcovers, to affirm that what it offered was Art, not ephemera; also to justify charging 5s., a book price, and ten times what the monthly *Strand* sold for. The prospectus said it would be "charming," "daring," and "distinguished"; also that it would "have the courage of its modernness, and not tremble at the frown of Mrs. Grundy." The formula is familiar; in Chicago, forty years later, it worked again for *Esquire*, which also charged a premium price. The word "modernness" is especially to be noted: moral values, it seems to say, are not immutable, and time is never on Mrs. Grundy's side. But while "modern" winked at emerging libertines, it was meant to be differently decoded by the purchasers Lane and Mathews were hoping for: solvent and conventional people who were yawning for something different. The sameness of reading-matter produced by the acre was beginning to tell.

Though the first number sold out three printings in a week, we know little about buyers who were satisfied. What survives is a strident record of denunciation. *The Times* spoke of "repulsiveness and insolence," *The Speaker* of "aspiring affectation and preposterous incompetence." The *Westminster Gazette*, detecting "excesses hitherto undreamt of," wished an Act of Parliament would "make this kind of thing illegal," but didn't suggest how such an Act might be worded.

The Yellow Book's editor, Henry Harland, was an expatriate American and a worshipper of Henry James, who noted in him "literary longings unaccompanied by the *faculty*." (Harland wrote *The Cardinal's Snuff-Box*, if you've heard of that.) Its art editor and chief illustrator was the cadaverous Aubrey Beardsley, not yet 22. So in the first number it came about that "The Death of the Lion," by Henry James, appeared between covers drawn by a man notorious for having illustrated Oscar Wilde's *Salome*. James managed to be absent from the publication-night party, and shrank from sending a copy of the volume to his brother, William: "I hate too much the horrid aspect and company of the whole publication. . . . It is for gold and to oblige the worshipful Harland."

Oscar Wilde may serve as emblem of the company James hated keeping. Wilde had been giving Art a bad name for some time, and though he'd been prudently barred from *The Yellow Book*, his reputation, soon to be confirmed in court, helped define what reviewers thought they detected there. And certainly there was something never quite wholesome in the demi-monde of Beardsley's imagining, rendered with such astonishing technique. Did he care for women, or not? That seems the wrong question. Aubrey Beardsley was likely asexual, though obsessed with what he took for sexuality: grimaces, costumes, pert faces, naughty play. But line: design: his sense of those is irrefutable.

Nor should his Burne-Jones strain be undervalued. From imitating Kate Greenaway* at 10, Beardsley by 18 had ascended untaught to a scintillant level of accomplishment. He visited and got encouragement from Sir Edward Burne-Jones, sometime pupil of Rossetti's. It was at Sir Edward's that he met Oscar Wilde; also there that he was confirmed as a third-generation Pre-Raphaelite, someone for whom human likenesses, especially of women, were iconic: were beings not observed but imagined; were figured forth, to some unstated, unsettling purpose.

Skill in the Pre-Raphaelite idiom had brought Beardsley his first commission. It was to decorate a book, and the kind of decorations that were wanted were the kind Burne-Jones made for William Morris's Kelmscott Press, most famously for the *Chaucer*, the great unreadable book—and expensive (120 guineas)—that helped affirm, against machines, the Book: a handmade work of high craft. Admirers would give a copy to W. B. Yeats on his fortieth birthday, doubtless guessing that he'd place it on a lectern. That was the way to revere the Kelmscott *Chaucer*, with its Burne-Jones reveries that nudged free from any special time the narratives Chaucer had been glad to particularize.

The over-decorated William Morris book may remind us how obsolete processes claim survival as Art. As TV has turned old movies into "cinema," so the rotary press and the monotype (an 1887 patent) had just made hand presswork an art form. It needed much ornateness to prove it was done by hand. Morris and Burne-Jones had even regressed to a time before printing; you were meant to be reminded of illuminated manuscripts. And once Art had consecrated the ornate, people who couldn't afford the Kelmscott prices were apt to want ornate books of their own. In 1892, which was well before the *Chaucer*

* Who perhaps never perceived her lasting influence on the unisex figures he used in supporting roles. When he came to her notice (and everybody's) she HATED him, in capital letters.

but after the first Kelmscott productions had made a stir, J. M. Dent, spotter of trends, envisaged possibilities in a pseudo-Kelmscott, to be made on steam presses for issue to the "general reader" in monthly parts at 2s. 6d., with a Large Paper edition on Dutch handmade sheets for cognoscenti. The text would be Malory's *Morte d'Arthur*, well publicized by the sham-medieval *Idylls of the King*, and Dent needed a pseudo–Burne-Jones at a lower fee. He got Beardsley, who spent eighteen months doing pseudo–Burne-Joneses by the hundred, at £250 for the whole job. It was congenial work at first, if not toward the end.*

So, installed by predilection and by long practice in a line of descent from Rossetti via Burne-Jones, Beardsley was skilled in envisaging the kind of drawing that *meant* something, though you might not be sure quite what. With Beardsley, you might not even want to be sure. The Victorian illustration had told a trite story, or even accompanied one. The Rossetti picture might tell a story you didn't know unless its text was handy. But a Beardsley drawing might seem to tell a story the respectable didn't want to specify. They roared and foamed about indecency, never sure what the indecency was exactly. *L'Education Sentimentale*, for example, in the first *Yellow Book*: a fat woman with a leaflet, a slim girl. It aroused diffuse outrage; Max Beerbohm (aged 22) was unique in spelling out what he saw in it:

> A fat elderly whore in a dressing-gown and huge hat of many feathers is reading from a book to the sweetest imaginable little young girl, who looks before her, with hands clasped behind her back, roguishly winking. Such a strange curved attitude, and she wears a long pinafore of black silk, quite tight, with the frills of a petticoat showing at ankles and shoulders. . . .

Max describes the picture by paraphrasing its "story"; he says nothing at all about its most striking gesture, the imbalanced balancing of assertive areas of black, and the delicate stipple that encloses domains of white. Part of the picture's theme is its own economy in creating a magical illusion: the illusion that we can see past ink and white paper. That was one thing Art was coming to mean: an isolating of its own devices, and a foregrounding of them. Beardsley never let you

---

* He did other jobs for Dent, whose passion for sets and series was unremitting. Even some little books collecting the *bons mots* of Goldsmith, Sheridan, Lamb, others—simply joke-books rendered vendable by history—had decorations by Beardsley.

forget what you were really looking at: paper, ink. Whatever else you saw was up to you: a pretty young face, for example, which your eye might collect from a single outlining stroke around minimal markings so exactly placed you read them as eyes, mouth, nostrils. "Fat elderly whore" likewise is something Max read in a tight cluster of pen-strokes. And in the "fat elderly whore," oddly enough, we may now persuade ourselves that we see another of Beardsley's variations on the face of Oscar Wilde, with whom he'd soon come to detest being associated. But Philistia detected Wilde's presence in quite another way. Philistia didn't *look*; it read symbolically.

We are circling round something elusive and diffuse: Art and its status in the nineties. For one thing, it was foreign; talk about art was imported from the Paris of the can-can, and went with bohemian ways, which might amount to no more than over-fancy attire but could run all the way to free love and absinthe. *English* writers had never finicked over verbal "effects" and minute revisions; James, who did, was (however intensely respectable) a foreigner, one moreover domiciled for some time in Paris. (Wilde, come to think of it, hailed from half-savage Dublin.)

Also, Art was self-conscious about its procedures, and not only was that in itself unsettling, but it drew attention to the artist's presence. People were comfortable when no artifice was detectable, as in best-sellers (which, as they didn't reflect, only a few seemed to have the knack of writing). When they could detect what seemed not to have been done without thought, then they scented self-advertisement, which assured them that the advertised self was unsavory: one reason hardly anyone could perceive the extent of Beardsley's visual innovation. What Dent had paid him for was Burne-Jonesy imagery people were used to.

No item in the first *Yellow Book* was so unanimously denounced as young Max Beerbohm's "Defence of Cosmetics," unnatural from its first word, which was "Nay." ("To seem to write with ease and delight," wrote Max much later, "is one of the duties which a writer owes to his readers, to his art. And to contrive that effect involves very great skill and care.")

Nay, but it is useless to protest. Artifice must queen it once more in the town, and so, if there be any whose hearts chafe at her return, let them not say, "We have come into evil times," and be all for resistance, reformation or angry cavilling. For did the king's sceptre send the sea retrograde, or the wand of the sorcerer avail to turn the sun from its old course? . . .

Once "artifice" has implied a Wildean context, "queen it" becomes a tricky verb. As for "retrograde," that would send plain people to the dictionary. ("Canute didn't make the waves turn back," is all the clause says.) What, in short, was this whippersnapper up to? He seemed to be offending Everyman's sense of crisis by shouting "Theatre!" at a crowded fire, and the worst part was that you could almost hear him snickering. To be in the same room with a joke you've missed is to be pestered by suspicions that you may *be* the joke.

What the young whippersnapper was up to is still not easy to say. "A Defence of Cosmetics" parodies a transvestite manifesto so finely you can take it for one if you want. Or perhaps it's what it seems to say it is, a praise of "artifice," after the example of Huysmans's Des Esseintes, who got as far as fancying real flowers so monstrous they looked artificial (fancy that!). Or (the standard "appreciative" reading) perhaps it's a genial mocking of aesthetes who praise artifice? That's presumably what they'd decided at Buckingham Palace when they knighted its author forty-five years later. When it appeared, he'd been a mere undergraduate at Merton College, Oxford.

Oscar Wilde of course had pushed artifice, for instance in *The Chameleon* of 1893: "The first duty in life is to be as artificial as possible. What the second duty is no one has yet discovered." So too had Arthur Symons, who praised a play of Maeterlinck's as "written for a theatre of marionettes," praised Mallarmé's early poems also as "written in a language which has nothing in common with every-day language." Symons's amazing skills as a verse translator brought into English the qualities of Verlaine and Mallarmé that he admired, and his *The Symbolist Movement in Literature* (1899) would one day liberate the young T. S. Eliot from thinking there was nowhere to go after Swinburne. But in 1894, in *The Yellow Book*, he too occasioned outcry, with a poem, "Stella Maris," which celebrated a night of passion snatched.

> . . . joy, not shame, is ours to share,
> Joy that we had the will and power,
> In spite of fate, to snatch one hour. . . .

Behind that, if you wanted a philosophy, you could quote Pater on moments seized simply for those moments' sake, and banish from your mind the fact that Pater had (temporarily) suppressed the chapter in question from his *Renaissance*.

There was simply no way to disentangle Art from morals, and the aesthetes who kept insisting that Art meant nothing beyond itself were being more than a trifle disingenuous. For they insisted too that living was itself an art, and if that was so, and Art was its own end, then you might do anything you liked. If Oscar was teasing when he wrote an appreciation of the poisoner Wainewright, citing De Quincey, who'd ranked murder among the fine arts, he was also ready to persuade impressionable boys that sodomy belonged with the arts as well.

The day Wilde was sentenced, Dr. Richard Garnett, chief editor of the *British Museum Catalogue*, is said to have predicted "the death of English poetry for fifty years," so complete had been the victory of the respectable over an egregious emblem of all Art could be made to mean.

And how did Wilde become an egregious emblem? The lawsuit that doomed him was, C. H. Sisson remarks, "no more than a row between an overblown wit and a tiresome peer." In Johnson's age, in Byron's, an affair like that would have passed with little remark, the overblown wit left to suffer alone. What was new in 1895 was the popular press, which had learned, like Wilde, to seize moments for those moments' sake. An avenging God is another connoisseur of moments—you undo a lifetime of good works by today's peccadillo— and a press made in His very image thundered its outrage in accents mimed from Jehovah's. The wages of somebody's sin was now circulation. What Dr. Garnett was gauging was how long, in the Great Pressmaster's eye, publishers and reviewers would need for putting behind them the trauma of Fleet Street thunderclaps.

Fifty years proved an over-estimate, but poetry did go into hiding for some two decades, and hospitality to unfamiliar poetry was in abeyance still longer. People who wrote it, people who took it seriously, remained suspect alike. In 1915 Arthur Waugh, father of Evelyn, grandfather of the Auberon we've already heard from, and himself a onetime *Yellow Book* contributor, recoiled from a verse anthology he was reviewing; words like "anarchy" and "red ruin" came to his mind, and he invoked the classic custom of teaching young men morals by displaying a drunken slave as a bad example. Such a poem as "The Love Song of J. Alfred Prufrock," said Waugh, resembled that slave. He might have said more openly what he meant: that in being "aesthetic" the poem was dangerous like Oscar. Eliot's own later postulation of a boundary between Art and the Event, between the man who suffers and the mind that creates, and his recourse to austere metaphors drawn from science, have since been linked with privacies he needed to conceal; but in 1919 Eliot saw no other possible way to free talk about Art in England from confusions still potent after a quarter-century.

Three publics, then, at least, the third unfocused and after 1895 demoralized. Such is a serviceable diagram of the England into which a new literature would attempt to insert itself.

3 : A NARRATIVE INHERITANCE

The techniques of a dominant genre evolve the way machines do, acquiring glitter and optional accessories, shedding surplus weight. As decades passed, readers and writers had educated one another into a vast consensus on the many small things that made narrative possible. They agreed on details such as that dogs "bow-wow," doors "bang," Cockneys drop the initial "h"; arbitrary agreements all, since none of these statements is true save in English. French dogs say "*riau riau*," Chinese dogs "*wang wang*." In Germany doors go "*bums*." As for Cockney speech, its notation is a detail of something more intricate, the need for a printed shorthand to represent gradations of class.

No one could write fiction about the English without attending to "class," briefly describable as the system that evolves on a crowded island for reducing the number of people with whom you need accept the bother of intimacy. Something similar emerged independently in Japan. English classes are marked by their speech, natives, as Wyndham Lewis put it, being "branded on the tongue at birth." Fiction required a notation. As with dog-barks and door-bangs, so with human noises: reduced and arbitrary codes evolved, acceptable in lieu of closer transcriptions. Being a "readable" writer or a fluent reader meant getting the codes right, and writers as well as readers learned them less by listening than by reading.

There were the conventions of naming. "Dinner" is an evening meal for a lord, a midday meal for a laborer. That's an easy one. Other nuances are trickier. How French, still, is a formerly French word? Who says "an hotel," respecting its origins? Who (lower down the scale) says "a hotel," domesticating it? And—crucial question—which of these is your reader? Does one offer "port," or "port wine"? (though never "claret wine"!). At what moment, among which of the polite, did "Thanks" supersede "Thank you"? After that, to whose ears, if any, has "Thank you" come to sound a bit aloof? As for the word "lady" and the word "gentleman," or the proper use of "Esq." on an envelope, those were by 1895 kaleidoscopic themes. The nouveau-riche and Americans had long complicated matters; gauging the degree of acceptance they merited was delicate. How, if not as "*Cher maître*," did one address a Mr. Henry James, late of old New York and of Paris?

Pronunciation was still more important. You represented it by tricks with spelling, and started from the odd convention that narrator and reader belonged to an unspecified "literate" class with no discernible coloration, like clear water. These two were understood to share standard spelling as a baseline from which to measure small deviations. For a first approximation, one major deviation was needed; out of dozens of London dialects, "Cockney" got agreed on as the standard non-standard instance, and a missing "h" became the code for Cockney. Bernard Shaw, a foreigner who listened carefully, dodged the consensus and wrote down Cockney so his actors could reproduce the sounds:

> Aw knaow you. Youre the one that took awy maw girl. Youre the one that set er agen me. Well, I'm gowin to ev er aht. Not that Aw care a carse for er or you: see? Bat Aw'll let er knaow; and Aw'll let you knaow. Aw'm gowin to give er a doin that'll teach er to cat awy from me.

That kind of thing being hard to read on a train, the dropped "h" was normally deemed sufficient. Such a consensus ignored the sound-snob's principal bane, vowel irregularity. In the real world it's your vowels that do you in. In a poem called "Class" (a word he couldn't pronounce acceptably) Charles Tomlinson recalls how "those midland *a*'s/ once cost me a job," and Arnold Bennett made noises quite as jarring as any Cockney's whenever he said "first class" to rhyme with "gas" ("How many thousands a year," his biographer wonders, "does one need to live that down in an East Anglian golf club?"). But the transgressions of a fictional northerner in Bennett's plight would have gone unrecorded if not unremarked, the alphabet's resources being scanty.

Thus a whole dimension of English social awareness was let slip through the story-writer's mesh; his odd fish were apt to be foreigners, for whom, as for the Cockney, there were agreed notations. Paper-and-ink Americans said "waal" and "reckon," Irishmen said "me" for "my" and (in the *Tit-Bits* order of fiction) "begorrah"; Frenchmen turned "th" into "z" and admired "zee prospect"; while in darkest Wiltshire, for a writer who was keeping his anthropologist's distance, a peasant might mutter of a wife, "Her be gwaain whoam." In this substitute reality-system, people who were different were *very* different. Anybody who could read understood the system, and whoever wrote to be read understood it too.

Moreover, sharing as they did the "neutral" idiom, writer and reader alike could be free, while the tale lasted, from the great debarring world where your speech marks you. In the paper universe and there alone, syntax and grammar suffice. On paper Arnold Bennett, his vowels inaudible, was a glittering man of the world. On paper Conrad was serenely eloquent, his thick continental diction removed like grime from a window; on paper H. G. Wells spoke with crisp authority, his Cockney squeaks filtered out. And the voice you heard when you scanned their words was your own: quite a fine voice, as you knew from a lifetime's intimacy with it. No matter, for now, if it had sometimes reduced social temperatures.

So much for details of the writer's craft. There were larger considerations. How to begin telling a story? If it was short, Philip Beaufoy knew how, with a spoken line: "Ivan, ask me no more." If it was longer, you set a scene, then got people talking. Talk was what readers hungered after: reality, immediacy. How long you dallied before getting to the talk depended on the length of the tale. A quite long tale began by instilling the requisite patience.

So, by the end of the nineteenth century, magazine fiction, which must seize attention or perish, had much technique of narrative and notation available for a beginner to assimilate, and when H. G. Wells in 1894 set out to compose his first romance, *The Time Machine*, he could know from reading other writers' tales exactly how to go about it.

The Time Traveller (for so it will be convenient to speak of him) was expounding a recondite matter to us. His grey eyes shone and twinkled, and his usually pale face was flushed and animated. The fire burned brightly, and the soft radiance of the incandescent lights in the lilies of silver caught the bubbles that flashed and passed in our glasses.

"That flashed and passed in our glasses": a born writer caught that rhythm, mimetic of bubbles twinkling. But Wells does not trust everything to native gifts. He's astute with technique that can be conceptualized: careful to visualize his scene, careful to light it, cunning with bits of verisimilitude that don't tax our patience by stolidly describing. "The incandescent lights" is such a touch; in 1894 that phrase located the scene in the present, and did it visually, the way all the rest was done. (Edison's light-bulb patent was in 1886.) While Wells wrote, the motion picture was being invented, the next century's narrative vehicle. Novel and film are a continuum. Though narrative scans time, it concentrates itself into scenes, and the novelist's vivid imagining of scenes confirms his authority over change and process. If authority over change and process was far from the thoughts of Mr. Philip Beaufoy at the Playgoers Club, he valued scene-setting as much as anyone: "a gloomy-looking room lit with a couple of candles, and presenting a thoroughly forbidding aspect." How incomparably better is Wells! But a Beaufoy reader might even graduate to Wells, by learning a little patience. Many probably did. Anonymous thousands loved *The Time Machine*, and so did Henry James.*

Twenty years later James Joyce would be writing *Ulysses*, a deep-space vehicle, we are apt to suppose, by contrast with H. G. Wells's Kitty Hawk planes. It's enlightening, though, to observe how many detailed processes Joyce did not need to invent, only to refine. The stream of consciousness itself is scenic. Look at "Circe."

Wells's format, the narrative of a man returned from a fabulous journey, is as old as the *Odyssey*, and so is his strategy, tale-within-a-tale. The Wells journey is a journey into the future, not over the sea but down the stream of history. And as the tale of the Cyclops and Circe and the Sirens was told by Odysseus at King Alkinoös' court, for Homer to tell of his telling, so Wells contrived a man who had heard the Time Traveller's tale and let him tell it to us. No, Wells was no student of Homer. How to do that could be learned from magazines, or from Swift, or from whatever came to hand. He had days of voracious reading till the light failed.

The future: that was a Victorian speciality. As they grew convinced that historical processes were orderly, people came to think of times to come as foreseeable: if not anyone's private fate, then surely all

---

* Wells made his debut in good company. The journal that serialized *The Time Machine*— W. E. Henley's *New Review*—was soon offering *The Nigger of the "Narcissus"* and *What Maisie Knew*.

mankind's awaiting world. "For I dipt into the future," wrote Tennyson, whose personal future included the royal laurels—

> For I dipt into the future, far as human eye could see,
> Saw the Vision of the world, and all the wonder that would be.

That was in 1842, and if future wonders might include aerial warfare as well as commercial aircraft, "the larger analysis" could hold out hope. In an ultimate Legislature of the World,

> . . . the common sense of man shall hold a fretful realm in awe,
> And the kindly earth shall slumber, wrapt in universal law.

(What a striking equation, peace with sleep!)

In 1891, a half-century later, William Morris, socialist and hand-craftsman, published *News from Nowhere*, a prose romance about a man who wakes up in what Morris deemed earthly paradise, a socialist England where human satisfactions are those of leisurely handicraft. The book may have helped spark Wells's imagination; it had been out only four years when he wrote *The Time Machine*. To be sure, there are radical differences. Morris the arts-and-crafts fanatic would not have fancied riding into paradise on a machine, nor was he novelist enough to devise some non-mechanical rationale for time travel, the way Henry James would do in *The Sense of the Past*. A mysterious awakening, like Rip Van Winkle's, sufficed. (No, Englishmen weren't readers of that quaintly American tale. But everyone knew Rip in Dion Boucicault's stage adaptation.)

Wells, though, amid mankind's greatest crescendo of mechanical marvels—underground trains, tunnels beneath the Thames, electric lights, and now there was talk of airships—Wells understood how the machine had become imagination's way to the marvelous. Machines play their jiu jitsu with natural laws; the airplane would fly, when it did, thanks to principles that had been operative since the beginning of the world. So Wells, whose wonderful, glittering machine needed principles to exploit, ingeniously invented some.

"There are really four dimensions, three which we call the three planes of Space, and a fourth, Time," the Time Traveller explains. ". . . Why not another dimension at right angles to the other three? . . . Professor Simon Newcomb was expounding this to the New York Mathematical Society only a month or so ago. . . . "

Hermann Minkowski, building on early work of Einstein's, would define a rigorous four-dimensional continuum only in 1908, but the constituent notions were around in Wells's young manhood, and Herbert George Wells was acutely aware of what was around. Professor Simon Newcomb (Mathematics and Astronomy, Johns Hopkins) was real enough, and he did read that paper, in December 1893.*

As his conception advances on Morris's, so does Wells's narrative technique. He locates his tale in a normal house in the London suburb of Richmond, and supplies a suitably skeptical group for the Time Traveller to tell it to; they include a Medical Man, a bemused Provincial Mayor, and someone called Filby whose knowing wink says "Balderdash." Also, he is careful to run the first marvel in particularizing slow-motion:

> We all saw the lever turn. I am absolutely certain there was no trickery. There was a breath of wind, and the lamp flame jumped. One of the candles on the mantel was blown out, and the little machine suddenly swung round, became indistinct, was seen as a ghost for a second perhaps, as an eddy of faintly glittering brass and ivory; and it was gone—vanished! Save for the lamp the table was bare.

This draws much of its plausibility from the fact that three-quarters of its words are monosyllables, the more powerful in a story that begins in top-hatted fit-to-print prose with someone "expounding a recondite matter." The hammer-force of little words—that would prove a discovery.

And Wells's long view is different from Morris's too; things will seem to get better but will really get far worse. The view above ground, the floral world of the Eloi, is but half the future, an insipid half. Soon the Time Traveller discovers, below ground, the Morlocks.

It is not the twenty-first century or the twenty-fifth, but the 803rd. "The whole earth had become a garden," as in the future William Morris imagined, except that its inhabitants aren't working at looms. They aren't doing much of anything, save "playing gently, bathing in the river, making love in a half-playful fashion, eating fruit and sleeping." They even enact Arcadian tableaux, "the male pursuing the female, flinging flowers at her as he ran." That is Life as Art,

---

* Since Wells conscripted him to make time travel plausible, it's amusing that in 1901 Professor Newcomb would be judging mere air travel very likely impossible. It would require, he said, "the discovery of some new metal or some new force." In '03 the Wrights were airborne.

unmistakable *Yellow Book* decadence. And they are, it turns out, succulent edible cattle for the carnivore Morlocks, who live beneath the earth. The way calves in a Kentish field seem not unhappy, they are happy.

Such conceits are wonderfully stable. Looking back, we're not disconcerted by a reminiscence of Swift, whose style, Wells said, helped him shape the book. The Eloi are degenerate Houyhnhnms, the Morlocks dominant Yahoos. Looking forward, behold Richard Adams, in 1972's best-selling *Watership Down*, as he shocks his readers by disclosing that the most salubrious beings his creatures meet on their journey are the kept foodstock of mutant carnivores, and blissfully indifferent to their coming fate.

In the nine decades since H. G. Wells wrote his story, we have grown accustomed to invented futures that are not at all reassuring. Many are like Wells's, not visions of the future at all but metaphors for the present. Scientific knowingness had not yet seduced Wells into dreaming. In the very year he was born the Frenchman Jules Verne (1828–1905) wrote a euphoric *From the Earth to the Moon*, and 103 years later the moon was visited, by a man from Ohio, without incident. Verne's romances, unlike Wells's, sketch the technical marvels of what has proved to be an actual future. ("Very English," was the aged Verne's comment on Wells. "I make use of physics. He invents.")

When Jules Verne dreamed technology's dreams prematurely, life among its huge toys seemed enormous fun. But when Wells sent men to the moon in 1901 they had no fun at all; Selenites needed smashing like eggs, the way English explorers had often had to smash natives. Likewise the Eloi and the Morlocks, despite Wells's talk about the year 802701, existed in 1894: beautiful idle people lunching at the Savoy, and a thronging misery that might as well have been underground for all the heed graceful folk paid it. (Its standard of eating, Lovat Dickson tells us, was "lower than at any time since the Middle Ages.") What has changed after eight hundred centuries is only that the Morlocks, no longer utterly miserable, come up nightly from below ground to snack on the Eloi.

Here Peter Kemp supplies the arresting observation that Wells himself had lived his early life below ground: until 13 "in a completely subterranean kitchen, lit by a window which derived its light from a grating on the street level." *That* was the way England treated a smart boy who'd been born the youngest son of domestic servants and could enforce no claim on a future different from theirs. A string had always jerked him back into subjection. One time, a pharmacist's apprentice, he'd almost begun to learn the Latin he coveted, and was suddenly translated by his mother to the Southsea Drapery Emporium, where he could work at a living proper to his station. His hairbreadth escape from such tyranny was via a scholarship to the Normal School of Science in South Kensington. He was five feet seven, and further disadvantaged by a Cockney accent atop a squeaky voice. His mustache, even, was wispy. Science became one more thing to fail at—he left the Normal School without a degree—and deep down, however glib with its terminology, he would never share its official professions of confidence. Science lights a match, then sees its own hands, then darkness: that was the closing figure of the first piece Wells published for the world to see.

So *The Time Machine*, beneath "scientific" trappings, was a fable of the England H. G. Wells knew, restoring a genre of imaginative writing in which a seeming portrayal of the remote discloses the here and now, through its glass, and darkly. Just so, the violent Rome of *Coriolanus* is London, 1607.

London, 1895: that was Dystopia. After *The Time Machine* an imagined London would shape one unpleasant hallucination after another. "Heart of Darkness," *The Waste Land*, *Brave New World*, *Vile Bodies*, *The Human Age*, *1984*, *A Clockwork Orange*: metaphor after metaphor for the ruinous working-out of enlightened hopes. There had been dark places in the many Londons of Dickens, but no precedent, not even in *Bleak House*, for the City as emblem of sickness beyond remedy: all promise canceled, everything gone to pot.

"Heart of Darkness," written just four years after *The Time Machine*, resembles it in so many striking ways we are not surprised to learn that Wells's romances were part of Conrad's reading. Conrad could draw on the French example of innovative vividness and psychological nuance—Stendhal and Flaubert, untranslatable masters—but Wells's example shows how there already existed in British popular fiction a set of narrative procedures, scenic, crisp, onto which these subtle techniques could be grafted. "Heart of Darkness" was not meant for "aesthetic" segregation; it first appeared as a three-part serial in *Blackwood's Magazine*, the work of a man who was commencing to earn a living with his pen and was studying other magazine fiction. Quite possibly it was *The Time Machine* that suggested, for Marlow's recounting of his fantastic voyage, a setting carefully delineated and an interactive audience just sufficiently characterized. And like the journey into the future, the journey into the Congo maps a journey we can take without leaving home: into "the heart of an immense darkness" which is every man's heart and is also—Marlow's first spoken words bid us realize—London itself, in its time "one of the dark places of the earth."

True, differences leap from the pages. Not only has *The Time Machine* no Marlow and no Kurtz, it is wholly devoid of characters who can persuade us they are real. The Time Traveller himself is but a pronoun. The narrative is seldom as good as its own best parts. Many scenes are scamped; the ending is facile. Joseph Conrad sensed a writer's responsibilities differently. His 1898 preface to *The Nigger of the "Narcissus"* opens with words about Art:

> A work that aspires, however humbly, to the condition of art should carry its justification in every line. And art itself may be defined as a single-minded attempt to render the highest kind of justice to the visible universe, by bringing to light the truth, manifold and one, underlying its every aspect.

After the debacle of Wildean aestheticism, those are bold words indeed; Conrad's foreignness, like James's, helped protect him. In the abstract they can sound hollow, and H. G. Wells would have brushed the whole issue aside; when Wells wasn't simply writing entertainments, the way he memorably did till about 1910, his concern was not with the truth of "the visible universe," which he would have thought a microscope helped you arrive at, but with arguing that something needed to be *done*: science made plain, the economy rationalized, long views taken.

Conrad wrote, a few paragraphs later,

> And it is only through complete, unswerving devotion to the perfect blending of form and substance; it is only through an unremitting, never-discouraged care for the shape and ring of sentences that an approach can be made to plasticity, to color, and that the light of magic suggestiveness may be brought to play for an evanescent instant over the commonplace surface of words: of the old, old words, worn thin, defaced by ages of careless usage.

"An unremitting, never-discouraged care for the shape and ring of sentences": what story-teller in English before Conrad would have thought of his obligation in that way? "The old, old words, worn thin, defaced by ages of careless usage"—jingling coins passed unregarded from pocket to pocket—the *words* in which a story was written had not previously been pointed to as a focus of concern. But when Konrad Korzeniowski tired of life at sea and settled in England to write, he was still finding English idiom rather difficult. Nothing forces your attention on nuances of usage like an unremitting struggle to make people understand you and not smile.

Flaubert had disciplined himself to write French as though it were a foreign language. Now for the first time a writer of comparable genius was doing the same with English. And for Conrad, English *was* a foreign language. In some ways, for better and for worse, it remained so. Look at this:

My task which I am trying to achieve is, by the power of the written word, to make you hear, to make you feel, above all to make you *see*. That—and no more; and it is everything. If I succeed, you shall find there, according to your deserts, encouragement, consolation, fear, charm—all you demand—and, perhaps, also that glimpse of truth for which you have forgotten to ask.

"My task which I am trying to achieve"—the ring of that isn't quite right, and he was often insecure with "shall" and "will." But time and again he would stumble upon marvels, adjectival and adverbial ones especially. "He was densely distressed" (in "The Secret Sharer"), like so many phrases of Conrad's, is unobtrusively exact. No native speaker would have thought of it.

It is striking how, about 1895, innovative books commence to be written by people who've had to learn the written idiom. H. G. Wells, for instance: the talk he heard growing up was the careful, anxious talk of servants mimicking the manners of "upstairs," and a letter of about 1887 exhibits what he first took for proper style. He is fishing for an introduction:

You are acquainted with men like Harrison, Bernard Shaw and the Huxleys who must from the active and extensive nature of their engagements of necessity employ fags to assist in the more onerous and less responsible portion of their duties.

You'd not read the first page of a story told in that language, and Wells apparently finished one whole novel in it, *Lady Frankland's Companion*, before he knew it was all wrong and burned the manuscript. The idiom with which he soon caught readers' ears sounded racily ironic, and that's striking too because today it seems so natural. But it was something he'd schooled himself to, after what he called "a cleansing course of Swift and Sterne." Of the details we know next to nothing.

Conrad's learning process is likewise undocumented. Subduing a foreign idiom was only part of it; he had also to master an English tale-writer's devices. The intricate problems of class notation he dodged with the aid of exotic locales: Malaysia, shipboard. About English aristocrats he knew even less than Dickens, so in his one London novel, *The Secret Agent*, his aristocrat is an English-speaking foreigner whose diction suffices by being dictionary-formal.

Conrad had himself made Marlow's journey to the Congo; he seems even to have based Kurtz on a man he knew there. But the most naïve reader is unlikely to suppose that Conrad meant to write out an account of a queer trip he had taken. There is too much "art" for that.

The tale, for one thing, much more strikingly than *The Time Machine*, is elaborately enclosed in another tale, the tale of its being told. And Conrad's framing story is more than a device for getting at the story of Kurtz. It brings home the emblematic meaning of Kurtz. Within sight of "a mournful gloom" which broods "over the biggest, and the greatest, town on earth," aboard a ship, that microcosm of efficient order, four men, once sailors, listen to a fifth, who is a sailor still. Besides "myself," they are a Company Director, a Lawyer, an Accountant: administrators of the prosperity which ensues when a dark place of the earth has been opened by men from the sea. London, we are soon reminded, was opened by navigators from Rome, as the Congo is now being exploited by entrepreneurs from Brussels. How unlike are London and the Congo, really?

Then there are the little shocks to rationality: the gunboat, for instance, lobbing shells into the bush: "in the empty immensity of earth, sky and water . . . incomprehensible, firing into a continent": so pointless it teases us with intimations of dark meaning. And there is Kurtz, so fascinating to Marlow, Kurtz with his fanaticism, his eloquence, his enlightened "ideas" (who would not endorse them?), his ignominious death, his dying cry.

Meaning? For Marlow, we are told, "the meaning of an episode was not inside like a kernel but outside, enveloping the tale which had brought it out only as a glow brings out a haze." A haze defined by a tale's glow, and around it all darkness: that is what "the glimpse of truth for which you have forgotten to ask" will resemble when you have glimpsed it.

Thanks largely to Conrad, the narrative inheritance entered the twentieth century's poetry; his example had much to suggest to T. S. Eliot about the power of a measured, faintly exotic eloquence, and about the use of scenes of hallucinatory definiteness, enacted without explanation, swiftly terminated. *The Waste Land*, the century's most influential poem, was to have been prefixed by an epigraph from "Heart of Darkness": the two sentences that precede Kurtz's death-cry, and the cry itself. The epigraph was canceled, but the poem, from its brooding beginning to its nightmare journey in Part V—not to mention the London Apocalypse in Part III—bears Conrad's genetic material on every page.

"Above all to make you see": he could do that by the mere placement of an adverb. Here's a Russian student who has just finished betraying a Russian nihilist in *Under Western Eyes*:

> He went back into his room slowly, shutting the door after him. The peaceful steady light of his reading-lamp shone on the watch. Razumov stood looking down at the little white dial. It wanted yet three minutes to midnight. He took the watch into his hand fumblingly.

What disturbs the equable narrative poise is "fumblingly." An awkward-sounding word, and inserted with cunning awkwardness, it strikes a reader with much the same surprise as the fact that his hand was unsteady must have struck Razumov. If—needless even to say—you'll find no effect of that order from end to end of "For Vera's Sake," it's because "For Vera's Sake," awkward from end to end, has no norm of equability for a little glitch of diction to jar against. "Seeing the picture, there came of a sudden to him who gazed on it a violent return of the old jealousy, and for an instant he wavered in his good resolve. But it was only for an instant, and then the better purpose triumphed." In that chaos you'd not notice a dead cat.

A facile contrast, true. Yet if we seek among loftier reputations for a predecessor of Conrad's able at will to make one word tellingly fumble, it can prove, Henry James excepted, a barren quest. When writers of English have placed diction under conscious control it has tended to be for ironic purposes solely—Arnold's chilling "Wragg is in custody" comes to mind—and diction used with ironic formality is overt diction, ourselves as aware of it as ever its author. But the fumble of Conrad's "fumblingly" depends on our not noticing at all any of the words whose calm sequence it terminates: "He went back into his room slowly, shutting the door after him"—what could sound more natural than that? And we have to reflect that it's a *contrived* naturalness, the author's control as steely for the duration of some fifty ordinary words as in the minute displacement they lead up to. This is prose at least as well written as poetry.

But it wasn't by mastery of minute effects that Conrad's writing drew notice; no, by its "style," a phenomenon seductive and magical for some of his reviewers, florid and adjectival for others. "Style" is a term reserved for conspicuous language, as when Conrad huffs and puffs toward an enchantment. "The sea was a miracle of calm, a miracle of azure": that last word is (of course) right, triumphantly. Yet it's unthinkable away from "art"; no one *says* "azure." A reviewer of *Lord Jim* was bothered by a gap between how people talk and the book's claim that Marlow was talking. He quoted sentences the book ascribes to Marlow—

> There is something haunting in the light of the moon; it has all the dispassionateness of a disembodied soul, and something of its inconceivable mystery. It is to our sunshine, which—say what you like—is all we have to live by, what the echo is to the sound: misleading or confusing, whether the note be mocking or sad. It robs all forms of matter—which, after all, is our domain—of their substance, and gives a sinister reality to shadows alone.

—and he added portentously, "It is not thus that men speak." Yet "It is not thus that men speak" is no way anyone speaks either, from which we may deduce that all writers without exception at the century's turn were being flypapered by a written idiom. And Conrad on the haunting light of the moon is up to Fine Writing for sure.

That made judgments of "style" very tricky. Thus, another anonymity said *Lord Jim* was "impossible in style," but detected "genius" and offered a prediction: "Mr. Conrad will do great things when he consents to follow advice." (Mr. Conrad had already written, unadvised, *The Nigger of the "Narcissus"* and "Heart of Darkness.") And C. E. Montague, himself a novelist (*Rough Justice* and *Right Off the Map*) said no one but Conrad wrote "at off times, quite so carelessly."

Montague might have been thinking of stuff like this:

> The roofs of the congested trees, writhing in some kind of agony private and eternal, made tenebrous and shifty silhouettes against the sky, like shapes cut out of black paper by a maniac who pushes them with his thumb this way and that, irritably, on a concave surface of blue steel.

But wait, that's not Conrad, that's Max Beerbohm's parody. Yet the kind of thing it parodies isn't much different:

> The ever-ready suspicion of evil, the gnawing suspicion that lurks in our hearts, flowed out into the stillness round him—into the stillness profound and dumb, and made it appear untrustworthy and infamous, like the placid and impenetrable mask of an unjustifiable violence.

That's unhappily what got taken for Conrad's Style: mystery, menace, double-barreled adjectives, in a continental suavity of cadence.

Let us now look at something quite different:

> I heard a light sigh and then my heart stood still, stopped dead short by an exulting and terrible cry, by the cry of inconceivable triumph and of unspeakable pain. "I knew it—I was sure!" . . . She knew. She was sure.

No, not Philip Beaufoy but Joseph Conrad, toward the climax of "Heart of Darkness," his grip on the great tale gone slack. But he had pored over English magazine writers, absorbed their narrativè inheritance, well enough to know how they brought off romantic climaxes. Alas. It's doubtful, though, if that's the sort of lapse C. E. Montague had in mind when he mentioned careless writing. By a routine novelist's standards that's *great* writing.

It is exactly when reviewers aren't looking, when Conrad is simply *telling* us, as when Razumov takes up his watch "fumblingly," that he's doing what no writer of English had ever done before: making the words mime the actions while the actions enact their own significance. Razumov has betrayed a killer just to make him go away, and now watches him leave:

> Gazing down into the black shaft with a tiny glimmering flame at the bottom, he traced by ear the rapid spiral descent of somebody running down the stairs on tiptoe. It was a light, swift, pattering sound, which sank away from him into the depths: a fleeting shadow passed over the glimmer—a wink of the tiny flame. Then stillness.

So Haldin runs out of Razumov's life (the sound "sank away from him into the depths") to a police trap and doom ("a wink of the tiny flame. Then stillness."). And that black shaft Razumov is gazing down is the blackness he'll gaze into for the rest of *Under Western Eyes*. That is Conrad at his most magical, the presented fact become the economic metaphor: writing never overtly symbolic but always in touch with larger meanings through the details that hold our attention sentence by sentence. Its tour de force is the first two-thirds of "Heart of Darkness," the example for Eliot of how presented fact could portend: "And each man fixed his eyes before his feet."

After "Heart of Darkness," Marvin Mudrick observes, "the craftsman in fiction could never again be unaware of the moral resources inherent in every recorded sensation; . . . what now appears an immemorial cliché of the craft of fiction has a date as recent as the turn of the century." But it went unobserved at the time. John Masefield for one liked Kipling and Stevenson better, and compared the narrative method of "Heart of Darkness" to "a cobweb abounding in gold threads." Masefield had been to sea, which was one of his qualifications, and would one day be named Poet Laureate, which suggests another.

Reviewers notice only the saliently noticeable, and when Conrad the supreme craftsman got their attention it was as late as 1914, when he published his first *tired* book. Something odd about it awakened the ineffable Robert Lynd (of whom more later); Lynd thought that Conrad ought to have been able to tell the story of *Chance* in about two hundred pages instead of 406. Conrad agreed that "by selecting a certain method and taking great pains" he might have written it out on a cigarette paper. Yes, the complicated methods of *Chance* were quite discernible, and C. E. Montague now outlined "Mr. Conrad's unmistakable method of telling a story":

> Some shadowy figure of a narrator opens the tale and then melts into the dimness behind it and lets the bulk of it come as a tale told by one of the persons whom he mentioned, and this second narrator, in turn, hands over the job, for a time, to one of his own creatures. . . . As the story of Flora de Barral draws to an end this coil is unwound; each discarded narrator comes back into place—in inverse order, of course,—and the shadowy first narrator puts in a last word. It is like one of those algebraical uses of bracket within bracket, even to three or four brackets of various shapes. . . .

That is not, as its reference to algebra might suggest, a sneer; it goes on to laud "the strong charm of this system of interpenetrative lights . . . where nothing comes to you as a fact directly and impersonally stated; every new point has a greater reality and thrill for that," and "the whole atmosphere in which the narrative moves acquires a strange and exciting luminousness."

Now, it was apropos of *Chance* that for the last time the critical machine of Henry James, by then 71, was set in motion. The boilers were fired up, the leather belts flapped; shafts spun, the whistle hooted at random; onto the pages of the *Times Literary Supplement*, which had not acquired its mature confidence in recasting solicited prose, clacked thirty-five hundred words of the most impenetrable encomium ever concocted, one great immigrant taking the measure of another. Out of its calculated murk one supremely quotable phrase could be spotted glistening: Conrad, so the Master said, was "absolutely alone as a votary of the way to do a thing that shall make it undergo most doing."

That gets cited as a supreme accolade, the old maker of labyrinths saluting an equal. But Conrad, who had more incentive than anyone else to reread the whole thing the seven times it requires, would recall "*the only time* a criticism affected me painfully," having divined the real thrust of such intricacies as

. . . the course, so far as three words may here serve, of his so multiplying his creators or, as we are now fond of saying, producers, as to make them almost more numerous and quite emphatically more material than the creatures and the production itself in whom and in which we by the general law of fiction expect such agents to lose themselves. . . .

Translation: the innermost brackets in that algebra of narrators enclose substance insufficient to have merited all the fuss.

The complications of *Chance*, James thought, were no more than gratuitous: about that he's pretty explicit. Yet, miraculously, the great public—"an inordinate number of common readers"—liked *Chance*. And, said James with thunderous irony, "Great then would seem to be after all the common reader!" He was writing in the year of *Tarzan of the Apes*. What the common reader was enjoying—James divined this too—proved to be not Conrad's cat's-cradle of a tale, no, but Conrad himself, his repute; for it was now a fine thing to be reading "the new Conrad."

"So potent is Mr. Conrad's name now," said the *Glasgow News* accurately, "that the book has already gone through four or five editions." Everywhere the press fawned. ". . . the spell, . . . the entrancement, which Mr. Conrad's writing produces"—*Daily Chronicle*. "It is a red-letter day in the life of a reviewer when a new novel by Mr. Conrad falls to his lot"—*Spectator*. "Joseph Conrad is one of the marvels of our literature"—*Daily Telegraph*. "Much nearer wizardry than workmanship"—*Punch*.

How do such things happen? Mysteriously, about 1914, he was a celebrity; and it was as works by a magician of genius that the weary contrivances of his last ten years would be hailed one by one. Even adverse reviews of *The Rover* (1923) illustrate the principle that an acclaimed master will always in time be seen to fall short of what he was acclaimed for.

We're starting to encounter historical fortuity: here, a great innovator belauded for his "style," for his "method," for everything save his great innovation. Conrad had come to London for the same reason Catullus and Virgil and Ovid came to Rome. London was the capital of the civilized world. That's hard to remember now. He studied, in a tongue painstakingly acquired, what, for better and for worse, the virtuosi of the capital had to teach him: "I knew it—I was sure!" and hollow tricks of cadence fine writers had long been swotting from Sir Thomas Browne. Though his forte was never the novel but the novella, he paid the rent by grinding out novel after novel as doggedly as any denizen of New Grub Street. And he may never have known that in *Typhoon*, in *The Nigger of the "Narcissus,"* above all in "Heart of Darkness"—all in a few years at about the turn of the century—he had altered the narrative norms of his adopted language forever.

In 1911 Lloyd George proposed a rapid fix for some of the Industrial Revolution's accumulated damage. In the most industrialized country in the world, 4d. deducted weekly (by compulsion) from your wages would be added to 3d. from your employer and 2d. from the taxpayer. For that you'd be insured against sickness. Over furious opposition, his National Insurance Bill passed. Thirty-three years later Britons would be hearing of "cradle-to-grave" security against everything save paid busybodies. Neither fiction nor poetry took stock of such matters; certainly not a novelist known to specialize in the taut autonomy of seamen.

4 : THE TONE OF THINGS

One distinction between poems and novels was that poems got printed with an irregular right-hand margin, and another was that novels contained overt information but poems did not. The sheer informative power of popular fiction should be reckoned with. Listen to a cab-driver in a novel:

> He ran as far as the corner, and then seeing my cab, he hailed me and jumped in. "Drive me to Halliday's Private Hotel," said he.

That is from *A Study in Scarlet* by Arthur Conan Doyle, and if you were set down in the London of 1888 it contains all the practical guidance you would need for taking a horse-drawn cab. It is even clear that you could expect the driver to find a hotel without being told its address. From another page you may glean the Londoner's colloquial name for such a cab: it is "growler."

Or perhaps your ambition in 1888 is to drive a cab yourself. How might you go about that, how would you be paid, what might be the singular difficulties of the calling? Again the cabby in the novel obliges:

> I applied at a cab-driver's office, and soon got employment. I was to bring a certain sum a week to the owner, and whatever was over that I might keep for myself. There was seldom much over, but I managed to scrape along somehow. The hardest job was to learn my way about, for I reckon that of all the mazes that ever were contrived, this city is the most confusing. I had a map beside me, though, and when once I had spotted the principal hotels and stations, I got on pretty well.*

* Note "reckon," by the way, to denote American speech. That was *Strand Magazine* realism.

On the whole inessential to the novel's plot, these bits of vicarious living lend it color and plausibility. They could also have, for the avid consumer of fiction, a cumulative educational value. Fiction, an essentially urban genre, taught many provincials how to cope with the city: how to order a meal, send a telegram, register at a hotel. Even now, a century later, the Holmes saga tells us how trains were looked up in a book called Bradshaw. Such information clings to the pages of fiction like lint.

Earlier, it had clung to verses likewise. Homer catalogued ships, and helped his hearers remember practical formulae like the way to address a priest. Millennia later the world of his translator Pope is densely particularized still. The game of ombre in *The Rape of the Lock* has even been reconstructed card by card. Less arduously, from a single line—

> And the press'd watch returns a silver sound

—we may learn how a fashionable lady got the hour, by pressing a little button and then counting.

But the curiosity, the avidity for detail, that Pope and his readers share was soon to become the wrong kind of attention for poetry, the province of which came to be the grandeur of generality: *subjective* generality too. With Pope dead just a few decades, we find Wordsworth still valuing information very highly, often as a means of persuading his reader that some incident he narrates has really occurred— "the point is two or three yards below the outlet of Grisdale tarn, on a foot-bridge by which a horse may pass to Paterdale—a ridge of Helvellyn on the left, and the summit of Fairfield on the right"—but we do not find such details in Wordsworth's poems; we find them in author's notes. Or he will specify in a title, as he won't in a poem: "Lines Composed a Few Miles Above Tintern Abbey on Revisiting the Banks of the Wye During a Tour. July 13, 1798." His pleasure in recording minutiae is clear, and his sense that they belong on his page. Yet somehow they cannot exist inside his poetry; more exactly, the poetry can no longer exist around them.

> I've measured it from side to side;
> 'Tis three feet long and two feet wide.

Those lines were in "The Thorn" once, but he wisely took them out.

Thereafter, for more than a century, whoever wrote a poem left out of it any trace of a considerable part of his mind. Though Shelley treasured factual lore—his special passion was chemistry—you can collect little meteorology from what he writes of "The Cloud," and though Tennyson had enough of the *Tit-Bits* sensibility to remember from Darwin how blue-eyed cats are generally deaf, his way of utilizing this information is to make chucklehead Gawain cry,

> I will be deafer than the blue-eyed cat
> And thrice as blind as any noon-day owl
> To holy virgins and their ecstasies
> Henceforward. . . .

—quite as though it were not science but a quaint old oath. For hard-and-fast verifiability we must return to, oh, Conan Doyle, who can name the dealers the Hound of the Baskervilles was bought from, Ross and Mangles, and their address, Fulham Road. It would not be surprising if they once existed.

Poetry, therefore, it came to be understood, doesn't *tell* you anything save that its author is excited or resigned or in some such state.

IMPRESSION DE NUIT

LONDON

> See what a mass of gems the city wears
> Upon her broad live bosom! row on row
> Rubies and emeralds and amethysts glow.
> See! that huge circle like a necklace, stares
> With thousands of bold eyes to heaven, and dares
> The golden stars to dim the lamps below,
> And in the mirror of the mire I know
> The moon has left her image unawares. . . .

That is by Oscar's pal Lord Alfred Douglas. Recognizing an octave, you brace yourself for a sestet. When it comes, you scent the nineties in its rhymes:

—breasts
—towers
—breath

—rests
—death
—flowers.

You recognize too how poetry feeds off poetry; we have here a hectic night-piece spun off a well-known early-morning sonnet of Wordsworth's—

> . . . The City now doth like a garment wear
> The beauty of the morning; silent, bare
> Ships, towers, domes, theatres and temples lie
> Open unto the fields and to the sky,
> All bright and glittering in the smokeless air. . . .

Wordsworth does tell us that in 1802 you could see ships from Westminster Bridge, but young Douglas doesn't tell us much of anything save that lots of lamps are aglow. If his poem led you to think the streets of London were aglow with amethysts and rubies, you'd be mistaken. We are talking of what came to be called Poetic License. Douglas might be describing a Nocturne by Whistler.

Art is feeding on art. Whistler titled his paintings as though they were pieces of music. (Nocturnes, as by Chopin. And when someone asked why his *Symphony in White* had so little white in it, Whistler demanded whether a Symphony in F was "a continued repetition of F F F.") Likewise *fin-de-siècle* poets titled their books as if they were paintings—*Silhouettes*, *Silverpoints*. Whistler having invented their visual world, they liked mists and twilights, which selected the details for them. Hence in the poets' city it always seems to be night:

> . . . Lamp after lamp against the sky
> Opens a sudden beaming eye,
> Leaping alight on either hand,
> The iron lilies of the Strand.
>
> Like dragonflies, the hansoms hover,
> With jewelled eyes, to catch the lover,
> The streets are full of lights and loves,
> Soft gowns, and flutter of soiled doves.

> Upon thy petals butterflies,
> But at thy root, some say, there lies
> A world of weeping trodden things,
> Poor worms that have not eyes or wings.
>
> . . .
>
> Men die and rot deep out of sight
> To keep this jungle-flower bright. . . .

Working out his vision of London as a huge exotic flower, Richard Le Gallienne in 1892 has sighted the Eloi and the Morlocks; has even located the latter "deep out of sight." But verse won't let him *do* anything with the perception. That will require a writer of prose fiction.

Le Gallienne's instinct was to work with hard little bits of detail, such as "poetry" resisted. When he called his poem "A Ballad of London," it was partly because "Ballad" implied light verse, and particularity had withdrawn into light verse.

> There was a Boy whose name was Jim;
> His Friends were very good to him.
> They gave him Tea, and Cakes, and Jam,
> And slices of delicious Ham, . . .
> And read him stories through and through. . . .

—H. Belloc in 1907; and it would have been hard to pack so much exact naming into a Swinburnian cadence. In Le Gallienne's "Ballad of London" you can detect him longing to be specific but being inhibited by "poetry." The lamps are being lit one after another, in the ritual that starts up the city's evening, and he hopes to make something of that perception. Then "The iron lilies of the Strand" says something vague about their shape, something too perhaps about their metallic coldness, and it closes off the stanza stillborn. ("Lily" is a poetry-word.) One test of an age is the use it can make of its minor talents, and of Le Gallienne (1866–1947), distinctly a minor talent, nothing at all coherent got made.

Nor, for all his genius at interpreting the French, did Arthur Symons come to much as a poet either. When on his own he did best with moods and landscapes:

ON THE BEACH

Night, a grey sky, a ghostly sea,
The soft beginning of the rain;
Black on the horizon, sails that wane
Into the distance mistily.

. . .

I cannot think or dream; the grey
Unending waste of sea and night,
Dull, impotently infinite,
Blots out the very hope of day.

—June 18, 1890.

As you can tell from the stanza, he's been reading *In Memoriam*—you can generally tell what Symons has been reading—and you wish he had Tennyson's skill at modulating the pace of iambics. But not only is Symons distinctly a minor poet; poetry itself has become a minor genre, in which to do little "studies," mood-pieces, agreeable trifles. The sole exception in his generation was William Butler Yeats, and what had saved him was the fortunate discovery of his "Irish" heritage. Yeats was a major talent; he was also possessed by a vocation, to create a soul for his country.

Something was happening to fiction too. We were calling it an essentially urban genre, and one reason is that both a novel and a city can be thought of as elaborately organized structures of information. We can know a great deal about people who live in cities without knowing *them* at all; an address in particular may be highly informative. With conspicuous exceptions such as *Wuthering Heights*, English fiction after Defoe had tended to exploit the special particularities of the urban: streets with names, districts of repute, houses made of brick or stucco, detached or semi-detached; places of business, real or imagined but namable; regular comings and goings, regulated hours. Into such a grid the equally discrete persons and doings of the story can be fitted. Everyone knows the address of Sherlock Holmes, 221B Baker Street, and the name of his landlady, Mrs. Hudson. No one understood the principle like Joyce, and Mr. Bloom's authentic front door with the knocker on it was preserved from the demolition of 7 Eccles Street. You can see it on display in the foyer of a Duke Street pub, with an informative placard adjoined.

Now, it was just that order of information that Henry James was at pains to dissolve out of his fictions; from the soft-focus Coburn photographs he commissioned for his New York Edition we might gather, without so much as sampling his words, that urban atmospheres meant far more to James than urban specificities. Atmospheres were what people perceived, so they were what mattered; impersonal specifics you could get out of Baedeker, the way Joyce would get them from Thom's Dublin Directory. Nothing is more conspicuous in *The Spoils of Poynton* (1897) than James's omitting to describe the spoils of Poynton. Conducing as they do to an atmosphere of taste and luxury, their condition is to be but semi-visible ("the glow of a Venetian lamp just showed on either wall, in perfect proportion, a small but splendid tapestry") or even merely palpable ("the very fingers of her glove, resting on the seat of the sofa, had thrilled at the touch of an old velvet brocade").

But about horrors James can be ferociously particular: about "the maddening relics of Waterbath, the little brackets and pink vases, the sweepings of bazaars, the family photographs and illuminated texts, the 'household art' and household piety of Mona's hideous home"; or the pathetic souvenirs of Mr. Vetch: "old brandy-flasks and match-boxes, old calendars and hand-books, intermixed with an assortment of penwipers and ash-trays, a harvest gathered in from penny bazaars." Inventories comport with his rhetoric of contempt, or of tolerant deprecation; we are to understand that the Brigstocks' pink vases claw at civilized attention in the manner of obscene words, while as for Mr. Vetch, who must reckon his resources to the penny, "the harvest of penny bazaars" is the best he can hope to reap. Yet reap he will, fancying as he does that he has "a taste for fine things." In the 1908 preface James designates "that most modern of our current passions, the fierce appetite for the upholsterer's and joiner's and brazier's work, the chairs and tables, the cabinets and presses, the material odds and ends, of the more labouring ages." Mrs. Gereth at Poynton and Mr. Vetch in West Kensington suffer alike from this passion, each a predator upon some past.

In emptying fiction of its cherished tangibilities, James must not be suspected of reducing it to the vacuity at which verse had arrived. Things and places do exist in his world—indeed, supremely exist—

but they exist only as people value them, or covet them, or take them blankly for granted, or are ruthless in *using* other people by means of them, as Mrs. Gereth condescendingly uses Fleda Vetch. His fictions throb with motive and perception, frustration and hollow triumph: in short, with the crises of human consciousness, something he was inclined to equate with human life. When he complains that someone else's book is deficient in "life," he means only that areas of awareness have been elided, the writer, out of haste to get on with the story, having missed fiction's supreme opportunity.

James yearned for a fiction of uncluttered dramatic pressure, three-dimensional moving X-rays to show globes of awareness impinging, yielding, collapsing: a fiction in which everything of interest would have to be intangible. To that end he even dissipated what had been the core of the prose-writer's craft, the grammar of firm subject, active verb, picturable object: man kicks dog, dog bites man. Many readers will not have so much as noticed that *The Spoils of Poynton* turns on a ruthless seduction (of the hero, by his fiancée): fancy a novelist throwing that away! But the Jamesian care is for such nuances as this (from a different book): "She was not, the mourning niece, in her first youth, and her vanished freshness had left something behind which, for Stransom, represented the proof that it had been tragically sacrificed": the center of that sentence is "for Stransom," not what she said or did but what Stransom made of it; and whatever it was, it "represented" a "proof." On that principle, the seduction in *The Spoils* matters only for what Mrs. Gereth and Fleda make of it.

A reviewer of 1895 was reminded of "a skein of wool after a kitten has played with it," and asserted that "English of the normal pattern" could say it all "as fully and with infinitely better effect." The judgment is understandable but untrue.

The late manner toward which he moved through his long career is not empty but replete, though with elements so hard to specify they've challenged critic after critic. Seymour Chatman's *The Later Style of Henry James* is taut and dense with observation and 135 pages long, and proves by its strictness of specification that the labyrinthine sentences of the last phase neither grope nor fumble but go about their business with a definite method. His clinching proof is interesting: you can tell a good parody of James from a bad one, because the accurate parodist (Max Beerbohm) appears to have access to the Master's very tool-chest.* The bad parodist is merely prolix, as though wordiness were all it came to.

The tool-chest's contents when we see them laid out resemble less the rich spoils of Poynton than Mr. Vetch's penny-bazaar cullings. Fine up-to-date edged instruments the Master had cast aside, in favor of what his infinite patience could improvise from old tin-tacks and loops of string. Thus dead metaphors and tired clichés abound, their staleness disguised by their air of lending zest to yet bleaker clichés. With these he could evoke the omnipresent social vocabulary but not have to reproduce its vapid talk. "He conveyed in every phrase that he had done with the flesh and the devil and was counting the hours till he should re-enter the true temple of his faith": such a sentence lets nullity sound nearly philosophical, which is what nullity is trying to be.

Often abstractions suppress some plenitude of listing: Chatman calls our attention to the moment when the "chatter, candlelight, plates, silver, jewelry" of a dinner party are subsumed into one large word, "phenomena": ". . . appearances insisted and phenomena multiplied and words reached her from here and there like plashes of a slow, thick tide." (Did the conversation bear quoting he'd no doubt quote it, but no Disraeli or Wilde is ruling *that* table.)

Sentences will prolong and prolong themselves, as though groping for exit, with "a qualifying element of deliberate self-parody" Arthur Mizener has well compared to the frontier tall tale. "What was dreadful now, what was horrible, was the intimate ugliness of Waterbath, and it was of that phenomenon these ladies talked while they sat in the shade and drew refreshment from the great tranquil sky, whence no cheap blue plates depended"—his characteristic terminal crash of sudden concreteness, an effect many remembered from his conversation, the delays and hesitations of which were intrinsic to the performance. "Wu-a-wait a little, wait a little, something will come," Ezra Pound mimicked him saying, the same afternoon he likened the unforeseeable last words' impact to that of a pile-driver.

Or, as studied vagueness multiplies the options, uncertainty may be left to accumulate. Ambiguities in the key terms, by Chatman's amusing computation, leave one twenty-eight-word sentence open to exactly 960 different defensible paraphrases.

---

* Reading Beerbohm had an odd effect on James: it left him unable to write with any ease, from anxiety lest he be parodying himself.

The James world is a world of disappointed hopes, not least for any reader who expects either of the two things readers feel entitled to: an easy read, a last page open toward a marriage. The marriages almost never come off, and the reading is seldom easy. Nor were James's own hopes better served. His first royalty check from the great New York Edition, in which he'd invested four years of rewriting and prefacing and most of his financial plans for old age, was $211.

The reviewer James's prose reminded of a kitten in yarn was H. G. Wells, who had just published *The Time Machine* and was hacking for Frank Harris's *Saturday Review* while he worked at making his name. His review (1 June 1895) was anonymous in the bad old English fashion, and James in the subsequent years of their acquaintance likely never knew that his forceful young friend had written it.

Now, Wells was by no means a Philistine reader. Two weeks later he hailed the unknown Joseph Conrad's *Almayer's Folly* ("a work of art" to "haunt the memory"), and he was quick to remark Henry James's "eyes for human beings." But the James prose bothered him, as Conrad's would soon bother him. The next year he would write of *An Outcast of the Islands* that the "wordy" Mr. Conrad's second story "is not so much told as seen intermittently through a haze of sentences." That resembles a trope he'd already applied to James, through whose "ground-glass style," he said, "you can just discern . . . men and women as trees walking." Wells was the representative story-reader, impatient when words slowed him down. For some purposes that made him an ideal reviewer, though at this distance we extol other purposes.

He had first seen James on 5 January 1895, the most miserable night of Henry James's life. That was the night they booed his play *Guy Domville*, and when he was led onstage they booed *him*. "A little white Christian virgin," James had called his play, destined for throwing "to the lions and tigers." Some of the dread carnivores held critics' credentials. These included Mr. George Bernard Shaw, 38, an unsuccessful dramatist who was reviewing for the *Saturday Review*; Mr. Enoch Arnold Bennett, 27, assistant editor of *Women*, where he did plays under the pseudonym "Cecile"; and Mr. Herbert George Wells, 27, who on becoming the *Pall Mall Gazette*'s drama critic only three days before had needed dress clothes fabricated overnight. Apart from the pantomime and Gilbert and Sullivan, *Guy Domville* was the fourth play he had ever seen. ("You won't be in the gang," said his editor; "You'll make a break.")

Each had ahead of him a career in letters that would coin more money than James ever saw in his life. In the face of the facile myths that surround that night, we should recall that these men of the future did not hoot. Shaw thought the play too good for "the handful of rowdies" who yelled. Bennett discerned "fitful beauty" and "gems of dialogue." And Wells (*Pall Mall Gazette*, 7 January 1895) called it (bating certain defects) "a play finely conceived and beautifully written." But already he had a reservation: the play was *too* finely written for the stage, which requires bold strokes. That would be, for years to come, the Wells problem with James: "Delicate work simply blurs and looks weak."

In 1898 they met, to be friends for a decade and a half. ("I bothered him," Wells remembered, "and he bothered me.") James first showed up on a bicycle, which was salutary. In those days a bicycle was something for which you took lessons, and the Master, having taken them, rode about the environs of Rye under a peaked cap and in knickerbockers and an exiguous jacket striped black and white. Machines in their next generation would abstract humankind from legs, but cycling was a gaily accelerated walking. Those were bicycle times, as we now know computer times; only Sam Beckett has preserved their élan. The Time Machine with its saddle was itself a transfigured bicycle. Wells's third novel, *The Wheels of Chance* (1896), had been all about bicyclists, and editing *Bicycling News* was an early upward step for the fellow who would one day own *The Times* and be known as Lord Northcliffe. Resentful coachmen still lashed out their whips at cyclists, who felt united in sporty camaraderie. Henry James could not have made a less mandarin entrance into the class-obsessed awareness of H. G. Wells.

He and Edmund Gosse had biked over to find out discreetly whether Wells, in ill health and author of six published novels, needed help from the Royal Literary Fund. (He did not.) James invited Wells to visit him at Rye, where he lived in Lamb House and distributed his energies among eight writing-tables. Numerous visits ensued, and they would have talked shop, the thing James most loved to talk though he'd few to talk it with. But this young man, though "cheeky," was quick and articulate; he showed signs of becoming the old sorcerer's diligent apprentice. By early 1900 James had gotten round to reading "the particular masterpiece entitled *The Time Machine*." "You are very magnificent. I am beastly critical—but you are in a still higher degree wonderful."

Later he expanded on his way of being beastly critical. "My sole and single way of perusing the fiction of Another is to *write it over*— even when most immortal—as I go. Write it over, I mean, *re*-compose it, in the light of my own high sense of propriety and with immense embellishments." He'd done this to *The First Men in the Moon*, "and the superstructure I reared upon it had almost no resemblance to, or nothing in common (*but* the subject!) with, yours." This book, of which Wells had fumbled the potential, would not leave hold of the Master's imagination, and he offered a thoroughly amazing proposal:

> It is, the whole thing, stupendous, but do you know what the main effect of it was on my cheeky consciousness? To make me sigh, on some such occasion, to *collaborate* with you, to intervene in the interest of— well I scarce know what to call it. . . . Our mixture *would*, I think, be effective. I hope you are thinking of doing Mars—in some detail. Let me in *there*, at the right moment—or in other words at an early stage. . . .

The mind gambols. . . .

> It was not altogether disagreeably unfitting, rather, given the case, all too unbeguilingly not to be evaded, that his lot, as it presented itself to Camshaft, was to be, at the final tick of the dread clock, to close fingers precisely *his* and to close them precisely on the trigger of the afterburner. Nor, amid such a wealth of unexampled impressions—of the *canali* and their implied, even—dared he guess?—tentacled, architects, of topographical ruddiness and mercilessness, of unthinkable orbital if not occipital precisions—could it fail to present itself as implacably *given* that the "touchdown" to ensue would be of a touchiness, of a perilousness even, such as no guardians of far-flung thin red lines had in whatever storied distentions of Empire been required hitherto by destiny to shoulder. . . .

But no, it wasn't the *writing* James had proposed to do; what he'd offered was to assist with a scenario from which Wells might write. A James scenario unblest by his mannerisms, brought to life through the "cheeky" prose of H. G. Wells: one would give a great deal to see that.

Alas, nothing happened. For some while it had been apparent that Wells with pen in hand was an artist only part-time. Bang at the new century's turn, he'd taken to frankly designing futures, better ones than the Time Traveller encountered, and moreover with hopes of getting them implemented. *Anticipations* . . . (1901) is not a novel but a book of didactic essays about where we might all be going if we put our minds to it: not to Mars but to a eugenically ordered World State with Free Love, lots of Education, and breeding by the under-qualified prohibited. Its resemblance to the Oceania of *1984* has been noticed, though in 1901 it could seem seductive. That book was what finally got H. G. Wells talked about all over Europe. In a year there were eight printings for countless thousands of readers, one of whom (Henry James) said coyly, "my world *is*, somehow, other," while another (Leopold Bloom) said nothing on record but by 1904 would be indulging Wellsian fantasies that extended to electric dish-scrub-bers, the abolition of old scourges—tuberculosis, war, lunacy, men-dicancy—and, triumphantly, "Free money, free love and a free lay church in a free lay state."

Thereafter, when James unwrapped yet another new book from Wells—there were frequently two in a year—he could never be sure that some didactic idea hadn't run off with the disciple's narrative conscience. He admired, surely envied, H.G.'s ability to carry readers with him, and not by having taken "the measure of the huge flat foot of the public"; no, by sheer infectious zest. But need the public be whirled on such a paper-chase?

The end came as late as 1914, and suddenly. In the very essay that gave Conrad pain, his survey of "The Younger Generation" for the *TLS*, James held Wells aloft in public by the tail, a naughty mouse. He had tired of the ever-renewing "cheek," of the vast talent that could throw off a near-masterwork like *Kipps* unheeding: that never cared or even knew what subjects it squandered. "A novelist very much as Lord Bacon was a philosopher"—that is, a dabbler with a reputation—Wells was lost within the wonders of his own mind. And the Master cranked up a great unforgettable unforgiveable sentence:

The more he knows and knows—or at any rate learns and learns—the more, in other words, he establishes his saturation—the greater is our impression of his holding it good enough for us, such as we are, that he shall but turn out his mind and its contents upon us by any free familiar gesture and as from a high window forever open. . . .

. . . as they did in Pope's age with chamber pots.

Uncushioned now by the "mere twaddle of graciousness" that had muffled his response to the new book Wells flung at him every few months, that was what he'd obliquely signaled to H.G., over and over. Uncushioned, though, it hurt, and we can't doubt he meant it to; there lay hidden in James an alarming strain of cruelty. The response of Wells is famous. He hurried some supplementary pages into a pot-pourri he'd accumulated during thirteen years, and rushed it all into print as *Boon*. He then left a copy for Mr. Henry James at the Reform Club. James received it on 5 July 1915. Just 150 days remained to him before the stroke that augured, he is said to have said, "The Distinguished Thing."

Struck by what he felt as the treachery of James, Wells had re-membered something undistinguished: his own fancy of a kitten and string, amid the twaddlings of "The Altar of the Dead." The never-forgotten sentences of *Boon* ran as follows:

> The only living human motives left in the novels of Henry James are a certain avidity and an entirely superficial curiosity. . . . His people nose out suspicions, hint by hint, link by link. Have you ever known living human beings do that? [Yes.] The thing his novel is *about* is always there. . . . It is like a church lit but without a congregation to distract you, with every light and line focused on the high altar. And on the altar, very reverently placed, intensely there, is a dead kitten, an egg-shell, a bit of string. . . . Like his "Altar of the Dead," with nothing to the dead at all. . . .
>
> His vast paragraphs sweat and struggle; they could not sweat and elbow and struggle more if God Himself was the processional meaning to which they sought to come. And all for tales of nothingness. . . . It is leviathan retrieving pebbles. It is a magnificent but painful hippo-potamus resolved at any cost . . . upon picking up a pea which has got into a corner of its den. Most things, it insists, are beyond it, but it can, at any rate, modestly, and with an artistic singleness of mind, pick up that pea. . . .

The wrong questions, the wrong answers, there's nothing like them. "The thing his novel is *about* is always there": that distilled H. G.

Wells's resentment at the Jamesian insistence on a producible theme. "I don't think," H. J. had written on *Ann Veronica*, ". . . that I even make out what your subject or Idea, the prime determinant one, may be detected as having *been*," not even though the book was "irresistible (and indescribable)." But H.G. held a novel to be "a discursive thing . . . not a single interest, but a woven tapestry of interests," so that your purpose could shift as you wrote. All you had to do was keep your reader from quitting; and hadn't he done that with James? Hadn't James often said so?

They were talking about utterly different things: H.J. about an ideal Novel he himself, even, had never succeeded in writing (time and time again he'd "foreshortened" middles and ends, having lavished too much on beginnings); H.G. about the artless pleasures of a discursiveness that held people entranced by telling them stories—had Jesus, he might have thought to add, spurned that? James responded to *Boon* with his final and most eloquent paean to Art: "It is art that *makes* life, makes interest, makes importance, for our consideration and application of these things, and I know of no substitute whatsoever for the force and beauty of its processes." That can carry us far past what he had made of Art.

Wells, to be sure, had no artistic future; save in part for *The Outline of History*, nothing he wrote in the forty years after 1905 stays read. But Henry James lacked artistic progeny; what he'd brought the novel to he alone could survive with: a dead end like Beckett's. He and Beckett are our virtuosi of the dead end, playing there each man hand after hand of his own intent necessary solitaire, intricate in its quasi-colloquial abstractions, minimal in its referentiality, inauthentic for anyone else to attempt. His etiolation, yes, Virginia Woolf would inherit, for the playing of her own variations, and she's had no descendants either. As for H. G. Wells, his inheritors are too numerous to contemplate or to examine: write in any names sufficiently audible and you'll not be wrong. Don't forget the BBC.

5 : AN EDUCATION

1 : *Yeats*

In September 1908 Ezra Weston Loomis Pound, M.A., arrived in London from the U.S.A. via Venice, where he'd had a book called *A Lume Spento* printed. His hope was to learn from William Butler Yeats, whom he thought the best poet alive. That would have surprised much of literary London, where they deemed Mr. Yeats an exotic. True, he lived in London, but so did all manner of strange people, including those Russian anarchists.

Yeats was known to dabble in the occult; also rumor had it that he believed in fairies. Max drew him, languid and long-toothed, in the act of presenting a bemused and worldly George Moore to the Faery Queen. Rumor didn't understand that the wild Irish *sidhe* had nothing at all in common with Tinker Bell. Nor did it grasp the special quality of Yeatsian belief; the Order of the Golden Dawn had eased him out when his tentativeness became a nuisance to enthusiasts.

In the mid-nineties Yeats had roomed with Arthur Symons (and thus learned all about the Symbolist Movement without having to wait for the book Symons finally published). But in '96 he took up with the lady he calls "Diana Vernon," the one for whom he wrote "He Bids His Beloved Be at Peace," full of trampling Horses of Disaster whose tumult only her peace can overrule. They moved with borrowed furniture to 18 Woburn Buildings, near Euston Station, where a cobbler lived on the ground floor and an old peddler who made watercolors lived in the attic. After she faded out of his intimacy he stayed on in the two-room walk-up. It was to be his address for twenty-four years, and the sort of address stuffiness could condescend to. There's a plaque on it now.

The previous year he had published the *Poems* he'd be known by for decades, and though its lyrics were everywhere marked with the subtlest craft of Yeats they were rather a tradition's end than the start of anything new. Yeats in 1895, as Peter Makin reminds us, could draw on skills his English predecessors had been elaborating for seventy-five years. Applying these entailed confinement within

> . . . a special area of images (tender, woven, mouse-grey, solitary, gold, silver, wandering, veils) and of diction ("chaunt," "high"; "boughs" and not "branches"; "seek" and not "look for," "cry" and not "shout," "breast" not "chest," "wend" not "go"). Also of sound: the consonants and vowels in these words, for example, help to select them as being suitable for collocation in patterns of the soft and keening alternating with sharp sudden cries.

And "it took most of the nineteenth century to get from Keats via Tennyson and Morris" to the cunning elaborations of W. B. Yeats.

The main reason for "boughs" and not "branches" is that nothing Yeatsian can be done with the *sound* of "branches." But "boughs" has an open vowel, which makes the syllable not only stressed but what Latin scansion calls "long." (In English classrooms they mentioned only stress, one reason effects that depend on quantity could seem "Celtic.") By cunning application of long syllables the pace of a line can be slowed and then released, so iambics won't march past on booted feet. You can catch the principle when there's but one long vowel in the line—

> Under a bitter black wind that blows from the left hand

—and the voice must linger on "blows" while the lips shape its terminal sibilant. You can study more extensive possibilities in something like this:

> . . . Come near, that no more blinded by men's fate,
> I find under the boughs of love and hate,
> In all poor foolish things that live a day,
> Eternal beauty wandering on her way.

If you try repeating that second line aloud—

> I find under the boughs of love and hate

you experience not only a dwelling of your voice on "boughs" but also a cadence shaped by the vowel-rhyme of "I find" and by the short and long vowels of "love and hate," a cadence nowhere repeated in the poem. Nor is *any* cadence repeated, and that's so exotic you may wonder if the sanctioned iambic pentameter is really in charge. (It is.)

Yeats's effects were hypnotic, seldom semantic. Lost in those intricacies of cadence the way the eye gets lost in Burne-Jones intertwinings, minds moved as through a thick, delicious syrup. "Dreamheavy" was a phrase the book itself supplied; it took substantial effort to make out what the words were saying. None of that was for the Everyman's Library public: for the *Yellow Book* public, perhaps. The first poets admitted into Everyman's Library were Browning and Tennyson, Coleridge and Burns and Keats. Next came Adelaide A. Proctor, and then Shakespeare. That made six accredited classics and one poet Everyman could understand every word of. Miss Proctor (1825–1864) had commanded sales second only to the Laureate's, a fact not lost on canny J. M. Dent. Her best-known poem was "A Lost Chord," which began,

> Seated one day at the Organ,
>   I was weary and ill at ease,
> And my fingers wandered idly
>   Over the noisy keys.
>
> I do not know what I was playing,
>   Or what I was dreaming then;
> But I struck one chord of music,
>   Like the sound of a great Amen. . . .

She says she's been hunting for it ever since; maybe only "Death's bright angel" will disclose it. Death was Miss Proctor's surest resource of pathos; her American edition had an "Introduction" by Charles Dickens, ending with a Little Nell account of how she herself died. "She said: It has come at last! And with a bright and happy smile looked upward and departed." That, like her verse, was improving and spoke to the heart.

Miss Proctor's was to be the norm of schoolroom poetry for two generations and more, teachable because what it said was deep-felt and easy to extricate. Mr. Yeats by unsettling comparison—

Red Rose, proud Rose, sad Rose of all my days!
Come near me while I sing the ancient ways:
Cuchulain battling with the bitter tide;
The Druid, grey, wood-nurtured, quiet-eyed,
Who cast round Fergus dreams, and ruin untold . . .

—yes, about Mr. Yeats there did hover that aura of *decadence*.

It hovered about Ezra Pound too. A copy of *A Lume Spento* made its way to the *Evening Standard & Saint James's Gazette*, where a reviewer found in it "wild haunting stuff, absolutely poetic, original, imaginative, passionate and spiritual. Those who do not consider it crazy may well consider it inspired. Coming after the trite and decorous verse of most of our decorous poets, this poet seems like a minstrel of Provence at a suburban musical evening. . . ." That would not have enticed any fan of Adelaide Proctor's. If you were someone it did entice, Mr. Pound's book could be had from John Lane or from Elkin Mathews, names we've met before. After founding *The Yellow Book* they had split up.* Their bookshops, across Vigo Street from each other, Pound considered "the two peaks of Parnassus." That makes his allegiance to aestheticism explicit. He had just turned 23.

John Lane and Elkin Mathews had been known for the books of poetry they published, often books with unusual proportions dictated by the fancy paper they could buy in odd lots. The Pound of *A Lume Spento* had imitated their kind of poet indiscriminately, now Symons, now Ernest Dowson, now "Fiona Macleod" (who was really William Sharp), with numerous echoes of Yeats and with Dante Gabriel Rossetti everywhere.

So he might expect to find his London publisher on Vigo Street, and in January 1909 Elkin Mathews accepted *Personae*. Books could be produced fast in those days; it was out in April, and got reviewed (". . . something of a haunting charm"—*Daily Telegraph*; ". . . discontinuous and meaningless exclamations"—*Nation*). By late October, Mathews had issued yet another collection, *Exultations*, from which it was clear that Yeats had formally entered the young poet's system of influences. This time the *Nation* was pleased enough to quote

---

* Lane seems to have thought his more prudent partner a drag. In 1916 Mathews would censor Pound's *Lustra*; earlier he'd been nervous about "The Ballad of the Goodly Fere," which he printed with a disclaimer.

> Pale hair that the moon has shaken
> Down over the dark breast of the sea . . .

and to judge him "less derivative" than previously, though that hair
and moon are Yeatsian and the second line remembers the Yeats of
"white breast of the dim sea." The reviewer's "less derivative" simply
meant "more like what I'm somehow used to."

The "pale hair" detail belonged to a ten-poem sequence from which
the *Nation*'s man might have quoted more:

I

> When your beauty is grown old in all men's songs,
> And my poor words are lost amid that throng,
> Then you will know the truth of my poor words,
> And mayhap dreaming of the wistful throng
> That hopeless sigh your praises in their songs,
> You will think kindly then of these mad words.

II

> I am torn, torn with thy beauty,
> O Rose of the sharpest thorn!
> O Rose of the crimson beauty,
> Why hast thou awakened the sleeper?
> Why has thou awakened the heart within me,
> O Rose of the crimson thorn? . . .

The cadence and the studied repetitions of Part I have their precedent
on many pages of *The Wind Among the Reeds*; the Rose of Part II is
a symbol on which Yeats had held the patent since 1893. On almost
every one of the ninety-seven lines some mark of Yeats is discernible.
The excellences, by and large, are early-Yeatsian, the incompetences
("mayhap," "within me") early-Poundian. Even Yeats's majestic way
with the epithet is imitated, "The innumerable voices" being a timid
echo of "O sweet everlasting Voices."

The echoes are so systematic we're clearly meant to perceive them
and take the whole sequence for impassioned homage. It even has a
Latin title, to remember the *Liber Inducens in Evangelium Aeternum*
Yeats had invented in 1897 in a story he published in Symons's *Savoy*.
Pound called his sequence, not without wit, "Laudantes Decem Pul-
chritudinis Johannae Templi," Ten Praises for the Beauty of Joan of
the Temple, "Joan" being the way Rossetti had Englished Dante's

and Guido Cavalcanti's Giovanna in translations Pound had read in Dent's Temple Classics. So that knot has curious strands: W. B. Yeats, D. G. Rossetti, early Italian masters, the tradition of Ideal Ladies on whom naming confers existence, and (not least) the indispensable acumen of J. M. Dent, whose bilingual editions, little heavier than our tape cassettes and elegant though cheap, were a students' resource for decades. With firm covers and a ribbon marker, they sold for a shilling. There's nothing like them now.

By April 1909, probably before writing "Laudantes," Pound had at last gained access to Yeats himself. The route is worth tracing: via Elkin Mathews to the poet Frederic Manning; via Manning to the novelist and salon hostess Olivia Shakespear; then, with the help of Mrs. Shakespear and her daughter Dorothy, at last to W. B. Yeats, back in London from months of Dublin theatre bother. At each stage there were social gatherings that observed the ritual of tea. It differs from the cocktail ritual in this, that over tea people formally converse. The ceremony of tea creates an oasis where a stranger can meet the distinguished at their leisure without being expected to have business he can state. Or so things were.

The editors of the Pound-Shakespear letters remark on the speed with which, at this moment in history, "an alien figure such as Ezra Pound . . . made his way so quickly to the center of things":

> The revolutionary spirit, both literary and political, was quickening year by year. At the same time, the late-Victorian structure of clubs, societies, literary hostesses, country houses, bookshops and serious journals was still in place, offering many opportunities to an ambitious young writer from the provinces.

They add that this world was destroyed in 1914–18. The unconnected must now play blind-man's-buff.

Nor need anyone have come from far to be a provincial in London. Given English susceptibility to class and accent, a Lawrence from the Nottingham collieries or a Bennett from Staffordshire of the potteries commenced by being quite as much the outsider as a fidgety youth whose vowels bespoke Pennsylvania. Like him, both made their way quickly. And if Lawrence met many of the cultivated only to detest them, still in having met them he was forming his values on knowledge.

So it was sponsored by Olivia and Miss Dorothy that Ezra Pound attained 18 Woburn Buildings, where the light was dim and the pictures Pre-Raphaelite. He was soon in regular attendance at the Monday-evening gatherings Yeats held in imitation of Mallarmé's *mardis*. Eventually he'd have learned how Olivia first entered those dim quarters as long ago as when the great bard settled there. For Olivia Shakespear had been "Diana Vernon."

In a milieu differently structured, one offering fewer rites to less secure people, that could have been so embarrassing a coincidence as to interdict access by the Shakespear route. Years later someone who knew Dorothy well would call her "impossibly English." That referred to her long-preserved Edwardian skill at ignoring stickiness in sticky situations. She drew on her social endowment all her long life, till she died, Ezra Pound's widow, aged 87, in 1973.

Now, it was in 1909, according to his own sense of himself, that one W. B. Yeats died. That was the Yeats of "Innisfree," the sinuous, otherworldly galoot of Max's drawings, the Yeats of *Poems* (1895) and *The Wind Among the Reeds*, the author of lyrics to croon and of faery plays like *The Land of Heart's Desire*, the dark, mystic, twilit Celt who'd beguiled the beguilable. His *Collected Works*, eight volumes, had appeared in 1908, a terminal moraine.

The death of newspaper record, 28 January 1939, was, so to speak, a posthumous deed performed by a second Yeats, who'd reconstituted himself from the antimatter of the first, and bought a Tower and lashed out at the world. Yeats II wrote lengthy memoirs of Yeats I, and they terminate in excerpts from a 1909 diary, with for coda an account of the 1923 Nobel Prize ceremonies, which set Swedish royal approval on Yeats I's deeds.

The Yeats Ezra Pound first met in April 1909 was just back from the funeral of J. M. Synge, the event that seems to have determined, in Yeats's mind, that 1909 was the end of one life of his also. And he had already published *In the Seven Woods*, a brief collection that could seem anticlimactic to admirers of his Celtic croon. Instead of songs made "out of a mouthful of air" it offers the studied bleakness of "Adam's Curse":

> . . . I said, 'A line will take us hours maybe;
> Yet if it does not seem a moment's thought,
> Our stitching and unstitching has been naught.

Better go down upon your marrow-bones
And scrub a kitchen pavement, or break stones
Like an old pauper, in all kinds of weather. . . .'

It goes on to itemize "bankers, schoolmasters and clergymen," noisy folk he'd not earlier have accorded so much as a mention, unless in a diary or an article. Now behold such words in a poem! His poetry is opening itself to much more of his mind. And though that speech rhymes, it pretends to be something "said," in idle end-of-summer talk. Yeats hadn't previously let a poem be speech; poems had wanted dim lights and intoning. What it says, moreover, is that to put plain talk on a page, "unpoetic" talk, you must toil till all seems casual. The curse that was laid on Adam was bitter hard work, and poets are not exempt.

This was a Yeats for whom *Exultations* would be a risible title to put on a book of verse, and the Yeats to whom Ezra's *Exultations* would soon offer homage was already disappearing into the yesterday that had claimed his predecessors, Morris and Keats. Pound would call him "a sort of great dim figure, with its associations set in the past." He'd come just too late to profit from the Yeats he'd admired since school days, just in time to glimpse what the next Yeats was bitterly learning. For that the art he had perfected had been the *end* of an English tradition was a fact Yeats was coming to terms with. It took Irish eyes to see something English ending.

And his angel was guiding him. For three years he'd been doing an un-English thing: reading Ben Jonson. Only someone *outside* like an Irishman, someone who in being uncoerced by English destinies might as well read any book as any other, would have done that with serious intent. Fancy Arthur Symons reading Ben Jonson! When last, for that matter, had any poet read Ben Jonson for the good of his art?

Struggling with a verse play in 1906, Yeats had been looking for hints in a dramatist less overwhelming than Shakespeare. That fall he reported, "I am deep in Ben Jonson." Being deep meant going beyond the obvious things, *Volpone* or *The Alchemist*. Eventually he was immersed in what no one had taken seriously before: the *Epigrams*, which aren't epigrams by modern criteria, and the two other sets of short poems, *The Forest* and *Underwoods*. Their language having no glamor, they were what his lyric muse needed.

They included the Ode to the Great House at Penshurst, the two Odes "to Himselfe," the "Fit of Rime Against Rime": clear masculine speaking-out against habit and slackness. Their poetry is so unlike his own in eschewing every opalescent word—no "pearl-pale hand," no "sorrowful loveliness"—that only by miraculous critical intelligence could Yeats have discerned poetry at all.

> Say that thou pour'st hem wheat,
> And they would Akornes eat:
> 'Twere simple fury, still thy selfe to wast
> On such as have no taste:
> To offer them a surfeit of pure bread,
> Whose appetites are dead:
> No, give them Graines their fill,
> Huskes, Draffe* to drinke, and swill:
> If they love Lees, and leave the lusty Wine,
> Envy them not, their pallat's with the Swine.

There's no "tune" in such verses, no sensuous "mouthful of air"; no pretty words even, "boughs" for "branches," or "wend" for "go"; no veils, no gold, no thrill of loneliness; no drawing-out of the sense variously from line to line. No, Ben's hard rhymes with abrupt consonants go to work as with ball-peen hammers, and a populace that dislikes the sound of it all gets itself crisply likened to swilling pigs. And somehow that impressed a man whose best notes had been of another order entirely, notes he had sounded so as to woo, not repel:

> Impetuous heart be still, be still,
> Your sorrowful love can never be told,
> Cover it up with a lonely tune. . . .

When had anyone ever before admired Jonson as a poet at all, save for the seventeenth-century men with swords whose songs derived deft assurance from his "Drink to me only with thine eyes"? And what they had cherished was but a small part of Jonson.

In a few years Yeats would be insulting middle-class Dublin—

> What need you, being come to sense,
> But fumble in the greasy till
> And add the halfpence to the pence
> And prayer to shivering prayer, until

* Draffe: the *OED* says "hogs'-wash."

> You have dried the marrow from the bone?
> For men were born to pray and save. . . .

And he would be praising Lady Gregory's house at Coole as Jonson had praised the Sidneys' Penshurst:

> How should the world be luckier if this house,
> Where passion and precision have been one
> Time out of mind, became too ruinous
> To breed the lidless eye that loves the sun? . . .

Eventually he'd even mock himself in a manner prompted by Jonson. That's worth examining at a little length, since one thing inconceivable in the 1895 Yeats is any hint that he's vulnerable to mockery. The model is "A Celebration of Charis," where Ben tells us how he fell madly in love at fifty. W.B.Y. was prepared to appreciate that when he commenced hankering after Maud Gonne's daughter Iseult. Jonson had been quick-witted:

> Farre I was from being stupid,
> For I ran and call'd on *Cupid*

(What a rhyme!) Cupid must shoot at her one of his benign arrows; unfortunately he gets paralyzed by her glance, and drops his bow. Impetuous Ben had just picked it up when the lady's eye let loose in his direction too her petrifying lightning—

> . . . that tooke my sight,
> And my motion from me quite;
> So that there, I stood a stone,
> Mock'd of all: and call'd of one
> (Which with griefe and wrath I heard)
> *Cupids* statue with a Beard. . . .

"Nyaah, nyaah," went the rude little boys. Though it's agreeably Chaplinesque, no Victorian would call it poetry. But Yeats liked it enough to imitate.

So in "Men Improve With the Years" (1916) Yeats is 51, and he's been turned into something just a little less ridiculous, "A weather-worn marble Triton / Among the streams." That means he is unceasingly drenched with cold water, and his cheeks are puffed out, and his lips are glued to a ludicrous sculpted horn whence not a sound issues. And a lady looks at him, and he looks at her, and nothing else can happen. It's all more oblique than Jonson, its sheer farce being left for the reader to envisage. Meanwhile W.B. must take, he says, what comfort there is in being

> Pleased to have filled the eyes
> Or the discerning ears,
> Delighted to be but wise,
> For men improve with the years. . . .

What a handsome devil he was once, and what a tunesmith! Still, wisdom must be something to have achieved. Everyone says so. And the cold water plashes.

During the decade after they met, Ezra Pound would be increasingly intimate with Yeats, and would watch this hard new manner develop. As Yeats grew to trust him, they would even almost collaborate. When Yeats published the collection called *Responsibilities*, the one that contains his assault on fumblers in the greasy till and other assaults, including the one that calls Synge's mockers "eunuchs," Pound helped him find a Confucian epigraph for it:

> How am I fallen from myself, for a long time now I have not seen the Prince of Chang in my dreams.

That says you have an obligation to keep your dreams lofty.

2   :   *Ford*

From above a fishmonger's shop in 84 Holland Park Avenue, Ford Madox Hueffer conducted *The English Review*; you pushed toward its stairway past suspended carcasses of rabbits, fowl, and game birds. Any hint of squalor conveyed by the address Ford sought to cancel with a small gilt plaque which said "English Review, Ltd." Though "Ltd." implied solvency and shareholders and statements, Ford's head for business was appalling. His minimum rate, a guinea a page, was high and frequently exceeded; he was always startled by the printer's bill; and he took in but 1s. 10d. per half-crown copy sold. At a time when a pound was still real money, the losses ran to £500 per monthly

number, which dissuaded the shrewder contributors from accepting
his offer to pay them with a percentage of the profits. They chose to
be paid "in money," even Wells, who'd at first saluted a "socialist"
idealism. Within eight or nine months Ford was ousted from control,
not long afterward from the editorship too.

But from the very first issue, December 1908, his editorial genius
was unquestionable. In presenting the best new writing, *The English
Review* was what *The Yellow Book* might have been had it not sought
to peddle naughtiness; also had the coming generation been a little
better defined back in '94. Ford's criterion for the "new" was the life
he discerned on the page, irrespective of established or avant-garde
origins. A mere glance at an opening paragraph could suffice him, as
it did for Lawrence's "Odour of Chrysanthemums." By such a criterion, neither were the elders defunct nor were their juniors "unsafe."
Ford published the elders: Thomas Hardy (now a poet), and Henry
James. He published the generation of '95, Conrad and Wells and
Yeats. And as soon as they sent him manuscripts he was publishing
the new men: D. H. Lawrence, Wyndham Lewis, Ezra Pound. Pound's
"Sestina: Altaforte" appeared in his seventh number, June 1909.

> Damn it all! This our South stinks peace.
> You whoreson dog, Papiols, come! Let's to music!
> I have no life save when the swords clash.
> But ah! when I see the standards, gold, vair, purple, opposing
> And the broad fields beneath them turn crimson,
> Then howl I my heart nigh mad with rejoicing. . . .

It says much for Ford's catholicity that you could read that in the same
magazine where you'd found "The Jolly Corner." It says much for
Pound too, that he'd learned so much already about exploding the
iambic line from within: "I have no life save when the swords
clash. . . ." "To break the pentameter, that was the first heave," he
recalled three dozen years later. In "Altaforte" it is decisively broken.
Most of the sestina he wrote at a sitting in the British Museum Reading
Room, where he'd taken his first stanza to check out a sestina's system
of permutations.*

Once again he could thank Edwardian London's incomparable fa-
cilitations; at Elkin Mathews's bookshop he'd met Ernest Rhys, "who

---

* Since "Altaforte" has been deplored for proto-fascist bloodthirstiness, I'll add Pound's 1913
statement that "a poem on such a theme [i.e., stirring up strife] could never be very important."

introduced him to May Sinclair, who introduced him to Ford Madox Ford." Later Rhys and J. M. Dent would commission his first prose book, *The Spirit of Romance*. Capitals do facilitate, and the London of those years was still a capital.

Yeats and Ford seldom saw each other. Ford called Yeats "a great poet, but a gargoyle," while Ford's very presence—"a large pink object"—could disturb Yeats enough to make him lose the thread of a lecture. Before long, Pound, as he would often recall, was seeing "Yeats in the evenings, Ford in the afternoons." It was Ford who imparted the best of his London education.

> and for all that old Ford's conversation was better,
> consisting in *res* non *verba*,
> despite William's anecdotes, in that Fordie
> never dented an idea for a phrase's sake
> and had more humanitas   jen

Tall, blond, hare-toothed, inclining to obesity, Ford looked and drawled like the kind of languid Englishman whose disregard for "poetry" is inbred. But his disregard was for what people were apt to intend by the word: an unnatural language meant to sound impressive. "I cannot read poetry at all," he even wrote. "I never really have been able to." That was because, so he claimed, in schooldays "the attempt to read Tennyson, Swinburne and Browning and Pope" gave him and his fellows "a settled dislike for poetry that we have never since quite got over." It's a normal English experience.

"Is there something about the mere framing of verse, the mere sound of it in the ear, that it must at once throw its practitioner into an artificial frame of mind?" That might have been addressed to Pound, for whose benefit too Ford might have made some stanzas he'd published in 1900:

> Under the lindens on the heather,
> There was our double resting-place,
> Side by side and close together
> Garnered blossoms, crushed, and grass
> Nigh a shaw in such a vale:
> Tandaradei,
> Sweetly sang the nightingale. . . .

That translates a song by Walther von der Vogelweide (1170–1230 circa):

> *Under der linden*
> *an der heide*
> *da unser zweier bette was,*
> *   da muget ir vinden*
> *schône beide*
> *gebrochen bluomen unde gras.*
> *   Vor dem walde in einem tal,*
> *tandaradei*
> *   schône sanc diu nahtegal.*

Walther's sheer antiquity could have excused much archaism. Yet "shaw" is the only uncommon word used by Ford, and it's one he could have heard countrymen utter; it means "thicket."

But Ford Madox Hueffer's early and fugitive books had not come Ezra Pound's way to set their example, and as late as 1909 Pound's translatorese still sounded like this:

> Sith no thing is but turneth into anguish
> And each to-day vails less than yestere'en . . .

Against such tushery Ford inveighed, even to the extent, one day in 1911, of rolling on the floor in protest. "That roll," Pound remembered, "saved me two years." The quickest way to comprehend its effect is by looking at a later Pound version from the same Provençal poet who'd spurred him to "yestere'en." Here's where he'd arrived by 1914:

> . . . Of Audiart at Malemort,
> Though she with a full heart
> Wish me ill,
> I'd have her form that's laced
> So cunningly,
> Without blemish, for her love
> Breaks not nor turns aside.
> I of Miels-de-ben demand
> Her straight fresh body,
> She is so supple and so young
> Her robes can but do her wrong. . . .

But Ford was not merely admonishing a young provincial whose personal sense of idiom could be shaky. He'd detected a national disease, ambiguously linguistic and social, a recurring disease like malaria or typhus that despite long periods of apparent health never really goes away. The relapse epitomized by Tennyson, Tennyson of the "subnauseating sissiness," of the "insupportable want of skill in the construction of sentences, the choice of words and the perpetual amplification of images," evoked his best denunciatory powers.

What is the sense of requiring the reader's attention for this sort of thing

>   Nigh upon the hour
> When the lone hern forgets his melancholy,
> Lets down the other leg, and stretching, dreams
> Of goodly supper in the distant pool,
> Then turned the noble damsel smiling at him . . . ?

What is the point of saying that it was midday, or three, or seven, in that ornithological imagery, if it is not to make the reviewers go into ecstasy over His Lordship's observations of nature? And what is worse . . . the self-indulgence generated by the refusal to contemplate reality ended in a complete literary slovenliness. You will find nowhere in the world such a body of ill-written stuff as in the English nineteenth-century poets; nor so great an inattention to form either of sentences or of stories; nor such tautology; nor yet such limp verbiage.

It is not surprising that Ford was frequently unwelcome in households where the Victorian pieties lingered. When he read in "The Lotos Eaters,"

>   All round the coast the languid air did swoon,
>   Dreaming like one that hath a weary dream

he felt impelled to ask what it really meant. "Did the air actually snort and grind its teeth as do those who suffer from a nightmare?" And when he found in Tennyson's dedication of his life's work "To the Queen" four lines "beautiful enough almost to have justified the existence of Victoria":

>   Then—while a sweeter music wakes,
>   And thro' wild March the throstle calls,

> Where all about your palace walls
> The sunlit almond blossom shakes

it caused him nearly physical distress to read the way it went on:

> Take, Madam, this poor book of song;
> For tho' the faults were thick as dust
> In vacant chambers, I could trust
> Your kindness. May you rule us long.

Yes, had chronology permitted, the late Laureate would have received a critique more explicit by far than the sight of a huge form rolling on the floor.

No, Ford did not like "poetry." Yet until 30 September 1914, when the Pound whom Ford had by then reeducated held the typescript of "Prufrock" in his hands, the one good modern poem of any length that Ezra Pound could point to was a poem by Ford, called "On Heaven." He hailed it (in *Poetry*, June 1914) as "the best poem yet written in the 'twentieth-century fashion.'"

> . . . And so she stood a moment by the door
> Of the long, red car. Royally she stepped down,
> Settling on one long foot and leaning back
> Amongst her russet furs. And she looked around. . . .
> Of course it must be strange to come from England
> Straight into Heaven. You must take it in,
> Slowly, for a long instant, with some fear. . . .
> Now that *affiche*, in orange, on the kiosque:
> *"Six Spanish bulls will fight on Sunday next*
> *At Arles, in the arena"* . . . Well, it's strange
> Till you get used to our ways. And, on the *Mairie*,
> The untidy poster telling of the *concours*
> *De vers de soie*, of silkworms. The cocoons
> Pile, yellow, all across the little Places
> Of ninety townships in the environs
> Of Lyons, the city famous for her silks.
> What if she's pale? It must be more than strange,
> After these years, to come out here from England
> To a strange place, to the stretched-out arms of me,
> A man never fully known, only divined,
> Loved, guessed-at, pledged to, in your Sussex mud,
> Amongst the frost-bound farms by the yeasty sea.

A long quotation; but "it is absolutely the devil," as Pound noted, "to try to quote snippets from a man whose poems are gracious impressions, leisurely, low-toned": that is to say, from a man who hangs nothing, nothing at all, on memorable phrases. "On Heaven" has hardly a memorable line. Everything in Eliot clings to the memory, as does everything that matters in Tennyson. (And from many years' desultory exploration of Ford's diffuse writings—eighty-one books— I cannot recall a single mention of Eliot.)

To render the proportion between England and Heaven, Ford offers the proportion between England and southern France. To set this on the page, he felt he had somehow to *evade* the English language. For English has "a literary jargon," whereas "In France, upon the whole, a poet—and even a quite literary poet—can write in a language that, roughly speaking, any hatter can use." Ford's "long, red car" (in 1913) sums up the lady, her stylish, willful independence, much as in a Pre-Raphaelite poem a caparison'd palfrey would characterize its rider; and the trouble it cost Ford to devise an idiom into which he could slip the word "car"—the diffuse, leisurely sentences, the intimacy with the reader, the colloquial ease, the many—too many—words: this was trouble taken that he might "render his own times in terms of his own times." He refused to call it trouble. Over prose he took trouble. As for verse, he gave an offhand English shrug: "as far as I am concerned, it just comes. I hear in my head a vague rhythm . . . and the rest flows out." No wonder he did not think highly of "Prufrock," if he supposed that it just flowed out, and if he noted, as he must have, that the word "etherised"—

Like a patient etherised upon a table

—is not accommodated by the language as "On Heaven" 's language accommodates "car," but smirks with grotesque shock. That, for him, was a fault.

He was a prose writer in all his intuitions. He thought in passages of speech, blocked out. The effects he cherished require time in which to take hold. Distrusting the speed of his own imagination, he disciplined it to construct explicit set-pieces, or else indulged its flashes as casual whimsies.

A powerful tradition reinforced his distrust of imaginative leaps. Along with Kipling of the brassy finish and Hardy of the studied awkwardness, he derives from Browning, who derived from Wordsworth, who despite his friendship with Coleridge is not to be associated with Coleridge but with Crabbe, and, standing behind Crabbe, the Augustans; and behind them all stands Ben Jonson. This is the "documentary" tradition, over against which, in the nineteenth century, stood the "aesthetic" tradition: Keats, Coleridge, Tennyson, Swinburne, Yeats. It was the aesthetic tradition that absorbed Symbolism, so far as English could absorb that highly French affair, and out of the aesthetic-Symbolist fusion stems Eliot.

The aesthetic tradition has so dominated critical thought that the documentary tradition goes unrecognized, and its writers get seen as inept aestheticians. There seems to be no historian of these affairs. A clear view of the matter was possessed by the late Basil Bunting (1900–1985; may he be in great peace), but he published no statement about it. The preceding paragraph is based on his conversation.

Bunting drew attention to an odd thing, that not only was Ford a Pre-Raphaelite by inheritance (Ford Madox Brown the painter was his mother's father), but so also was Kipling, whose uncle was Burne-Jones. So if both were documentary it was by deep-felt reaction. And young Ford one day (said Bunting) had not been to Sunday school, and young Kipling was appointed to repeat to him the teachings.

"If you are *good*, Fordie," began Rudyard, "you will go to a place on the clouds; and there will be harps. You will sit on a cloud and sing praises unto the Lord, and that is what you will do for ever and ever. You will wear a kind of white dress. And there will be creatures like mama but with great wings. . . ." And Ford's face grew longer and longer. "But," continued young Kipling the realist, "if you are *bad* . . . you will go to a   *much   worse   place*."

Which may have been one reason for "On Heaven."

Only by great effort, apparently, could a writer of English arrive at natural diction. We've heard Yeats complain of the "stitching and unstitching" it cost him to make a line seem "a moment's thought." French writers incurred less trouble; when they toiled, it was for *le mot juste*, the "natural" words having come naturally. But the English that popped into a writer's head was apt to have popped there from half-remembered literary sources. So the style of a novelist giving no thought to style would never be "plain prose," whatever that is. Ford explained how it would be a mélange of styles.

In his pedestrian passages such a writer—unpretentious, widely trusted—would sound like *The Times*, where the unit is a vacuous semi-metrical phrase like "proposals of a far-reaching character." Thus (said Ford), "if the hero went anywhere he hailed a hansom or repaired to his tailor," in three- or four-word gobbets that, alas, wrote themselves.

We may want to test that on the nearest work of fiction. Let us try "For Vera's Sake"; does that comply? It does indeed:

> "He hailed a hansom, and was quickly driven in the direction of the house he was seeking"—Philip Beaufoy.

What is more, when he got there he "gained admission." And if Beaufoy doesn't convince, here's Arnold Bennett, stylist: "She informed George Cannon of her mother's indisposition."

Next, said Ford, when the writer required a descriptive passage, "he used the phraseology of Shakespeare, as it is found in the pages of Charles Lamb. . . ." Again our man obliges, even to a pseudo-Jacobean "whilst":

> "Faces round the table grew blacker, whilst stifled curses rose thickly on the air"—Philip Beaufoy.

(And compare "The sky was a crimson battlefield of spring, but London was not afraid"—E. M. Forster.)

And, Ford concluded, "for his emotional passages, strong situations, or tragic moments . . . he and his characters had recourse to the phraseology and the cadences of the Authorized Version or the Book of Common Prayer." Sure enough, the theatrics of our exemplary hack exude a reek of the Book of Common Prayer:

> "Vera, it is sweet to die in your service since it is not permitted to me to live therein"—Philip Beaufoy.*

("Dear girl, there is a troublesome business ahead of us, and nothing but the most absolute honesty and plain speech will see us through"—E. M. Forster.)

Since Ford was talking of unobtrusive gentlemanly writers, the

---

* Did Beaufoy have school Latin, or had he simply listened to patriotic oratory? "It is sweet to die in your service" recycles the translatorese for *"dulce et decorum est pro patria mori."* *Tit-Bits* could witlessly touch surprising heights.

Philip Gibbses and the C. P. Snows, who between the wars provided genteel England with its verbal environment, we find we have made with his aid this interesting discovery, that the norm of workaday English narrative writing approximated to that of Philip Beaufoy. If "For Vera's Sake" seems ludicrous and cliché-ridden, that is only because brevity keeps its effects compact, like those of a Symbolist poem. Diffused and distributed through the atmosphere, Beaufoy prose was the pollution everyone lived with. Whether that is still so is a question best left for now as an exercise for the reader.

The impulse behind Beaufoy prose—prose written after all for the simple readers of *Tit-Bits*—can be traced as far back as the Norman Conquest, when simple-hearted snobbery acquired the option of saying common things *à la française*. In noble kitchens chefs prepared "porc" and "mouton," while outdoors the grunting and browsing went on being done by beasts the rude countryfolk called "pigs" and "sheep." Soon no respectable person would eat pig; he'd consume pork. Likewise needlewomen made "drapery" of cloth and genteel revulsion turned graveyards to "cemeteries." No such words were available before the Conquest; after it they seeped in from the talk of the conquerors, and to use them was to elevate your discourse. By "Anglo-Saxon words" we still mean rude, blunt words, and we'd rather attend the theatre than go to the playhouse.

Soon writers' diction was being routinely elevated, if not by an author then by a middleman; where Thomas Malory about 1470 had written ". . . asked hir why she sate sorowing," the printer Caxton in 1485 offered buyers something fancier: ". . . demaunded of her wherfore she made suche lamentacion." Small words like "ask" and "sorrow" were being ousted by words not only longer but exotic; "demand" and "lamentation" aren't Saxon but French. This French disease would prove incurable.

Caxton knew better than Malory what a leisured public wanted; it wanted style, and style meant Gallicisms. So early descended the plague of copy-editors, who profess to know what "the reader" will expect. Soon writers were Gallicizing without help, propagating a paper-English no one spoke. When Beaufoy's man didn't "get in" but "gained admission," *Tit-Bits* browsers saw no violation of idiom, though never in their normal lives would they dream of "gaining admission." And every century or two since Caxton, the mind of England has turned over in bed, faintly roused by some cry that the words we see fit to write ought to be the same ones we use without pencil-chewing.

An heroic remedy, more than once proposed, was to shun all save the Anglo-Saxon roots and make up a word-hoard that tongue had never fondled. In the 1840's "foreword" got coined, so men of learning would no longer have to write "prefaces." In 1855, in a talk on "English as it might have been" (i.e., if the Normans had stayed in Normandy), R. C. Trench sighed for "unthoroughfaresomeness," the rich nutty thing we might have rolled on our tongues had "impenetrability" and other Latinisms not seduced our forefathers. Sheer crankery could even propose to remake every compound that had entered English during eight centuries, writing "inwit" for "conscience," "flameprint" for "photograph," thus achieving not transparency of style but a posturing romantic nationalism. As Pound's "Seafarer" showed in 1912, strict Saxon diction can be powerfully poetic—

> . . . Bitter breast-cares have I abided,
> Known on my keel many a care's hold . . .

—but its feel of artifice is undeniable.

Saxon cranks flourished in the later nineteenth century, when all over the British Isles schoolmasters and housewives and lighthouse-keepers were filling out citation slips for the *OED*, and lexicographers lived in paradise. There's a striking analogy with the Nationalists who wanted Ireland to revert to the old Irish tongue. Those were busy after 1893, when the Gaelic League was founded, and they had their work cut out for them. The Gaelic non-theological vocabulary did not much exceed the needs of stone-age farmers, and for conversing with any fluency in a Dublin where people took "trams" and exchanged "snapshots," words had to be invented quite as strange as "inwit" and "flameprint."* It was either that or relapsing to lives of "poetic" simplicity, as in *News from Nowhere*. Either way, we're talking politics, not style.

Cranks would have us believe that all problems are simple. But, alas, there's no rule of thumb for "natural" English, one reason achieving it can be so troublesome. Many found it hard even to see what the problem was; Ford had detected something more elusive than the long-familiar issue Wordsworth raised. When Wordsworth called for "the real language of men," he was castigating a well-defined Poetic

---

* The Irish for "tram" was declared to be just "trama," but a photograph was a "grianghraf," "sun-script." Nowadays they usually say "fótograf," much as in Germany "Telefon" has ousted "Fernsprecher." Gadgetry's words are transnational.

Diction. It was something anyone could recognize the moment it was pointed out; you had only to look inside a well-defined structure called a Poem, and there it was. If you didn't care about poems, then you had no reason to take notice of Wordsworth's fuss. And if you did care for poems and the Poetic-Diction kind was what you liked, then you didn't like Wordsworth's kind—in his lifetime most people didn't— and that was all there was to it. And if you did like Wordsworth's kind, its language was never so natural you'd not notice it was there, because rhythm and solemnity would never let you forget that you were reading a poem.

But what Ford reproved was far less well defined: several inter-related dictions used at random, each of them so pervasive it wasn't easy to get them recognized as dictions at all. That was like exhorting fish to be conscious of water, and when he talked of "style" and the toil style demanded, the fish understood him to be advocating fancy stuff, "fine writing."

Ford's own example could be inconsistent as well; he wrote too much, since he always needed money, and despite his conscience often wrote too fast, in an easy avuncular jargon he'd learned to call up with as little effort as, we may suppose, Philip Beaufoy called up his.

But his best prose (in Pound's words) "lay so natural on the page that one didn't notice it." Pound also recalled trying to condense on the back of an envelope something of Ford's, and finding to his young surprise "that I couldn't make the note in fewer words than those on Ford's actual page."

3 : *The Short Poem*

It was chiefly novelists who stood to learn from Ford; Graham Greene for one did, and I'll make the flat though unfashionable statement that Conrad too gained by collaborating with him. A Ford poem, though, despite that exemplary diction, was apt to be diffuse and even whim-sical, as though it embarrassed him, as it doubtless did, to be using verse at all. In that as in much else he was English. So Ezra Pound got the balance of his London education in yet another quarter, among poets who wanted to rethink the English Short Poem. That led to Imagism and to much else, including, perhaps, Ted Hughes, Poet Laureate.

Here there's no focal figure, no Yeats, no Ford; just an ambience created by the possibility of a few ill-assorted men meeting. That is in itself an interesting sign. There had been a London where one could meet The Poets—Pope, Gay, Swift, Addison, lesser talents. The Poets moreover were largely in agreement, if not about who was accomplished, at any rate about what accomplishment amounted to.

But where were the 1910 poets, and what were they agreed on? Yeats was at 18 Woburn Buildings when he wasn't in Ireland, but wherever you found him he was making a point of being outside the public consensus. Thomas Hardy was away in his big forbidding house at Max Gate near Dorchester, and though a poem of his had led off the first issue of *The English Review*, there were few who thought of him as a poet at all. He had built his big forbidding reputation on the "pessimistic" and "outspoken" novels he stopped writing after 1895. He'd been writing poems since about the year Yeats was born, and by 1910 had just published his third collection. Exhibiting their lapses is all too easy—

> . . . Once engrossing bridge of Lodi,
>   Is thy claim to glory gone?
> Must I pipe a palinody,
>   Or be silent thereupon?

Yes, he was "awkward"; fine individual achievements—"Neutral Tones"; "The Darkling Thrush"—seemed accidental. The astonishing sequence of 1912–13, haunted page after page by the dead wife he'd been estranged from—no one could have foreseen him rising to that. What Hardy and Yeats may have found to say to each other I have no idea.*

Other people were known on account of a poem or two. Henry Newbolt had written "Drake's Drum." Arthur Symons had written this poem or that (but after 1910 he was mad off and on). Or there was Edward Storer, whose *Mirrors of Illusion* (1908) contained

STREET MAGIC

> One night I saw a theatre,
>   Faint with foamy sweet,

---

* Pound would cherish a letter in which Hardy advised him that *Homage to Sextus Propertius* (1917) might be less circuitously entitled *Propertius Soliloquizes*. That would have shifted the emphasis from "treatment" to "subject." Though he didn't make the change, he saluted the principle.

And crinkled loveliness
Warm in the street's cold side.

—remarkable for being the entire poem. Yes, "foamy sweet" is poetic in the worst sense. Diction, Ford's speciality, is Storer's undoing; like many of his generation he thought a poem had to be made of yummy words. But he'd glimpsed a poem he wasn't able to write; had seen the possibilities of speed and brevity: of what young James Joyce among classmates in Stephen's Green had used to call, somewhat grandly, the Epiphany.

Such a man repays notice, slight as his talent was, for his witness to the ubiquity of an idea. He talks of "pictures" and "scattered lines" and "suggestions," groping to convey the quality of a poem that shall register some brief experience we don't have words for: a new *kind* of short poem, necessarily short. The importance of this idea consists in the fact that other people had glimpsed it too. Pound would call them, collectively, "the 'School of Images,' which may or may not have existed." Insofar as a "school" existed, it met off and on, most informally, in a Soho restaurant. No manifestos were issued, and what got talked about became public only in part, amid wranglings about what "Imagism" meant and whose idea it was. But "images" don't define the radical novelty of something like this:

The after-black lies low along the hills
Like the trailed smoke of a steamer.

That was found by the biographer of T. E. Hulme (1883–1917), in 1960, among Hulme's notes. It seems not to be an excerpt but an entire poem, and if that is a judgment we make with some confidence now, we do so as heirs of those Soho restaurant gatherings. To call it a poem would have been preposterous as late as 1910. But of course we're familiar with Pound's "In a Station of the Metro."

Or consider this, another poem by Hulme—

Old houses were scaffolding once
                    and workmen whistling.

—also unpublished by him; but the six he did publish are almost as short; "Above the Dock" has but four lines. Hulme's poems on the whole do not impress; like Storer he's interesting now for the way he seems to take for granted the autonomy of a poem that is very short, and is concerned with a single perception. That was new.

If the brevity and the snapshot perception were new, an older necessity was also at work. Perception tends toward inventory, and we note the focus on nouns: houses, scaffolding, workmen. The new short poem would have to turn on its nouns, and somebody would have said "Imagism" if Pound hadn't. "Images" are the things nouns prompt you to think of, such as "Petals on a wet, black bough." And here we are in touch with something profound. Ever since—let us say—the Civil War, the mental habits of England had been displaying a tropism toward the noun.

That *something* began to happen thenabouts, something of poetic import, has been widely agreed; Eliot, for instance, alludes to "a dissociation of sensibility." Whatever that was, it was the kind of event no one knew about at the time, much as no one was ever aware of living through the Great Consonant Shift that changed "piscis" to "fish," "pater" to "father." And as we can identify the Consonant Shift, so we may imagine our own great-great-grandchildren speaking of our twentieth century as the time when the Great Verb-Noun Shift consolidated itself after some three hundred years. They may want to relate our poetic upheavals to that.

An early symptom had been Dryden's sense that Shakespeare needed rewriting. There was talk of decorum and of the unities, but if we examine Dryden's dealings with cadence and line we find him busy at something he was perhaps hardly aware of: unraveling Shakespeare's lines that turn on verbs, reweaving them around nouns. "As for her person," wrote Shakespeare of Cleopatra,

> It béggar'd all description; she did líe
>
> In her pavilion—cloth of gold of tissue—
>
> O'erpícturing that Venus where we sée
>
> The fancy outwórk nature.

I've marked stresses selectively: not the meter's obligatory five per line, but the higher-pitched ones we place to clarify sense, and they fall on "beggar'd," on "lie," on "o'erpicturing," on "see," on "outwork" (with emphasis on the second syllable). But when Dryden offers

> . . . Where shé, another sea-born Vénus, lay,

followed by

> She lay, and leant her chéek upon her hánd,

though he has twice maneuvered "lay" to where meter will stress it, yet "she" and "Venus" and "cheek" and "hand" are words that get a rising inflection. *She* is a *Venus* (apposition); *cheek* is on *hand* (rap-prochement); Dryden is an early instance of a new mind that prefers opposed nouns to single verbs, if only because a stressed verb lets possibilities hover, unpredictable. And to the extent that an effect is unpredictable it can feel uncontrolled, a venture into the random, which isn't Augustan.

Verbs may take us anywhere. "I see . . .": anything at all may follow "I see." But Dryden was accommodating to a taste we share, a taste for the programmed rather than the fortuitous, taking its pleasure in planned, not improvised, effects. That helps explain his interest in dramatic unities, lacking which we never know where we'll next be—Rome? Alexandria?—or whether the next act will shift us to next year.* And runs of but a few words too may prize forethought, equil-ibration, engineering: needless to say, revision ("A line may take us hours maybe"). To catch our time's resonance writing must contrive, and show off its contrivance. "Happiness, too, yes, there was that too, unhappily," writes Sam Beckett, making "happiness" *foresee* "unhap-pily." That was not a spontaneous line. Yeats too served a taste for the foreseen; ". . . And all dishevelled wandering stars" owes its mournful weight to our sense of a weighty line conceived and worked out as a whole: not like Shakespeare's way of letting us imagine that his speakers are just happening on the next word, as exhilarated by it as are we.

By 1916 Pound was uneasy; he was drawing attention to verbs, and welcoming Ernest Fenollosa's assurance that nouns were degen-erate verbs, the verb-force still latent within them. One means of releasing it was the cadence of live speech. "In a Station of the Metro" seems verbless, but the pause between its two lines works like a silent verb. It's the moment of awed surprise, and creates a person present and alert.

Yes, most poetry implies a speaking presence; but by Dryden's time,

---

* And measured by unities of time, place, action, Yeats's plays (though not Synge's, except *Riders to the Sea*) are positively neo-classical.

rather suddenly, orality had receded, to be recovered as *synthetic* orality. And 1910's poets weren't writing, like Dryden, for the theatre; they were writing for the printed page. If the modern short poem offers speech as its salient criterion, it must presuppose print even so. For it's *seen* before it is *said*.

Short poems had tended to be short because governed by a tune, or because constrained by a set form, like the sonnet. Even a sonnet is not as short as it looks; Donne once got a slow apocalypse into a sonnet, a feat Yeats would repeat in "Meru." The sonnet may also be described as a bag you must fill with rather more than a hundred words, however few you may need. But now behold something different: the snapshot poem, as brief as its occasion, free to stop when it's done because its "form" is being contrived *ad hoc*. The preoccupation with that idea in London, among men of less than overwhelming genius—Storer, Hulme, F. S. Flint—suggests a foreign origin. Paris?*

Quite possibly, the Paris of Monet, where the Impressionists had turned away from historical tableaux as sharply as the Soho poets were turning now from dreams of some new *Idylls of the King*. Degas in backstage glimpses of the ballet, Manet in the bar of the Folies-Bergères, Monet with his wife and child in the garden at Argenteuil, had invited respect for brilliant unsentimental re-creations of the ordinary. When Wordsworth encountered the otherwise unexceptional, he made drama of "O / The difference to me." These poets of a century later were trying out the painter's role, the observer's, less to feel themselves altering than to learn how their art might.

And they were living in the world of the snapshot photographer, who for about a generation had been finding in his prints much he'd been unaware of when he pressed the button: the deacon's untied shoelace, the anonymous cat's face in the rose-framed window, the moment's contours of a windblown veil. What I've elsewhere called the Impressionists' esthetic of the glimpse is inextricable from what John Kouwenhoven points out—the way, in a snapshot, the hierarchy of forms is "ordained by the indiscriminate neutrality of light." Painters select and synthesize; impartial light, frozen, confers equal im-

---

* Yes, yes, the Japanese models, the *haiku*, the *tanka*. In those years of dilettante orientalizing, they certainly had their effect. But perceiving their applicability as models meant being already held by the idea that an English poem could be small.

portance on what they'd routinely ignored. Ways of seeing changed, and a moment's accident contained elements to prize.

> Like a skein of loose silk blown against a wall
> She walks by the railing of a path in Kensington Gardens. . . .

Then there was Verlaine's ability to empty a fine poem of anything worth paraphrasing—

> *La lune blanche*
> *Luit dans les bois;*
> *De chaque branche*
> *Part un voix*
> *Sous la ramée. . . .*
>
> *O bien-aimée . . .*

—which says only, O well-beloved, that the white moon shines through the woods, and voices come from every branch (and it's "branch," not "bough"). Two more stanzas have little more to say, and the last line of all is simply, *"C'est l'heure exquise"*: in this moment, perfection. If that seems feeble in English, it is partly because no musical English exists for its particular simplicities; partly too because English readers expect a huffing puffing engine of thought.

It is here that *vers libre* becomes pertinent. If poetry, in Eliot's famous phrase, "can communicate before it is understood," it can also communicate before it is even read. After Milton and Wordsworth, a sonnet could announce by its look on the page that like the late Mr. Gladstone it was prepared to *say* something: that a book was writ of late called Tetrachordon, that the world is too much with us. The look of a poem is what communicates first. The look of *The Excursion*, long unbroken columns, says to be braced for heavy rumination, and the look of *In Memoriam*, numbered groups of short stanzas page upon page, says that the dolefulness will go on for some time, though not in a steady wail but in stoical episodes. So the first thing to be modified might be the way a poem looked on the page: if it was brief and its lineation irregular, that would suggest wording shaped by some moment's uniqueness. "Free verse" was called for.

Prompted by its novel look, a few readers and then more would learn what attention to pay. The line, as Charles Hartman argues in his admirable *Free Verse*, was the primary fact from which readers could get started. If the line is arbitrary "verse" is meaningless; but "if lineation helps to enforce attention, it serves as a prosodic device, whether the line is metrically organized or not."

So if Everyman thought *vers libre* a French anarchy like absinthe and the can-can, a few dreamers in London were seeing opportunities. Flint had guessed that the future was open "to the poet who can catch and render . . . the brief fragments of his soul's music." By August 1909, Hulme was comparing prose to an algebra of x's and y's which can go on and on, but poetry to a handing over of sensations bodily, "to make you see a physical thing, to prevent you gliding through an abstract process." Now fragments are by definition brief, and the essence of sensations is brevity. To catch perception on the wing like that you'd not want an interposed formality of tum-tum. Claude Monet had made pictures of appearances, not of salon directives, and English *vers libre* might be a poet's response to Monet.

The history of "free verse" seems to be unwritten; it's to be hoped the job won't be ventured by a dull dog. Milton arrived at irregular lines in *Samson Agonistes* by imitating Greek choruses. Richard Aldington said he'd done the same thing as a schoolboy. But by his time the phrase *vers libre* was in circulation, which means it was felt to be a French discovery. Yet in France they'd been aware of Walt Whitman, who'd respected the decorum of Prophetic Books, and notably the 1611 English Bible, when he shaped *Leaves of Grass* on their vatic analogy. So "free verse" could mean, among other things, Milton's

> Which shall I first bewail,
> Thy Bondage or lost Sight,
> Prison within Prison
> Inseparably dark?
> Thou art become (O worse imprisonment!)
> The Dungeon of thy self; thy Soul
> (Which men enjoying sight oft without cause complain)
> Imprison'd now indeed. . . .

or Whitman's

> I will make the poems of materials, for I think they are to be
>   the most spiritual poems,
> And I will make the poems of my body and of mortality,

> For I think I shall then supply myself with the poems of my
> soul and of immortality. . . .

—models so curial they weren't of the least use for what some were
wanting in England about 1910, a verse responsive to the run of casual
speech.

What they were not wanting was to be unread; but an unpredictable
measure nearly guaranteed that. Poetry, for Everyman, meant rhyme
and meter, certainly meter.

It was easy
—all too easy—
   for any dabbler
      to cut lines into little snippets
and pretend they were verse:
"unmetrical sprawling lengths," as the *Cambridge
         Review*
said of something of Pound's. Poetry's three elements were "thought,
words, and metre. . . . That is the beginning and end of the whole
affair," so let us have no more of "lengths chopped off anyhow." (In
chancing to die young, that reviewer, Rupert Brooke, would become
the golden lad of pre-war poesy.) By now the issue seems trivial;
but *vers libre* more than anything else may have been what sealed
poetry's future in England as a hermetic art. How to rationalize it in
elementary classrooms, the way the measure of *Hamlet* is rationalized
still?

"Free verse" came to be thought of as an American anarchy. Its best
practitioners did in fact tend to be American, partly out of a new
American interest in capturing speech rhythms they'd learned need
not be British. But shouldn't *vers libre*, a French discovery, have been
exploited by the islanders for whom, since Chaucer's time, French
examples had been catalytic? It's hard to resist diagnosing a failure of
energy, corresponding to the absence of any readership. Poetry: who
cared, really? Not Everyman.

Hulme's interest in writing poems, never strong, had petered out
well before his untimely death. Flint is remembered now for excerpts
from his articles. As for Storer, Tancred, Joseph Campbell . . . no
one need feel obligated to make an anthology. Yet if all now seem
minor characters in another story, the story of Ezra Pound, that does
not lessen the value of the milieu they helped create. "And pass on
the tradition," Pound wrote long after:

there can be honesty of mind
         without overwhelming talent
I have perhaps seen a waning of that tradition

They peopled a London long since supplanted by a lesser and a trivializing capital.

6 : THE LAWRENCE BUSINESS

Gouty and emphysemic, so long deposed from London eminence that Olivet, Michigan, would seem a haven, Ford Madox Ford earned small checks at 63 by spinning yarns for the *American Mercury* about how it had been in the distant golden days. In 1909! Twenty-seven years ago . . . That had been the year the young woman called "E.T." had sent him at *The English Review* a story by a shy friend of hers. It was called "Odour of Chrysanthemums," and Ford had tossed it toward the "Accepted" basket upon finishing the first paragraph. What could have made him so sure? He re-creates the process:

"The small locomotive engine, Number 4, came clanking, stumbling down from Selston," and at once you know that this fellow . . . is going to write about whatever he writes about from the inside. The "Number 4" shows that. He will be the sort of fellow who knows that for the sort of people who work about engines, engines have a sort of individuality. He had to give the engine the personality of a number. . . . "With seven full wagons" . . . The seven is good. The ordinary careless writer would say "some small wagons." . . .

"It appeared round the corner with loud threats of speed." . . . Good writing; slightly, but not *too* arresting . . . "But the colt that it startled from among the gorse outdistanced it at a canter." Good again . . . Anyone knows that an engine that makes a great deal of noise yet cannot overtake a colt at a canter must be a ludicrously ineffective machine. . . .

"The gorse still flickered indistinctly in the raw afternoon." . . . Good too, distinctly good. This is the just-sufficient observation of Nature that gives you, in a single phrase, landscape, time of day, weather, season. It is a raw afternoon in autumn in a rather accented countryside. . . . Yet there has been practically none of the tiresome thing called

descriptive nature, of which the English writer is as a rule so lugu-
briously lavish. . . . And then the woman comes in, carrying her basket.
That indicates her status in life. . . .

This man knows. He knows how to open a story with a sentence of
the right cadence for holding the attention. He knows how to construct
a paragraph. He knows the life he is writing about in a landscape just
sufficiently constructed with a casual word here and there. You can trust
him for the rest.

This writer whom you could trust was a miner's son named Lawrence, a 24-year-old schoolteacher in Croydon on the southern edge
of London, and he had somehow escaped the gentrification of diction
against which Ford was accustomed to preach: that taint of Original
Beaufoy. No one in a D. H. Lawrence story hails a hansom; hardly
anyone talks like the Book of Common Prayer, though at times he
will jolt us to a realization that the Book of Common Prayer can talk
like them. He's been called uneducated, though he wasn't; if he'd
aspired to Oxford like Hardy's Jude Fawley, and unlike the obscure
Jude gone there, the difference would have amounted to no more than
airs he had no need of. The life of his remote community had baptized
him with sound sense, and its local school equipped him with skills
and information. (English public education, H. G. Wells remarked to
Ford, was "the best in the world.") Lawrence's knowledge of French
and German had made him for a few months a valued clerk in an
elastic-stocking factory, and in the Croydon classroom "it amused him
to write scandalous tags of Latin verse for his boys to copy, because
this showed how completely the headmaster had forgotten his own
Latin."*

Another of his stratagems was to have the boys write stories to be
sent to papers that paid; some were accepted, it's a fair guess by the
Boys' Own Paper or perhaps even *Tit-Bits*, and "from henceforth," his
headmaster recalled long after, "the despised 'composition essay exercise' assumed an unexpected value in their eyes." In that sentence
we may observe this headmaster writing fluent Beaufoy like most
educators; such notions of style help us understand how they ranked
Lawrence in English when he himself was a high-school student in
Nottingham: thirteenth in a class of twenty-one. But he did take the
Mathematical Prize that year.

---

* This anecdote of Helen Corke's is a little obscure. The headmaster would see the verses but
miss their scandal?

There were decencies he seemed not to understand. A teacher once had to tell him that "stallion" was a word we don't use. Then his way of teaching poetry disturbed the calm; he got the boys reading it out loud! Sixty boys would be chanting, sometimes in unison:

> The Assyrian came down like the wolf on the fold,
> With his cohorts all gleaming in purple and gold. . . .

Also

> . . . On this I ponder
> Where'er I wander
> And thus grow fonder,
>   Sweet Cork, of thee. . . .

Even, in simulated Scots,

> Go fetch to me a pint o' wine
> An' fill it in a silver tassie. . . .

Noisy pedagogy, dubious selections. As for his art classes, they stressed spontaneity and enjoying what you were doing. A student still-life that looked insufficiently dead upset an inspector enough to prompt discreet investigation.

Lawrence wrote as he painted, without show of premeditation, and in that he resembles, yes, Marie Corelli. Fortunately, he was far more intelligent; also he had grown up in Eastwood, Notts, not Bayswater. Eastwood ways to say things stayed in his head, and in his Eastwood people he had a subject. Marie Corelli had no subject save her fantasies of herself, but D. H. Lawrence knew a life, lived by thousands, that had never been transmuted into fiction. All his first work is guided by a saving obsession with bringing news of what he knew at first hand.

This "obsession," a word that will have to do for now, is what not only guides but propels his power. Here Mrs. Leavis has a helpful observation:

> But there is something else to the great names of popular fiction—
> Marie Corelli, Florence Barclay, Ethel M. Dell, Gene Stratton Porter,
> Hall Caine—than sympathetic characters, a stirring tale, and the absence

of the disquieting. Even the most critical reader who brings only an
ironical appreciation to their work cannot avoid noticing a certain power,
the secret of their success with the majority. Bad writing, false sentiment, sheer silliness, and a preposterous narrative are all carried along
by the magnificent vitality of the author, as they are in *Jane Eyre*. . . .
They were in many ways remarkable persons.

Now "magnificent vitality" fits the best of Lawrence—he wrote, like
the great best-sellers, at white heat—and all that kept him from best-
sellerdom was his disinclination to provide the rest of the formula,
"sympathetic characters, a stirring tale, and the absence of the disquieting." We may explain the startling fury he could arouse, the shrill
accusations of "perversity" and "sheer filth," by supposing readers
who sensed that they held in their hands a best-seller manqué. An air
of contrivance attends the fuss stirred up around the baroque low-
temperature *Ulysses*, of which the most famous assailant was *The
Sporting Times*, known from the color of its stock as "The Pink 'Un."
The Pink 'Un was simply on the watch for Our Daily Scandal. That
The Rainbow should have been prosecuted is more understandable.

It was prosecuted, in 1915, under the Obscene Publications Act of
1857, in the Bow Street Police Court, where Methuen & Co. were
ordered to show cause why 1,011 copies, 766 of them still unbound,
should not be destroyed. Sir George Methuen, a "be-knighted gentleman" in Lawrence's phrase, "almost wept before the magistrate. . . .
He said he did not know the dirty thing he had been handling, he
had not read the work, his reader had misadvised him"—in short,
he all but implored the moral bobbies to apply their torch to his re-
grettable mistake forthwith. The similarly be-knighted Sir John
Dickinson, examining magistrate, directed them to do exactly that
after seven days; he also chided gently his repentant fellow-knight
for not having withdrawn the book once reviewers had spoken their
displeasure.

Was that not what reviewers were for, to detect aberrancies? And
Robert Lynd had detected "a monstrous wilderness of phallicism,"
Clement Shorter "an orgy of sexiness" that omitted "no form of vi-
ciousness, of suggestiveness." That should have sufficed to alert the
dozing Sir George. Lynd and Shorter were what used to be called
"bookmen." They lunched with authors and they romped on Fleet

Street. Lynd in particular the public took to its heart as "Y.Y."; it even warmed to the "delicious humour" in this encoding of "Wise." Weekly under his chummy pseudonym, decade in, decade out, he wrote for the *Nation* and then for *The New Statesman* what Leonard Woolf was to call "an impeccable essay . . . like an impeccable sausage, about anything or everything or nothing"; regular collections of these, with ingratiating titles like *The Pleasures of Ignorance*, were hard-bound and bought and cherished. On achieving exactly the Biblical quota of years, he died in 1949. An effigy hangs in the National Portrait Gallery, and the *DNB* preserves an admiring tribute to the witlessness that enabled his copious triflings.*

These bookman-essayists who made books from their endless articles had become points of reference in the London scene. Leonard Woolf's jibe at Lynd conceals an allusion to three collections of Hilaire Belloc's: *On Nothing* (1908), *On Everything* (1909), *On Anything* (1910); not to forget plain *On* (1923). Lynd's titles (which also included *The Green Man* and *In Defence of Pink*) echo phrases of G. K. Chesterton's, whose *The Defendant* (1914) defended Penny Dreadfuls, Skeletons, Nonsense, Planets, and Rash Vows, and was itself a collection of reprints from *The Speaker*. G.K.C. also had a weekly piece in *The Illustrated London News* for fully thirty years; to his admirers' relief, they've not all been collected yet. He and Belloc had powerful minds, which their contrived personalities hid from the periodical public and also often inhibited from real use; other London bookmen, unencumbered by minds, had mastered the manipulation of tone, a sonorous way of saying that they kept their readers ever blissfully reassured. Their readers in turn, ineffably inert, kept the bookmen from ever casting a fond eye, save with infinite precaution, on anything new. This readership was drawn from the Everyman's Library public, cherishers of good old unexamined things. Dent even extended his endless list of series with a Wayfarer's Library, to collect in ephemeral hardbacks the effusions of bookmen; lists of recent additions to Everyman's could be found on the jacket flaps.

When a bookman wasn't extolling Nothing gracefully, or rooting out degenerates and highbrows, when he was chewing on an author he'd have us respect, he was apt to say why that author was "worth while." Either a good writer told a rattling good story, or understood

---

* "He was at his best as a light essayist. In this field he was unique. He went on week after week, year after year, with little effort turning out essays on trifling everyday topics . . . delightful because they are the quintessence of a delightful personality."

the Virgilian tears of things, or possibly both, so in bookmen's en-
comiums all worth-while writers sound alike. Here is Arthur Waugh,
bookman, appreciating someone worthwhile, whose identity it is a
challenge to try to guess:

> The world, he seemed to say, is full of sorrow and tribulation, but
> the soul of man justifies itself by its patience and endurance. Purity,
> innocence, the simple heart, are its only lasting possessions. They will
> inevitably be misunderstood; but even so they are abundantly worth
> while. For a man must be able to respect himself before he can be at
> peace with the world.

Who is this laureate of the simple heart? Waugh's apostle of patience
and endurance, of self-respect amid sorrow and tribulation, is . . .
Henry James! To eradicate the distinctions by which one mind is
known from another, thus keeping the world of letters companionably
homogenous, was the bookman's paid task, and no light one. During
his lifetime Arthur Waugh alone "noticed" (i.e., reviewed) some six
thousand books. Moreover, that was but Saturday-morning work; on
weekdays he managed a publishing house, Chapman and Hall, which
had published Trollope and had once employed George Meredith,
who rejected, on its behalf, Marie Corelli.

Like figures on a wallpaper so smoothly hung no one doubts there
are walls behind it, the bookmen whose names were known to Everyman adorned an unnoticed decor no one thought to question. Its
constituent propositions could seem odd if you looked at them one by
one, the way they weren't meant to be looked at. In 1914 a biweekly
called *The Egoist* began exhibiting snippets from the *Times Literary
Supplement*, as, for example:

> The position of Keats among our poets is no longer questioned.

> Too often we find ourselves saying, "It may be so, but on the other
> hand it may not."

> Tennyson's art and craft for long forbade Mr. Catty new effort.

> If Homer is authentic, so is Milton, though with a slight difference.

> To him, as to all Yorkshiremen, the horse was a noble animal.

Mr. Abercrombie has judged the great epics; and as his judgment coincides generally with that of the secure world, it is the best of testimonies to its soundness. [Read that again.]

Truly, "Men have been tired of the merely intellectual pastime called thinking."

The chief pillars of Shakespeare's fame are not his English historical plays.

At a moment like this we should try to think clearly.

Being a crank paper, *The Egoist* never had more than 185 subscribers, notwithstanding its "serial story," *A Portrait of the Artist as a Young Man.* The sales of the *TLS* were climbing toward fifty thousand.

Thus mass literate taste was kept gyroscopically stable, and mere poets or novelists were kept in place to serve the social and other interests of bookmen. When Gerald Gould, a minor bookman, had W. B. Yeats to dinner, Yeats was bidden to perform a true office for a poet, which was to chant his host's small son to sleep. ("Ah, I shall speak him some verse . . ." were words the son remembered all his life; moments later he was being sluiced by the syrupy envoweled Celtic flow, and cringing in his crib hating it.) For a bookman all was grist. On the birth of his son, bookman Gould had himself published a poem, achieving in the course of it two memorable lines—

> And now we have a boy—like me, they say,
> Also I think a little bit like you.

—which two fellow-bookmen, the Messrs. D. B. W. Lewis and C. Lee, enshrined in an Anthology of Bad Verse, a collection which in turn yet other bookmen did not fail to promote. ("Let us enjoy the fun to be got out of *The Stuffed Owl.* There is plenty, plenty of it.") "Let us enjoy the fun": the bookman's leitmotif. As Wyndham Lewis remarked of his countrymen's habits, "If you cannot think, you can always laugh." The Englishmen in his apocalyptic novel have "not the vigour to think about a sock," but are laughing uncontrollably at the stars.

* * *

So it was into a treacly milieu that the fiction of D. H. Lawrence had to be launched, with results poor Sir George Methuen would have foreseen had he read *The Rainbow* with any attention. He might not have thought it indecent (Gerald Gould for one did not think it that, "just bad—dull, monotonous, pointless," dull enough for a little bookman's joke: "The most improper thing about it is the punctuation"), but he'd have scented such an author as had once had to be warned about the word "stallion." Here's a passage Sir George likely skipped, from the second page, about something as aseptic, normally, as a family and its land:

> They felt the rush of the sap in spring, they knew the wave which cannot halt, but every year throws forward the seed to begetting, and, falling back, leaves the young-born on the earth. They knew the intercourse between heaven and earth, sunshine drawn into the breast and bowels, the rain sucked up in the daytime, nakedness that comes under the wind in autumn. . . . Feeling the pulse and body of the soil, that opened to their furrow for the grain, and became smooth and supple after their ploughing, and clung to their feet with a weight that pulled like desire . . .

Altogether too many words of the "stallion" family; one or two might have passed as accidental, since even *The Times* might occasionally have need for the word "intercourse," but such a coagulation bespoke dirty-mindedness.

What it does bespeak, of course, is an effort to make lyrical the dumb upwelling fecundity on which all farming relies, thus stating one theme for a novel that will course through several Brangwen generations; we needn't judge it altogether successful to respect that. Never mind. Though fertile soil was well enough in its place, Everyman wasn't having it mixed up with themes you didn't mention. So on Everyman's behalf, somebody imperturbable—legend said, the public hangman—trashed the 1,011 copies, and Methuen in his rectitude recalled and destroyed 184 more.* The case was to have endless consequences from its sharp reminder to the printer that he bore by law a responsibility equal to the publisher's. Those unbound sheets, after all, had been seized on the printer's premises.

---

* So of the twenty-five hundred printed, about half actually reached readers. Of these, five hundred were shipped to the insusceptible colonies; Lawrence to his surprise in 1922 was shown one in the Mechanics' Institute Library in Perth, Australia.

Indecency's typesetters in the past had accepted, like housebreakers, with open eyes the risks of their lucrative enterprise. But nowadays "literature" was booby-trapped, so you could be handling porn and not know it. Thereafter honest dull printers would be England's most effective censors, fearful of involvement with anything they weren't confident they understood clear to the bottom, and publishers in turn could always point out how, broad-minded though they themselves were, they must safeguard an all-important relationship with a printer. So the next year Ezra Pound's innocent *Lustra* was bowdlerized, for one thing because the Greek word *phaloi* (helmet-spikes) might be misunderstood, and a couple of years later the firm that had typeset the very first installment of *Ulysses* for *The Egoist* got cold feet and refused its imprimatur even with deletions, and by 1921 the printing of avant-garde works in English had been systematically transferred to France, thus making British Customs the island's last bulwark of decency. It was on Customs that the public had to rely for protection from the full outrage of *Ulysses*, and when a young Cambridge instructor, F. R. Leavis, sought formal permission to import one copy, the percentage of female students at his lectures was reported to the Vice Chancellor by the Public Prosecutor.

Women in Love, the quasi-sequel to *The Rainbow*, was written by 1916, but it was four years before anybody published it. That was a three-guinea edition "For Subscribers Only": in its price, seven times the going rate for a novel, we behold the old *Yellow Book* dodge of enhancing naughtiness with luxury's aureole. Later Martin Secker took his life in his hands and issued trade editions of both books. For some reason nothing happened save spiteful reviews ("A loathsome study of sex depravity leading youth to unspeakable disaster"—*John Bull*). By then, having judged in 1919 that "England of the peace was like a corpse," the Lawrences had been long committed to more or less permanent exotic exile—Sicily, Mexico, Taos. . . . When D. H. Lawrence died in 1930 he was in the south of France.

No English writer is harder to see steadily; we're distracted by so much that he seems to be standing for. His daemon and his moment in history made him a figure whose very name can portend. "Laurentian" is a totem. But of what? It's a trouble to specify exactly, though the word "life" will embed itself somewhere in the attempt. Life! Even F. R. Leavis, evangel of a fiery discipline of responsiveness to the actual written words, made of D. H. Lawrence a preposterous all-purpose emblem, to stand for "life" against everything that got on susceptible nerves: machinery, Americans, T. S. Eliot's piety, the *TLS*, Bloomsbury, Two-Cultures talk, grammatical but empty noises made by the educated. If it's testiness you want a sanction for, then Lawrence is your man.

A nervous reach toward the emblematic is latent in Lawrence's most casual sentences. "A large bony vine clutched at the house, as if to claw down the tiled roof": that seems to offer more than it reports. Has tile intruded into the domain of vine? Or is that bony vine death's arm? "The pit-bank loomed up beyond the pond, flames like red sores licking its ashy sides": the very cosmos, thereabouts, obscenely chilblained. Mechanical death, machine-deadness, is one of his commonest tropes. "The small locomotive engine, Number 4," that caught Ford's attention as it came clanking and stumbling is itself an emblem, in that early story, of industrial England affronting the timeless realm.

The timeless realm lies back of his sustaining myth. Agricultural people are a people without history, a respect in which we may delude ourselves into counting them blessed. But industrial eras are reckoned in befores and afters: before and after steam, before and after nickel steel (hence the bicycle-chain and Henry James in knickerbockers), before and after brick and soot disfigured the hills. Industrial men are interdependent specialists; if the train stops, if the coal stops, everything stops. (Civil war is more or less permanent, its bomb the strike.) As specialists, they're new-minted *individuals*, each defined in contrast to everybody else. And with labor for sale, each competes with everybody else:

> The wages of work is cash.
> The wages of cash is want more cash.
> The wages of want more cash is vicious competition.
> The wages of vicious competition is—the world we live in.

In delimiting self and not-self they're strenuously verbal; when you see a lot of talk on a Lawrence page, as often as not he's dropping his characters through an air-pocket. And whether talk be empty or substantial, new befores and afters govern lives: before and after sexual awakening; before and after marriage. (How eventless marriage could seem, when the farmer, heigh ho, took a wife!) Also time off the job is something to be killed, by reading the papers, by jawing, by getting drunk....

The story that began with Engine Number 4 ends with a miner dead on his parlor floor. Before they carried him in dead, his wife had been waiting for them to carry him in drunk. That was his usual reason for being so late. The parlor is a room with no fireplace, seldom used. Now it must be made ready for a corpse.

> She turned away, and calculated whether there would be room to lay him on the floor, between the couch and the chiffonier. She pushed the chairs aside. There would be room to lay him down and to step round him. Then she fetched the old red tablecloth, and another old cloth, spreading them down to save her bit of carpet. She shivered on leaving the parlour; so, from the dresser drawer she took a clean shirt and put it at the fire to air. All the time her mother-in-law was rocking herself in the chair and moaning.

In a story by Flaubert, this spreading of cloths to save the carpet would be observed with a sardonic eye; in Lawrence it is bleakly practical. There you have one clue to his magic, that he can install you so quietly in a woman's practical intelligence that must assimilate shock by *seeing* to things. "Her bit of carpet," which is what she'd call it, is a value to conserve; there's no irony in saying so. And the clean shirt she puts at the fire: the sentence began, "She shivered on leaving the parlour," after which "so" offers a connection: she shivered, so she put a shirt at the fire. So? So shivering prompted her to some fireside business? So she felt if the parlor was cold he (dead!) would need a warm shirt there? We cannot say, nor could she; she's sleep-walking below articulation. Expressive unspecified connections are Lawrence's métier.

> Elizabeth sank down again to the floor, and put her face against his neck, and trembled and shuddered. . . . Life with its smoky burning gone from him, had left him apart and utterly alien to her. And she knew what a stranger he was to her. In her womb was ice of fear, because of this separate stranger with whom she had been living as one flesh. Was this what it all meant—utter intact separateness, obscured by heat of living? . . . She looked at his face, and she turned her own face to the wall. For his look was other than hers, his way was not her way. She had denied him what he was—she saw it now. She had refused him as himself. And this had been her life, and his life. She was grateful to death, which restored the truth. And she knew she was not dead.

Also: "They had met in the dark and had fought in the dark, not knowing whom they met nor whom they fought." Whether metaphorical dark or the dark of the bedroom—it's like Lawrence to leave that unspecifiable—they have lived together and had children and never known each other; in that story, published when he was 26, one theme of his emerges clearly, the dilemma of individuality, its curse of consciousness. For can we conceive of a better intimacy for these people? So long as "conceive" is the operative verb, we can not. Conceptions, judgments, opinions, those are what interfere, when they cannot carry the instinctual life with them. His trashiest writing—of ganglia and dark centers—attends his efforts to get a terminology for the instinctual life. When he triumphs, it's by leaving it implicit, catching bits of behavior with electric intensity, no motives or reasons offered.

In *The Rainbow*, which Roger Sale rightly calls an historical novel, a canal and then a railway and then a colliery and "red, crude houses plastered on the valley in masses" make their appearance in the 1840's, leaving Marsh Farm "remote and original, on the old, quiet side of the canal embankment, in the sunny valley where slow water wound along in company of stiff alders, and the road went under ash-trees past the Brangwens' garden gate." That defines Marsh Farm as it had never been defined when it was indistinct from a countryscape like itself. It is now (in Sale's word) "pastoral," and its Brangwens can emerge from prehistory. In Tom Brangwen the emergence is only commencing. He says to the strange woman with the child, "I came up to ask if you'd marry me. You are free, aren't you?" She is. Then she says she doesn't know. Then she says ("impersonally"), "Yes, I want to." It's the strangest courtship in English fiction; that it is made plausible, and that the bond between these strangers can seem to survive and deepen despite scant dialogue, scant incident, is a wonder that might have arrested the genteel bookmen who preferred to work up indignation. Were they really as angry as they professed to be, or did they merely anticipate Everyman's certain bewilderment, accustomed as Everyman was to a different schematism? For here's another schema:

Vera drew herself up proudly as she replied, in a firm tone, "Yes, I do love him, and without shame I confess it. Who can control love? It gives itself sometimes to the least worthy—it pardons all faults—it even loves such faults because they are part of the beloved. I love Slavinski,

and it shall be my life's task to seek to reclaim him—aye, and at the eleventh hour, perchance, a woman's love may save him ere it is too late."
                                                    —Philip Beaufoy

There you have a cartoon version of decencies *The Rainbow* flouted. (Flesh out its absurd rhetoric, and lo, a best-seller.) If its words explain quite as little as Lawrence's do, they keep Vera and Slavinski in acceptable roles, he fallible, she nobly shouldering a life's task; and inexplicable uncontrollable love is conceded to make sense, though its sexual dynamism is evaded. But Ursula and Skrebensky in *The Rainbow*—! Here's her sense of him when, back from war, he's asked to see her:

> What did he want? His desires were so underground. Why did he not admit himself? What did he want? He wanted something that should be nameless. She shrank in fear.
> Yet she flashed with excitement. In his dark, subterranean male soul, he was kneeling before her, darkly exposing himself. She quivered, the dark flame ran over her. He was waiting at her feet. He was helpless, at her mercy. She could take or reject. If she rejected him, something would die in him. For him it was life or death. And yet, all must be kept so dark, the consciousness must admit nothing.

A risky phrase back there, that says what he did when he was kneeling; you may have to read twice to make sure it's not literally meant. Then they talk of nothing much (" 'How long,' she said, 'are you staying in England?' 'I am not sure—but not later than July, I believe.' ") Yet within a few more pages, under a tree in the night,

> She was caught up, entangled in the powerful vibration of the night. The man, what was he?—a dark, powerful vibration that encompassed her. She passed away as on a dark wind, far, far away, into the pristine darkness of paradise, into the original immortality. She entered the dark fields of immortality.

It is possible to find such rhetoric as absurd as Beaufoy's, and Lawrence's best critic, Roger Sale, warns us how "To read *The Rainbow* one must stop at every murky or mysterious passage and see the kind of sense it makes." He remarks too that unsympathetic readers often guide us better than devout ones, refusing as they do to be put off "with a passage from a letter or an essay offered as exegesis as though such passages could serve as substitutes for a passage in the novel." The business of finding and collating such substitute passages has generated many thousands of printed pages, behind all of which hovers anxiety lest the prophet not be making sense without acolyte help. No, "The rule on this point is clear: if the context of the novel does not make a passage clear, then the result is jargon, private language, inferior."

"Private language" is any language we don't share. Sale adduces the English tradition of "visionary authors—Milton, Blake, Shelley, Swinburne"—who were driven to invent their own system of symbols, meaning "either greater vagueness or greater cultist insistence, or both." The word to mark is "cultist"; Sale mentions "quarrels between staunch admirers willing to operate inside the fearful symmetries . . . and amused or alarmed detractors who stand outside and insist that all writing make sense." He is right to add that "with *The Rainbow* one can stand implicitly with the detractors and still be 'inside' the book."

We might take another route to a similar conclusion. Without piling New Jerusalem on a camel's back, can we think Philip Beaufoy's language visionary? " 'Yes, I do love him, and without shame I confess it. Who can control love? It gives itself sometimes to the least worthy— it pardons all faults—it even loves such faults because they are part of the beloved.' " That may fairly pass as "visionary language," since it's hard to decipher it as anything else. Yes, yes, debased, debased; it is what evangelical Christianity had come to, having trickled down into the *Tit-Bits* idiom.

Chief of sinners, Lord, am I

—so Vera might imagine Slavinski chanting; and if Jesus will understand, can Vera do less? Lawrence's "pristine darkness of paradise" is no less Biblical; likewise his "dark fields of immortality," with "darkness" and "dark" to advise us of switched polarity. If his rhetoric is new-minted, Beaufoy's worn, they've stamped comparable metals, unmistakably from the reign of King James. We remember Ford observing how the Authorized Version would infiltrate the English storyteller's solemn moments. Then the Beaufoys rely on its idiom to say something for them. Lawrence is different in having something new that he wants to say.

A best-seller manqué: we are back to that. His power was a popular power: a power the populace could recognize, however he might pervert it. Hence the screams.

But he could scream too. There was his Prussian Officer side, the dark side that indulged fantasies of cruelty, often tacit but sometimes utterly explicit, as in the passage from *Studies in Classic American Literature* no admirer of that respected work ever mentions:

> The poles of will are the great ganglia of the voluntary nerve system, located in the spinal column, in the back. From the poles of will in the backbone of the Captain, to the ganglia of will in the back of the sloucher Sam, runs a frazzled, jagged current, a staggering circuit of vital electricity. This circuit gets one jolt too many, and there is an explosion.
>
> "Tie up that lousy swine!" roars the enraged Captain.
>
> And whack! whack! down on the bare back of that sloucher Sam comes the cat.
>
> What does it do? By Jove, it goes like ice-cold water into his spine. Down those lashes runs the current of the Captain's rage, right into the blood and into the toneless ganglia of Sam's voluntary system. Crash! Crash! runs the lightning flame, right into the cores of the living nerves. . . .
>
> It is a natural form of human coition, interchange. . . .

Now that is beneath *Tit-Bits*; that's close to rubber-shop porn. And Lawrence screams exultation, the way he'd done a few years earlier in the essay called "Education of the People," where we find him yelling, "Smack the whimpering child. Smack it sharp and fierce on its small buttocks. . . . Good God, spank their little bottoms: with sharp red anger spank them and make men of them." As for any mother who prefers to "smirk and yearn," she must have "ten hard, keen, stinging strokes on her bare back, each time." It's amazing how this stuff gets passed over in silence.

He'd drafted "Education of the People" in 1918, for the *Times Educational Supplement*, which sent it back. His biographer suggests a motive: "to establish himself as something of an authority on education in order to obtain an administrative post in that field." D. H. Lawrence, bureaucrat—what a thought! And if he's advocating the tradition of the cane, he hasn't the administratorese quite right.

Whether or not the flagellation ecstasies were in the draft on which he pinned such hopes—he reworked the version we have after giving England up—their sudden shrillness cannot but alarm. Could he gauge his own tone, ever? But he's certainly not pandering to dark fantasies: look at the contexts. *Studies in Classical American Literature* and "Education of the People" are didactic works both, by an author revaluing middle-class values. And in the course of making a sober, defensible point, he suddenly loses control, like a being possessed. There are instabilities in everyone. Lawrence seems often not to know which of his own it's productive to give rein to. Some of the stories, even, tread volcanic ground as if heedlessly; "The Prussian Officer" is one of those.

The common overstatement that he could not revise, only rewrite, points to a truth, that the writing was apt to record the psychic state he had conjured himself into while doing it; to get *The Rainbow* right he rewrote some of it seven times, recommencing rather than edit and retouch. That does suggest surrender to a daemon.

Yes, an instinctive, like Marie Corelli. Dickens too was an instinctive. Like Dickens, unlike Corelli, Lawrence was an instinctive of genius. Unlike Dickens, he went unstabilized by public norms, oscillated into wild anger, left England, ranted. You can't imagine that happening to Dickens; the millions who awaited his weekly installments kept Dickensian passions in check. Yet—here we encounter again the emblematic status of Lawrence—there was available to him no such public as Dickens had. For public norms had been enfeebled; symbiosis with a literate body could be enjoyed and exploited only by hollow best-sellers or by hearty bookmen. Deprived of even the illusion of speaking to a public, to any but a *Daily Mail* public such as you'd cow by shouting, after 1920 he ran wild into pseudo-science, pseudo-anthropology: polarities, dark centers, dark gods. The dippiness traceable as far back as Blake, the Messianic crankiness conspicuous in Milton, these were part of the literary tradition he inherited, as they are part of the inheritance of any English writer, whose job has been dealing with such a heritage, and with isolation. (And it is a Protestant heritage; Eliot was right about that.)

A sense of the past, something Blake had little of, can steady the Messianic imagination wonderfully. Uniquely, in *The Rainbow*, Lawrence had glimpsed a history, as it were a hand from the past emerging, unclasping, to display the modern plight. From the prehistoric Brangwens to passion-tossed Ursula, generations of progressive individuation ran clear. Like an anchor thrown down into the past, that book made him able to write the book he'd started on, restarted seven times, burned a thousand pages of: the here-and-now book that became *Women in Love*. And he wrote *The Rainbow* out of first-hand knowledge of a rural England where three eras could still be visited: where some tilled as in the Middle Ages while others got lowered by cables down the mineshafts, and others again heard college speculation about whether "life" possessed any special quality. ("We don't understand it as we understand electricity, even, but that doesn't warrant our saying it is something special. . . . May it not be that life consists in a complexity of physical and chemical activities . . . ?") That's a long way from "the intercourse between heaven and earth": almost as long as the novel.

In the urban world there's much falsity, much to irritate. "A complexity of physical and chemical activities," indeed!

> You've no more use for the solid earth
> and the lad you used to be.
> You sit in the boughs and gibber
> with superiority.

Yet he's not nostalgic for the lost timeless realm, knowing perfectly well as he does that, save for the pits his father toiled in and the schools ratepayers were supporting in the post-timeless money economy, he himself would not have so much as learned to read and write.

The vision in those two interdependent books lapsed into "prophecy" and trust in "strength." People needed "proper ruling," by some Prussian Officer. "One great chosen figure," "supreme over the will of the people"—that was what Europe needed; so wrote "Lawrence H. Davison" in a book called *Movements in European History* which Oxford, of all presses, published in 1921. Why Oxford required a pseudonym seems unexplained; worry, perhaps, about *The Rainbow*'s notoriety? If so, Oxford was rejecting association with the author's major credential, his great triumph of historical vision.

If it hadn't been for the war . . . That may have been what drove D. H. Lawrence half mad. After it he leaves in abeyance the historical sense that had guided him, once, to one unique vision.

7 : A POCKET APOCALYPSE

"In or about December 1910," said playful Virginia Woolf, "human character changed." She pointed to a shift in "all human relations"—between "masters and servants, husbands and wives, parents and children"—a shift so profound that it had altered also "religion, conduct, politics, and literature."

But all in one month? Such mutations take decades. Awareness that they've occurred, though, can be sudden. An event of late 1910 was the Post-Impressionist exhibition, where one English visitor got so hysterical he had to be led outside and walked.

That unfortunate fellow—his name has been lost—saw a portent. A few square feet of color, signed "Paul Cézanne," had jarred his eyes open on something very unpleasant, something not to be put behind on merely leaving the gallery. Whole orders of former certainty were vanished. Irremediable novelty had leered in his face.

To reconstruct such a shock from this late in the century, we have to peer back past other critical years, whose events today loom much larger. One of them is 1922, Annus Mirabilis, the year of *Ulysses* and *The Waste Land*: the formal dawn of International Modernism. In each of the Three Provinces that event is a boundary: in Ireland, between O'Casey's plays and Beckett's; in America, between a Dreiser's fiction and a Faulkner's; in England, between *The Old Wives' Tale* and *To the Lighthouse*.

Or, far more profoundly, 1915, after which there would be No More Parades. What had commenced in August 1914 had looked like just one more war, of the kind Europe had taken in stride for centuries. But by the next summer anyone could see that something very terrible was going on. D. H. Lawrence was one of many who recalled a good life lost:

I can't tell you with what pain I think of that autumn at Cholesbury—the yellow leaves—and the wet nights when you came to us, and Gilbert and the dogs—and I had got pork chops—and our cottage was hot and full of the smell of sage and onions—then the times we came to you, and had your wine—those pretty wineglasses on your long table. Something inside one weeps and won't be comforted. But it's no good grieving.—But there was *something* in those still days, before the war had gone into us, which was beautiful and generous—a sense of flowers rich in the garden, and sunny tea-times when one was at peace—when we were happy with one another, really—even if we said spiteful things afterwards. I was happy, anyway. There *was* a kindliness in us, even a certain fragrance in our meeting—something very good, and poignant to remember, now the whole world of it is lost.

Lawrence is astute in locating the change in "us"; when "the war had gone into us," *we* changed, and that changed our world. It's hard to think of any precedent for so decisive a change of mood: for the shared sense of a whole order of things disagreeably mutated. And it is important to note the baleful synchronicity whereby, and especially in England, the structure of agreements into which modernism was just commencing to insert itself got dissolved exactly when it did. When the war was over, that left what was left of modernism looking oddly rootless and willful.

Which brings us back to the date Virginia Woolf designated. Between 1910, when Ford lost control of *The English Review*, and August 1914, when all Europe plunged toward suicide, not much of public import happened in literature. But in those years the English public found itself confronted over and over with modernism plain and stark: something it couldn't put down, as in *Yellow Book* days, by invoking piety and the marriage bed. Deprived of that rhetorical resource, it could only scream. The confrontations took place not beneath reading-lamps but in galleries: on art-dealers' premises: at forums where propagandists for the visual sought to ease Everyman into the new century. Before long there was no more hysteria, but the first shock remained hard to forget.

The 1910 Post-Impressionist exhibition was organized by Roger Fry, almost 44, a painter of tasteful pictures who until a few months before had been European buyer (Goyas, Guardis, Murillos) for New York's Metropolitan Museum. In 1904 he had turned down a more visible post, the directorship of the Met, in part because it would have meant more proximity to Pierpont Morgan than he wanted. J. P. Morgan thought an art-expert's job was to reinforce "his own wonderful sagacity," and not even opportunities to ride in a private car with a fireplace where fat logs were ablaze in snowtime could be worth, for Fry, a career of dancing to that tune. As European buyer he'd danced to it part-time till a Morganitic sneeze blew him away; then he'd done occasional buying on commission for such lesser millionaires as Frick. Rejecting fakes, authenticating Bellinis, arbitrating prices, such had been his paid role in a milieu that rattled with money now that buying paintings was a way to buy status if you bought the right ones, the right nodes in a web of relationships: a web art-relators like himself had spun and kept in repair.

Since 1906 at least, a secret Roger Fry had cohabited with this Fry who tended the web. The hidden Fry was increasingly absorbed by paintings with, at present, no collectors' value at all: Cézannes, for instance; Matisses. Virginia Woolf, who first met him about the time he brought back the bold French pictures from Paris, recalls the new Fry at a preview:

> There they stood upon chairs—the pictures that were to be shown at the Grafton Gallery—bold, bright, impudent almost, in contrast with the Watts portrait of a beautiful Victorian lady that hung on the wall behind them. And there was Roger Fry, gazing at them, plunging his eyes into them as if he were a humming-bird hawk-moth hanging over a flower, quivering yet still. And then, drawing a deep breath, he would turn to whoever it might be, eager for sympathy. Were you puzzled? But why? And he would explain that it was quite easy to make the transition from Watts to Picasso; there was no break, only a continuation. They were only pushing things a little further. He demonstrated; he persuaded; he argued; the argument rose and soared. It vanished into the clouds. Then back it swooped to the picture.

There you have the veteran art-relator in action; "no break, only a continuation"—between G. F. Watts and Picasso! G. F. Watts, whose *Hope*, a brooding allegorical female, hung in sepia reproduction on ten thousand post-Victorian walls! . . . Either Roger Fry saw very deeply, or he talked to keep his hearers' minds off what they saw. Note that Virginia Woolf identifies the Watts by its subject, "a beautiful Victorian lady"; that is not how you'd specify a Picasso. Indeed, which Picassos were in question she doesn't say. They were pretty tame actually, from his "pink" and "blue" periods: in the tempo of most painters, a lifetime ago. By 1910 the Catalan Proteus was far into Cubism, *Les Demoiselles d'Avignon* of the brutal masks already four years behind him. As for the other artists, by and large the work on display was nearly a generation old.

Writing in 1940, Virginia Woolf is cautious still. She's committed to Roger Fry, and she'll not seem allied with Philistia, not she. Yet to vindicate Fry's 1910 judgment she mentions the prices Cézanne and Matisse came to fetch, and adds that "opinion too is on his side"; and that's all. A lack of passion is detectable. Bloomsbury, on normal occasions scornful of money and of "opinion," saved its passion for bright uneventfulness, over which it would huff and puff till the literati took it for daring. Richard Cork remarks that Fry "was out on a limb of his own making"; in 1910 he'd simply caught up with Cézanne (1839–1906): as though someone in 1995 should "discover" Beckett, and bring *Godot* to the notice of Pago Pago. Yes, it's all strange. Fry may well have had misgivings of his own. No wonder he talked so much.

In November 1910, with the show hung in the Grafton Gallery, there was no way for even a non-stop Roger Fry to evangelize every visitor; more than four hundred people came every day, and they thought Cézanne, Gauguin, Van Gogh, Derain, Matisse, Picasso "outrageous, anarchistic and childish." The nonsense raged for three months. A Dr. Hyslop gave his opinion that the painters were clinically insane; his speech about that drew enthusiastic applause. Old Wilfrid Scawen Blunt (poet, diplomat, Arabist) wrote in his journal of "that gross puerility which scrawls indecencies on the walls of a privy": words carrying the authority of a man who'd known seventy busy years of visiting privies, including the kind they have in Irish jails. *The Times* saw "a rejection of all that civilisation has done." The man who'd had to be walked in the fresh air could blame his hysterics on Cézanne's portrait of Mme. Cézanne, of which he'd undergone the rude impact uncushioned by any words of Roger Fry's to show him how like it was, really, to a lovely Watts.

Yet in merely assembling the show Roger Fry had made a statement, and from a man of taste and learning he sank in genteel esteem to a brutish self-advertiser. In that role he had an appointed adversary.

As D. H. Lawrence would enrage the bookmen, so donnish Fry in November 1910 woke the sleepless ire of Tonks.

Tonks? Tonks, Henry Tonks (1862–1937), a symbolic Victorian product, his father a brass-founder of Birmingham, his mother's people in the wine trade like Ruskin's. He commenced a career in medicine and advanced as far as being senior medical officer at the Royal Free Hospital with F.R.C.S. after his name. Then came a conversion which the *DNB* handles cautiously: "Since youth Tonks had had a certain interest in art and towards 1890 this interest became very strong." It's quite like Fry discovering Cézanne, and one thing that ensued was that Tonks began to paint. He proved to be "essentially English in outlook, loving a beautiful and elegant subject," and became about as good a painter as Roger Fry. Both of them painted better than, say, W. B. Yeats, though Yeats's father, J.B., and Yeats's brother, Jack, painted rings round the pair of them. (The chief employment Jack Yeats found in England was illustrating comic papers.) But Tonks's painting was essentially a sideline. Of more moment was the fact that by '94 he was assisting the Slade Professor of Fine Art at University College, London. There Tonks defended cinquecento Rome with the fervor of a late convert. He had, Wyndham Lewis remembered, "one great canon of draughtsmanship, and that was the giants of the Renaissance. Everyone was attempting to be a giant and please Tonks. None pleased Tonks—none, in their work, bore the least resemblance to Michelangelo. The ladies upstairs wept when he sneered at their efforts to become Giantesses." That can be put in quite another way, as the *DNB* assures us. There we read that at the Slade, and especially after 1917, when he'd risen to the Professorship itself, Tonks conducted "a most vigorous defence of the traditional spirit in art in general, and in draughtsmanship in particular, at a time when futurism, abstraction, and so on, were assailing all that he held most dear." (Futurism, abstraction, and so on—you know, all that rot.) "I shall resign if this talk about Cubism doesn't cease," Tonks told George Moore; "It is killing me."

There is more to be said about his vigor than obituary phrases convey. At the time of the offensive exhibition, 1910, Tonks had circulated caricatures "in which Roger Fry, with his mouth very wide open and his hair flying wildly, proclaimed the religion of Cézannah," and when Fry died in 1934 Tonks said it was "as if a Mussolini, a Hitler, or a Stalin had passed away." That was fighting the good fight *à la* Tonks, and so fiercely did Tonks fight it that, according to the

DNB, "the present [1945] strength of the traditional movement is, in a considerable degree, due to his work." Forty years later we're free to ponder such strengths as the commemorator may have had in mind.

For when Tonks's celebrant says "the traditional movement" he tells us more than he means to. Movement? Could it be that by mid-century tradition, whatever that was, could be thought of—and by its well-wishers—as only a movement among movements? If so, it was no longer *tradition*; it was an ideology, a sheaf of prejudices. But if that's odd, it is equally odd to think of Roger Fry arguing that Picasso was just a continuation of Watts; odder still to think of Fry having to argue, since what he said (if true) should have been evident from the pictures. Perhaps there was a way to look at pictures of which Fry possessed the knack and his hearers didn't; perhaps, even, Fry saw things Picasso wouldn't have (for fancy Picasso taking the measure of *Hope*!). But leave off fancy. There *was* a crisis in painting. And the crisis was not made by the dourness of Tonks. What points to a longtime crisis is the necessity for Fry.

For the middleman, the art-relator, when did he come in? With Ruskin, possibly, defending Turner against Philistia.* By 1834 at least, painting could no longer survive without a critic's aid. And that was also true of poetry, as Wordsworth's 1800 *Preface* and Coleridge's *Biographia* made clear. As far back as that we may detect an avant-garde, its advances covered by critical cannonades. From Wordsworth to Pound, the innovative poet (Browning excepted) would double as his own critic, making poems under one hat, reeducating the public under the other. Painters (Wyndham Lewis excepted) have tended to let experts handle their public relations, and since a picture is an object in a way a poem is not, the most useful painting-experts have doubled as dealers. For a career in art, your first requisite is a good dealer. The talk of so well placed an art-relator can coin you money.

Thus history created a role for Roger Fry, and also for Henry Tonks, the counter-Fry. After he'd met Virginia Woolf and Clive Bell, Fry's milieu was Bloomsbury and his public its avant-garde readership: a *literary* set. Tonks the Slade Professor meanwhile admonished young painters, such of them as chose to come up through the system. Many whom he'd admonished defected, among them Wyndham Lewis and

---

* Nor was Ruskin infallible, as we know from the libel Whistler sued him for. Fry likewise professed to make little of Wyndham Lewis.

Augustus John. But many more stayed loyal to Michelangelo's mouth-piece. So in England "professional" painting became one thing, hunk-ered down in a fortress called Burlington House, and "enlightened" taste—taste with access to a language-arsenal—became something else entirely.

So it's clear how the 1910 Post-Impressionist show counts as a literary event. Pound mocked the revulsion in a two-line poem he called "L'Art, 1910":

> Green arsenic smeared on an egg-white cloth,
> Crushed strawberries! Come, let us feast our eyes.

His French title registers the public perception that all this offensive stuff was foreign. His poem's words seem to say what Philistia was saying. Yet by its very brevity and shocking diction, the poem an-nounces its own allegiance to the new. "Come, let us feast our eyes" can be read unironically: what can feast the eyes need not be good fare for stomachs, and to confuse these feastings is to drift into Tonks-ian yearning for some "beautiful and elegant subject" that shall guar-antee a picture worth looking at, a poem worth reading.

But for some years, since the advent of Cubism at least, "subject" and picture had inhabited different worlds; "the distinction between art and the event," as Eliot later put it, "is always absolute." His "always" claims very much; it would move into separate domains the *Iliad* and Trojan warriors, the Sonnets and the Dark Lady. That implies that the moderns were recovering an ancient understanding, so long obscured that its recovery could detonate like a revolution. If that's so, then out of Pound's small poem can be winkled, with good will, a better truth than Roger Fry had to offer when he tried to place Picasso just a little farther on along the rutted road trodden by George Frederick Watts.

Nineteen thirteen was the year of Jacob Epstein's "The Rock Drill," a construction that incorporated a real drill. Drill and driller share a sculptural idiom of geometric carapace: either *he* is a machine, or *it* is human, or (more likely) both pertain to the domain of forms whence praying mantises emerged and lobsters and kindred artifacts of God the Engineer. The structural logic of exoskeletal beings—insects or crustaceans—was not hidden beneath soft flesh but was manifest. The same was true of armor, and of machines. Art was beginning to prize such unpadded exemplars.

You could begin to think of "free verse"—unfortunate name—not as a non-form derived from prose but, rather, as an aid to assembling forms; a way to build up a poem from its skeleton—indeed, to *exhibit* the skeleton, the phrasal and the rhythmic units. Did not rhyme and meter conduce to adipose deposits?

> . . . Lo! sweetened with the summer light,
> The full-juiced apple, waxing over-mellow,
> Drops in the silent autumn night.
> All its allotted length of days,
> The flower ripens in its place,
> Ripens and fades, and falls, and hath no toil,
> Fast-rooted in the fruitful soil.

Might not Tennyson have less lavishly written,

> Summer, the apple mellows.
>   Autumn, it falls.
> Flowers open, fade, die;
>   that is all they need do

—and on finding there was rather little to that, mightn't he have sought firmer substance, not lusher language?

Also the word "hard" was coming into vogue. We find it in Pound's 1912 prediction that the best poetry of the coming decade would be "harder and saner . . . as much like granite as it can be," and with "fewer painted adjectives impeding the shock and stroke of it." His "The Coming of War: Actaeon" (1915) bears that out almost literally:

> . . . Gray cliffs,
>   and beneath them
> A sea
> Harsher than granite,
>   unstill, never ceasing;
> High forms
>   with the movement of gods,
> Perilous aspect;
>   And one said:

"This is Actaeon."
Actaeon of the golden greaves! . . .

Gray cliffs, granite—those are natural forms; but their still austerity
is like architecture. The adjectives serve to convey information about
this visionary landscape: that its cliffs are high, its seas harsh. Three
words from an unknown speaker suffice to identify Actaeon, who saw
a forbidden vision and was torn to pieces by his own hounds. Cliffs,
sea, "forms," the mythic victim: from these and from its stark reticence
of language the poem's emotion derives. Compare this altogether different austerity:

> Sombre and rich, the skies;
> Great glooms, and starry plains.
> Gently the night wind sighs;
> Else a vast silence reigns . . .

—stress after stress falling on the modifiers, "sombre," "rich," "great,"
"starry," "gently," "vast": from these words the poem's emotion is
being wrung. For is this dark sky of itself somber and rich, this silence
in itself vast? No, those are showman's words to insist that an ordinary
nightscape is portentous. Yet Lionel Johnson, whose "By the Statue
of King Charles at Charing Cross" the quatrain introduces, was a poet
celebrated for Stoic reserve: that illusion his reserved stanzas could
create in those glory days of pentametric gush, and his dependence
on epithets could go unnoticed. It's not from the night and the statue
that his poem emanates, but from his theatricality of utterance. . . .
Gautier, from whose analogies of cutting and carving Pound took the
word "hard," might have been a better model for quatrains than any
Lionel Johnson found:

> *Carmen est maigre,—un trait de bistre*
> *Cerne son oeil de gitana.* . . .
>
> Grishkin is nice; her Russian eye
> Is underlined for emphasis. . . .

Another source for the criterion of hardness, as for Epstein's interest
in machines, was the modern city: London, which for some decades
had been changing from a clustering of shelters into a huge machine.
The electrification of London Transport had commenced at about the

century's turn, to suck vast numbers of people underground for delivery at various orifices. Its subterranean rumblings were soon answered by notes from above. Heralded by horns and barbaric percussion, machinery was invading the open streets. Automobiles, black and predatory, demanded wholesale repaving lest suspensions be knocked to pieces, and thousands of square miles of cobbles gave way to macadam. Below, webs of water-pipes, sewer-pipes, gas-pipes needed constant renewal, the pavement sometimes no sooner laid than torn open. Stone drills blattered beneath urban windows, valves sounded their 4/4 ta-pocketa, backfiring exhausts exploded. Though England had led mankind into industrialization, its Satanic mills were elsewhere, north and west, and most Londoners' experience of the Machine Age had been limited to the locomotive. That held lordship in its temples, the great stations, but so bucolic in some respects was the city elsewhere that public goats wandered loose to scavenge its alleys. (Near Piccadilly, in 1884, Joseph Pennell, the artist, watched a man scare a goat off by opening an umbrella; it fled into the open door of a club.) And now there were tubes, motor-buses, motor-taxis; telephones too. Machinery confronted you in London everywhere you looked.

> At the violet hour, when the eyes and back
> Turn upward from the desk, when the human engine waits
> Like a taxi throbbing waiting . . .

—so Eliot, in *The Waste Land*, after the War. But in the last prewar years it was only painting that brought news of change: painting that leaped like lightning from country to country, Paris–Moscow–Munich–London, unchecked by Babel's barriers. And by 1913 designs rectilinear as a city grid, busy and cacophonous as Oxford Circus, brought the unwanted news that Constable's England and Jane Austen's was gone forever.

What Roger Fry had displayed in 1910 was tame painting by the lights of 1913; as we've noted, it was even old in 1910. Yet, though no one had been forced to go to the Grafton Gallery, word of atrocities on display drew hundreds, who came, it seemed, to be alarmed, and were. They duly screamed their outrage, most of them people who'd showed no sign in their lives of special concern for pictures. (Had the screaming been matched at all by concern for pictures, every painter in England would have had a patron.) No, the fuss was not about painting. It was about the news this strange painting brought to the most innocent: that you could no longer rely on the men with brushes to affirm the worth of things. The office of painting had been to reassure you that chrysanthemums and handsome ladies in gowns were valued today as yesterday and always; by extension, that on an island whose factories and ships had long made wealth, the elegant norm was still the countryhouse and its pretense of cherishing ploughmen and the soil. That was what really underlay so much fierce attention to the treatment of *subjects*. Though sensible people needn't care about pictures—though painting, for that matter, was an art in which nothing much ever happened—the painters in their very uninventiveness had affirmed long continuities of worth. But the wild men of Paris were scorning this consensus about the worth of what they looked at. To displace a woman's eyes, even as mildly as Cézanne displaced things, was to devalue her. Somehow the world had changed, the social world, the world in which you knew where you stood and where everybody else stood, the cook, the dustman, the painter, the painter's themes. Something—God knew what—was undermining all that. If you can't trust your eyes, you can trust nothing. And it was eye-art that was misbehaving. The painters had commenced to lie like poets.

Soon the word-arts were counter-mobilized. By 1914 Clive Bell, 33, had published *Art*, a piece of graceful twaddle still reprinted. It offered the perplexed exactly what they needed, a good phrase with "all the magic of a slogan." That was *significant form*, defined by Bell as "arrangements and combinations that move us in a particular way," and it was the *one* thing that all successful works of art possessed in common—"Sta. Sophia and the windows at Chartres, Mexican sculpture, a Persian bowl, Chinese carpets, Giotto's frescoes at Padua. . . ." In each of these, "lines and colours combined in a particular way, certain forms and relations of forms, stir our aesthetic emotions." They offered significant form. That was all there was to it, and by including the Persian bowl Clive Bell had cleverly undercut the whole problem of "subject." Clearly a bowl, considered as a work of art, has no subject save itself. Even Tonks would have had to concede that much, fume though he might over disparities of scale between the bowl and, say, Michelangelo's *David*.

Toward the age of Michelangelo, in fact, Clive Bell was distinctly cool—an age when "the power of creating significant form becomes the inexplicable gift of the occasional genius," genius-worship being "the infallible sign of an uncreative age." No one ascribes the Persian bowl to genius, though exceptional discernment may be ascribed to the connoisseur with the taste to fancy it. Having been born no more susceptible to bowls than anyone else, such a person may even have undergone an experience akin to religious conversion, seeing the world thereafter with reopened eyes. The analogy between connoisseurship and religion runs through *Art* from end to end; the book's real hero is not the maker of significant form but the person who responds to it, and that this person is uncommonly gifted is one thing Bell is sure of. It's for want of his gifts that the many hanker after familiar subjects and take pleasure in an art of representation. He, though, when he encounters significant form, is transported "from the world of man's activity to a world of aesthetic exaltation"; he is "lifted above the stream of life" like an adept of pure mathematics. Pound would depict him in *Hugh Selwyn Mauberley* (1920):

> A Minoan undulation,
> Seen, we admit, amid ambrosial circumstances
> Strengthened him against
> The discouraging doctrine of chances,
>
> And his desire for survival,
> Faint in the most strenuous moods,
> Became an Olympian *apathein*
> In the presence of selected perceptions.

Such existences are enabled by a sure income (the Bells had money from a coal mine).

After Clive Bell's smart handbook had become available, with its version of fourteen hundred years of European art (on the whole, a long downslide recently arrested by Cézanne),* anyone literate could learn how to go through the motions of connoisseurship, and guess in what accents to murmur "significant form!" Hooting at "distortions" could be left to the penny press. Bell enjoyed a long reputation as a sage, though the merits of *Art* are on the whole those of an articulate undergraduate's long essay. As late as 1958 he answered a question about the greatest colorists in the history of art: "Why, dear boy, Titian, Matisse and Duncan Grant." Lord. Yes, he knew what tone to take, what corners could be safely cut, and in knowing such

---

* "This alone seems to me sure: since the Byzantine primitives set their mosaics at Ravenna no artist in Europe has created forms of greater significance unless it be Cézanne."

things he exactly judged his public. When he wrote the book he was a decade down from Cambridge, and a few years married to Vanessa Stephen, with whose sister, Virginia, he'd pretty heavily flirted before she annoyed him by marrying Leonard Woolf. (Vanessa meanwhile was disporting with Roger Fry.) Woolf naturally thought Bell "a fat, round body" with a "little, round, fat mind." We're on the verge of the Bloomsbury Years: of that "House of Lions," in Leon Edel's phrase, that so frequently resembles a basket of squabbling kittens.

Yes, the hero of *Art* is the connoisseur, and certainly not the artist. With the artist Clive Bell is most comfortable when he's anonymous, like the architects of Ravenna. That's at bottom a democratization, since you too might hope to become a connoisseur the way you'd become a Methodist, by such sudden illumination as could befall anyone. It befell Roger Fry, who'd been destined for science; it befell Clive Bell, whom fortune seemed to have marked out for mindless grouse-shoots. As for becoming an artist, the best way was to be born into such a culture as sustained the maker of the Persian jar; *Art* is full of praise for nameless craftsmen. But, failing that, you'd need to be a "genius," and genius is not created by some flash on a road to Damascus or to the British Museum. No one knows where it comes from, and Bell thought it rather vulgar. When, in 1913, Roger Fry founded the Omega Workshops, an odd, mad scheme for surrounding people with beauty—chairs, rugs, china—he insisted that his impecunious workmen stay anonymous, though, being a connoisseur, he was never anonymous himself in the *Athenaeum*. Also people who dealt with Omega knew they were dealing with Fry. And that was too much for the principal genius Fry had backed into his stable: Wyndham Lewis.

Which is the shortest way to tell a Byzantine story, the upshot of which was that Lewis broke from Fry and Omega, rallied his own supporters at the Rebel Art Centre, and planned a huge magazine called *Blast* to support a movement for which Ezra Pound at the last moment came up with the right name: Vorticism. *Blast* finally appeared in late June 1914. Lewis was solely responsible for about half its pages. And since Lewis had published stories in Ford's *English Review* before ever anyone heard of him as a painter, we're back to literature at last.

He was one of the great originals of language. "The man with the leaping mind," he minted sudden phrases, and by 1914 had evolved a posterish style which didn't force him to spell out their connections.

CHAOS OF ENOCH ARDENS
> laughing Jennys
> Ladies with Pains
> good-for-nothing Guineveres

—that's a lurid glimpse of Victorian fetishes, caught by the Lewis searchlight. How to make *sentences* out of such elements seemed at that time a subsidiary problem; "anything less essential than a noun or a verb," he recalled decades later, "prepositions, articles,—the small fry—as far as might be I would abolish." In *Blast* he relied on typography, not syntax: whole pages arranged in a job-printer's bold display fonts, disjunction their normal state. A little later his novel *Tarr* rammed phrases into a syntactic compactor, to make what were nominally sentences but resembled, page by page, a fevered translation from the Slavic. Yet whatever problems it dismisses unsolved, the early style of Wyndham Lewis can rise to unique eloquence:

> But life is invisible, and perfection is not in the waves or houses that the poet sees. To rationalize that appearance is not possible. Beauty is an icy douche of ease and happiness at something *suggesting* perfect conditions for an organism: it remains suggestion. A stormy landscape, and a pigment consisting of a lake of hard, yet florid waves; delight in each brilliant scoop or ragged burst was John Constable's beauty. Leonardo's consisted in a red rain on the shadowed sides of heads, and heads of massive female aesthetes. Uccello accumulated pale parallels, and delighted in cold architecture of distinct colours. Korin found in the symmetrical gushing of water, in waves like huge vegetable insects, traced and worked faintly, on a golden pâte, his business. Cézanne liked cumbrous democratic slabs of life, slightly leaning, transfixed in vegetable intensity. . . .

In its affirmation of particular worlds for individual minds, its refusal to locate a Cézanne just a little farther along the same road as a Watts, nothing could less resemble the reassuring patter of Roger Fry or Clive Bell, which in making unfamiliar art assimilable implied that all art was alike, including the potter's, in conferring aesthetic ecstasy.*

The reverse of genteel, the rhetoric of *Blast* was so strident it was difficult to be sure what it was saying. To an art-world abounding in isms, it seemed to be proposing a new addition, Vorticism, the disputes of which with Futurism or Cubism seemed nonsensically arcane. Yet what was being proposed was of some moment: nothing less than a distinctively English art, to comport with London's distinction as a world capital and England's status as a maritime nation. One page affords a point of entry:

BLESS ALL PORTS.

PORTS, RESTLESS MACHINES of

	scooped out basins
	heavy insect dredgers
	monotonous cranes
	stations
	lighthouses, blazing
	through the frosty
	starlight, cutting the
	storm like a cake
	beaks of infant boats,
	side by side,
	heavy chaos of
	wharves,
	steep walls of
	factories
	womanly town

BLESS these MACHINES that work the little boats across
clean liquid space, in beelines.

That's an inventory of visual motifs, at once mechanical and maritime: it points toward an art of sharp, vigorous angularity such as the *Blast* Manifesto thought indigenous to a northern and maritime nation. ("The English Character," said the Manifesto, "is based on the Sea.") Cézanne's Provence, by contrast, was southern and sunny, its Mediterranean a bathers' lake. Cubism's guitars and apples bespoke both the south and a salon-culture. It made little sense to base an art for

---

* In *The Caliph's Design* (1919) Lewis mocks "the arcane masturbatory tone in which some of them chant in the newspapers of their experiences: 'Connoisseurs in pleasure—of which I count myself one—know that nothing is more intensely delightful than the aesthetic thrill' . . ." As he adds, "Unsatisfied sex accounts for much."

the maritime north on any of that. "The Modern World is due almost entirely to Anglo-Saxon genius,—its appearances and its spirit. Machinery, trains, steam-ships, all that distinguishes externally our time, came far more from here than anywhere else." Industrialization, an English speciality, had "reared up steel trees where the green ones were lacking; . . . exploded in useful growths, and found wilder intricacies than those of Nature." That is accurate history, routinely ignored. The English like to believe that their genius is literary, though in language too their bent is technical: toward syntactical sureness, like skill with a rivet-gun. And the great *OED* wasn't made by litterateurs.

True, Monet had indulged ecstasies of steam in the Gare Saint-Lazare. Not serious steam, though: a kind of salon-steam, romantic, with the light coming through it. And the Italians, in "their Futuristic gush over machines, aeroplanes, etc.," were "the most romantic and sentimental 'moderns' to be found." A half-dozen pictures in *Blast*, by Lewis, Edward Wadsworth, Cuthbert Hamilton, hinted at an idiom for northern starkness: lines savagely straight, an energy of the diagonal, human figures (for the present) suppressed, an urban subtext of grids, traffic, blocks, steel frames. That was a beginning for a considerable movement, and despite rumors that it came to little, Richard Cork, its historian, has amassed enough visual and textual material to fill two large volumes. By 1987, when the Royal Academy (yes!) mounted a show of British Modernism, it was crystal-clear that the opposition all along had stemmed from Bloomsbury—from Roger Fry and Clive Bell. That show never reached New York, where Modern Art's mentors had been taught that Vorticism was a provincial ripple.

The reverberations of *Blast* #1 (June 1914) were soon obliterated by the guns of August. Plans for a quarterly were an early wartime casualty. A second issue, much thinner, got published in 1915. There was never a third. It would soon be possible to pretend—it was even successfully pretended for sixty years—that nothing had happened really save an eructation of Lewisian spite.

That was another impression the 1987 show undermined. Once pictures by Lewis, Nevinson, Spencer, Nash were gathered for the first time into one room, it was manifest that in working toward abstraction they'd foreseen a theme the War would grimly enforce: men reduced to automata, nature to harsh lines jabbing (ruined landscapes like parodic cities), community to indifference within a common plight, most sentience to a numb wait while some apocalypse got around to happening. Thus Flanders, 1916, foreshadowed London, 1956. Artists being "the antennae of the race," Vorticism had made a visual vocabulary ready. Those English war-pictures are like no others painted in Europe.

But the post-war oracles were blind and dumb. Nineteen nineteen would see Clive Bell and Roger Fry invested with authority among the "advanced," Tonks ensconced at the Slade, Pound preparing to leave for Paris, T. S. Eliot literally underground in a bank, and Lewis, unwilling to paint what nobody would buy, facing a decade of writing polemical books.

8 : ARMAGEDDON

Paul Nash, the painter, surveyed a continental landscape: "The rain drives on, the stinking mud becomes more evilly yellow, the shell holes fill up with green-white water, the roads and tracks are covered in inches of slime, the black dying trees ooze and sweat and the shells never cease. They alone plunge overhead, tearing away the rotting tree stumps, striking down horses and mules, annihilating, maiming, maddening, they plunge into the grave which is this land; one huge grave."

That was, for four years, the normal look of Flanders and much of northeastern France, where, by November 1918, of every ten Englishmen under 45, one had died and two more had suffered wounds: two million English casualties alone. The system that chose officers from the educated classes, then sent officers ahead over the top, ensured that those groups suffered the heaviest losses: the toll of intelligentsia was disproportionate. At random: T. E. Hulme died; the sculptor Henri Gaudier-Brzeska died—

> Charm, smiling at the good mouth,
> Quick eyes gone under earth's lid . . .

the poet Wilfrid Owen died—

> What passing-bells for those that die as cattle?
> Only the monstrous anger of the guns . . .

the painter-poet Isaac Rosenberg died—

> The wheels lurched over sprawled dead
> But pained them not, though their bones crunched. . . .

One day, 1 July 1916, saw sixty thousand British casualties, a record till 21 March 1918, when they lost 150,000 in "the largest engagement fought since the beginnings of civilization." By the time it was ending, half the British infantry were younger than 19. The gas, the high explosives, the Mausers, the tanks, decimated a generation. How much art they killed, how much literature, there is no guessing. Eliot's hernia kept him in London; Pound, his astigmatism. We're fortunate.

Toward the end of it, Bolshevism engulfed Russia. A year after that, fire and sword and ideology had a new ally, pestilence: the influenza pandemic that killed twenty million worldwide. Mankind had known nothing like that since the Black Death. And by the time the whole complex disaster had subsided, London itself felt like a no-man's-land, from which to look back toward an order as irrecoverable as a dream. Wyndham Lewis remembered, long after, the distant world he and T. Sturge Moore had shared:

> How calm those days were before the epoch of wars and social revolution, when you used to sit on one side of your work-table and I on the other, and we would talk—with trees and creepers of the placid Hampstead domesticity beyond the windows, and you used to grunt with a philosophic despondence I greatly enjoyed. It was the last days of the Victorian world of artificial peacefulness—of the R.S.P.C.A. and London Bobbies, of "slumming" and Buzzards cakes. As at that time I had never heard of anything else, it seemed to my young mind in the order of nature. You—I suppose—knew it was all like the stunt of an illusionist. You taught me many things. But you never taught me *that*. I first discovered about it in 1914—with growing surprise and disgust.

There Lewis might be echoing D. H. Lawrence—"Something very good, and poignant to remember, now the whole world of it is lost." And one could multiply such quotations.

England's hereditary enemy had always been France. But here we were allied with the French, and fighting the Germans. And our King bore a German dynastic name, Saxe-Coburg-Gotha (hastily changed to "Windsor").* The Kaiser was his cousin. Also, though the shooting of an archduke had somehow started it, that did not explain what the war was all about. What sense did it make to protest, to the extent of uncountable deaths, the violation of what a German was reported to have called "a scrap of paper" concerning Belgian neutrality?

The leisure in which Everyman might have pondered such questions got quickly preempted. Framed copies of the scrap of paper—a treaty of 1839, signed by England, France, Prussia, Austria, and Russia— were indignantly hung in schools, to affirm that it *was* the reason, and people began hearing a German word, "Junker." That sounds nasty to plain English ears; it grunts and swaggers and relishes decapitated babies. Gallant England was saving little Belgium from Prussianism— from the Junkers!

Bernard Shaw, by then 58, was skeptical. The guns had been firing only a hundred days when his *Common Sense About the War* appeared, thirty thousand words to decry Junkerism all round. A Junker, Shaw's *Encyclopädisches Wörterbuch* had disclosed, was simply Germany's word for what England called a country gentleman. England too was ruled by Junkers; it was a war of Junker vs. Junker. So "Let us have no more nonsense," said Shaw, "about the Prussian wolf and the British Lamb. . . . We cannot shout for years that we are boys of the bulldog breed, and then suddenly pose as gazelles." It was a power war, a balance-of-power war; as for Belgian neutrality, Britain, by sending in troops, had violated that quite as much as had Germany in proposing to march through. But the German marchers got represented as "Huns," another word much in vogue; it seemed that an amiable and innocent people could only be nerved for war "by enormous overdoses of self-righteousness and moral indignation."

But in late 1914 an Irishman whose gaze toward Germany trembled with anything more complex than lust for blood seemed treasonous in London. Shaw insisted that the war, once engaged in, must be won, but how that proposition could be combined with his claim that gentlemanly rulers had bungled it into being was more than the press or even his associates could grasp. His editor, Dan H. Laurence, is right in calling *Common Sense About the War* "the most audacious and courageous action of his life." "Former friends cut him dead. . . . Booksellers and librarians removed his works from their shelves."

---

* Likewise, Ford Madox Hueffer became Ford Madox Ford, and off in Canada the town of Berlin, Ontario, renamed itself Kitchener.

One socialist colleague (Robert Blatchford, editor of *The Clarion*) even described *Common Sense* ("insensate malice and dirty innuendo") as "the meanest act of treachery ever perpetrated by an alien enemy residing in generous and long-suffering England."

"An alien enemy": rage had let Blatchford expose the deepest English prejudice, one that exceeded genteel anti-Semitism. Though every Irishman was a U.K. citizen, the Irish had long seemed treacherous animals indeed, most dangerous when (occasionally) they were clever. They might smoke clay pipes upside down, which was all right, or amusingly ornament hearthrugs and croon lyrics like "Innisfree." But let one of them venture an independent thought and instantly he became what at bottom he was, an alien enemy, fondling his dearest maxim: England's difficulty, Ireland's opportunity.

So Shaw had to play the man on guard, repelling with good humor all attackers, even the blind sharks his blood agitated. He claimed to be the one sane man in a land of sentimentalists. Day and night he relished his own rationality. He spelled matters out, a,b,c; he claimed that he was never wrong about anything, and eventually came to believe it. In the process he turned into "GBS," a man whose most exhilarating writing, the *Letters*, wouldn't be published until decades after he was dead, by which time the plays he'd staked his fame on seemed historical curiosities.

"In the right key one can say anything," Shaw wrote; "in the wrong key, nothing: the only delicate part of the job is the establishment of the key." Like all great comedians, he had a principal key he'd spent much of a lifetime establishing. It permitted him to say perhaps not anything, but surely any number of outrageous things, all composed in his own tonality of bright percussive knowingness: Toccatas in Shaw Sharp Major.

War has just deprived the playwright St. John Ervine of a leg, and Shaw offers consolation: "For a man of your profession two legs are an extravagance. . . . The more the case is gone into the more it appears that you are an exceptionally happy and fortunate man, relieved of a limb to which you owed none of your fame, and which indeed was the cause of your conscription; for without it you would not have been accepted for service."

It's hard to imagine who else could have carried that off; or this (to H. G. Wells): "My dear H.G., I am all right about Russia. The longer

I live the more I see that I am never wrong about anything, and that all the pains I have so humbly taken to verify my notions have only wasted my time." Or this (to a journalist he'd never met): "Dear Sir, Your profession has, as usual, destroyed your brain."

A heartless egotist? That has become the cliché. But though any smarty might contrive to insult a stranger—a journalist at that—by imputing brain damage, what would any smarty find to say next? Such an insult he might scribble across a letter he had no intention of answering. Shaw used it, though, to launch a detailed answer, a thousand words in pungent explication of what it was the journalist hadn't been noticing. So expository energy redeems his opening sally, which says, Why must I always explain the world to people whose alleged job is keeping an eye on it? That does for the explanation what pepper can do for soup: prevents it from seeming an academic exercise.

As we grow saturated in his correspondence, Shaw's insults, like his boasts, turn transparently genial. Pick up the third volume of his letters (1911–25), and within a few pages here's GBS responding to Gilbert Murray's translation of *Oedipus Rex* with a brief outline meant to expose the defects of Sophocles.

> . . . Edipus—Then—then—I—Oh Lord! (Exit)
> Chorus—   Ah me, no chappy
>   Call I unhappy
>   Until—
> . . . Edipus—(rushing in and scattering rose pink
> from his eyes all over the orchestra) Woe, woe! Pain!
> Ah me! Ai! ai! ai! Me miserable!

> Stupendous applause. The Messenger & Edipus take six calls and finally reappear with Sophocles between them. Immense enthusiasm.

> Chorus—   Talk of bliss
>   After this!——

Murray replied that he and his colleagues found that difficult to read without tears; he seems not to have commented on Shaw's assertion that Sophocles was the sort of man the English like: "the brains of a ram, the theatrical technique of an agricultural laborer, the reverence for tradition of a bee."

"The sort of man the English like"—that's a useful clue. An Irish playwright in exile among the slow-witted English, whose idea of a playwright was the amiably incompetent Sophocles: such is one description of the role Shaw elected to play. And the first mistake they made about this Irishman was expecting sentiment and blarney. For, no, he glittered with competence and logic; those underpublicized Irish traits he even exaggerated, in a way that alarmed his most famous Irish contemporary, W. B. Yeats—no mean logician himself, as *A Vision* shows if you'll only concede its premises. Yeats once had a dream of a sewing-machine, a sewing-machine that clicked and perpetually smiled, and he realized that it was Bernard Shaw.

Another thing Shaw claimed to notice about the people around him was that not one of them had the least idea how to go about doing anything, so that he had to be always telling them. His machine-like reserves of energy were fortunate, seeing that he felt obliged to explain, for instance,

—punctuation, to Lawrence of Arabia (an aspiring writer "no more to be trusted with a pen than a child with a torpedo");
—articulation, to the actress Molly Tompkins ("Get out the words from which the audience can guess the rest; . . . The others . . . are useful only for rhythm");
—the production of vocal tone, to the musician Arnold Dolmetsch ("You round the back of your throat and throw the column of air into vibration without forcing it out; and when you want to make a crescendo . . . you pull down your diaphragm, arch your soft palate, and enlarge the instrument generally, but you don't blow");
—the whole art of rehearsing plays, to the producer Augustin Hamon. (Here Shaw knew exactly what he was talking about.)

On the scaffold, had it come to that, you'd have heard Shaw coaching the hangman. Late in 1915 "his attitude regarding the war" caused several members of the Dramatists' Club to want him expelled, and they didn't even know how to go about that. So he had to outline in full to the secretary a proper procedure for expelling a member, and then watch the leaves fall from the calendar while they tried to follow it. (After a week he'd tired of the game, and resigned.)

GBS naturally attracted biographers; one of these, with the improbably romantic name of Thomas Demetrius O'Bolger, surfaced about 1913 in Pennsylvania, where among other peccadilloes he professed English. O'Bolger (1871–1923) spent the last ten years of his life trying to make something publishable of his Ph.D. thesis, "The

Real Shaw," and took up unconscionable hours of the real Shaw's time. He'd surmised that there was something less than normative about Shaw's mother and father; that his mother in particular had taken up with a figure named Vandaleur Lee, even moved herself and the children in with Lee, thus massaging the psyche of young GBS toward all manner of cynical irregularity.

Enough of an Irish gentleman to defend his mother's honor, Shaw sent O'Bolger lengthy accounts of his childhood in which Vandaleur Lee (whose name he consistently misspelled) figured as a neglected genius into whose London house Mrs. Shaw had moved with her brood for the most rational of reasons: as rational as the reasons, also set forth, whereby GBS himself later married a woman of means, and quite honorably.

Lee seems to have been a how-to man like GBS; his speciality was voice production, which he taught Mrs. Shaw. Shaw's father certainly didn't like him, but Mrs. Shaw "went her own way, which happened to be the musical way of Lee, just as Lee went his, and my father could only look on helplessly, just like Mr. Jellyby in Bleak House." Lee turned into "an amusing humbug" (not unlike GBS). O'Bolger may have been on to something. But, worn down by Shaw, he never got to publish it.

Shaw's way was at any rate "the musical way." We've heard his words on getting the right key, in which you can say anything. More arresting, though, is a paragraph in a letter to O'Bolger which describes an essentially eighteenth-century musical upbringing: "Beethoven was modern and disturbing to us. . . . The modern realistic expression of erotic emotion was [to Shaw's mother] . . . unladylike and indecent," as it surely was to GBS.

More: "My deliberate rhetoric, and my reversion to the Shakespearean feature of long set solos for my characters, are pure Italian opera. My rejection of plot and *dénouement*, and my adoption of a free development of themes, are German symphony. My clown and ringmaster technique of discussion cannot be referred to French music: it is plain Molière; but I daresay I learned something from Gounod as well as from Fra Angelico as to the ease with which religious emotion and refined sexual emotion can be combined."

Indeed he did, to the bafflement of the English, among whom he spent nearly all his life. A people for whom literature marches step after step like the alphabet won't feel prepared for such irrational nonsense. They didn't stomach it when T. S. Eliot (following Wagner) did it in *The Waste Land*. They stomached it from GBS because his lines were so funny (unwilling to think, still they could always *laugh*), and they stomached GBS himself because in his gallant energy he was always three skips ahead of where the flyswatter had struck.

Shaw "introduced into England," so we are routinely told, "the theatre of ideas." That can be put differently. The world his words delimit, the words of his letters and pamphlets as well as his plays, is a world of abstractions and outlines: a caricaturist's world. A good caricature is a brilliant simplification, so stark, so deft, so linear and two-dimensional, that how it keeps up relations with its living model—how he's even recognizable—is far from obvious. Shaw's very cool talk about some of the horrors of post-revolution Russia, about superfluous *rentiers* and middlemen being shot by the thousand—in the heat, as it were, of a brisk and overdue housecleaning—tends to posit that liquidating a human being is like erasing an unsatisfactory part of a drawing, to redo it in a style more in keeping with the style of the rest. In not being horrified by some of Shaw's sentences we're conceding some such analogy; the act of erasure is intellectual, bloodless. It resembles the loss of St. John Ervine's leg.

For look at a sentence from that letter to Ervine again:

> The more the case is gone into the more it appears that you are an exceptionally happy and fortunate man, relieved of a limb to which you owed none of your fame, and which indeed was the cause of your conscription; for without it you would not have been accepted for service.

The feat he's performing here is making an amputee smile. He's cajoling Ervine to regard his own body as a caricature, with a superfluity happily erased. In a get-well letter, that is amusingly insolent. Though he'd not stop missing his leg, and Shaw knew that he wouldn't, Ervine would be entertained by the gambit. Likewise, Professor Murray's mention of "tears" conveys pleasure in a caricature that left his beloved *Oedipus* unscathed. It wasn't, Murray could feel sure, the "real" Sophocles his correspondent was knocking senseless.

And such is always Shaw's gambit, in books and plays that address not a crippled friend but a public, regarding themes that imperil the quality of its existence. He shifts lives and deaths and passions to the plane of diagram, where the most violent happenings threaten nothing real. That is "the theatre of ideas."

He entertained many thousands, yes. And, yes, he helped prepare them to accept, for better or worse, the social revolutions yet another war would be bringing. One side-effect, though, is undeniable. As one of England's most visible intellectuals in the last years print and stage still dominated, before the BBC and its radio Brains Trust, he confirmed Everyman's very reassuring notion that a life of the mind— a life other than the average sensual life Shaw affronted with his vegetarian crankery—though boring at worst is simply amusing at best. Everyman could shut a book of Shaw's more certain than he'd ever been that highbrow talk-talk isn't really *about* anything. Especially after a war that had swept away so many old things, the old things were the best.

If art's inner landscape had changed by the end of the war, the world of Everyman's perception was disoriented too. Those machines were popping and snorting wherever he looked. Where vehicles smaller than trains had been horse-powered, by 1919 they were petrol-powered. As recently as 1905 most Londoners had never seen a tram or a motor-bus. That year the electric lines first ventured north of the Thames, to commence obsolescing the horses Europeans had relied on since Troy's time. In London alone there had been a quarter-million horses. But fifteen years and, lo, horses were gone, and Sherlock Holmes's hansoms, the horse-buses, the carts, the drays, the carriages, the turds and their sweepers.

Though London had no such thoroughfare as the Champs-Elysées for broughams to promenade on—though the French were historic specialists in ostentatious horsiness (*cheval-erie*, chivalry)—Englishmen had always been proud to vie. To fight the Great War both peoples had mobilized cavalry divisions, and had shuttled their troops in *"quarante et huit"* railway cars, built for forty men and eight horses. Hurrah for the gallant steeds! But soon the horses were being used chiefly to haul guns through a muck in which wheels sank. After caterpillar treads eventually conquered muck, there was no place mechanized vehicles couldn't go. In the post-war streets, on pneumatic tires, they went everywhere. London's omnibuses now snorted and gave off fumes, and private cars were starting to proliferate. Pre-war there'd been just a few of those, rich men's toys, resented mainly for the dust they'd kicked up on the quiet old dusty roads. And now, for their convenience, even the country roads were being macadamized.

It was difficult to remember how, pre-war, glimpses of the new machines had partaken of a certain romance. A London Transport poster of 1914 had offered a cheap Sunday fare to Hampstead—for just 4d. (return), via Underground, you could

TAKE YOUR SON AND HEIR
WHERE THERE IS SUN AND AIR

WE CARRY DOGS AND FOLDING MAILCARTS

Its picture of the holiday delights of Hampstead took you into a nineteenth-century country fair: pony rides, dogs, cockshies, kites, balloonmen, happy children running, indulgent parents carefree. Apart from nuances of costume, just two details bespoke a modern world where the Underground was convenient: past a big house went a single open touring-car; distant in the sky hung a single biplane. The sensibility the picture appealed to had no difficulty assimilating those: glimpses of novelty were part of the fun. By 1919 "fun" was no longer the word, either for the cars that were choking the streets or for the winged machines that had filled French skies and dropped death.

Pre-war too, people still spoke in Homer's way, face to face; the telephone was a business instrument. (Alexander Graham Bell himself never had one; he'd as soon have put a cash-register in his house.) Post-war, the telephone was turning up in furnished flats, and within a few years, to T. S. Eliot's ear, it was beating the flat-folks' time like a metronome:

TELEPHONE: Ting a ling ling
Ting a ling ling
DUSTY: That's Pereira
DORIS: Yes that's Pereira
DUSTY: Well what you going to do?
TELEPHONE: Ting a ling ling
Ting a ling ling
DUSTY: That's Pereira
DORIS: Well can't you stop that horrible noise?
Pick up the receiver
DUSTY: What'll I say!

"Are you there?" was what people instinctively said into a phone; some were still saying it as late as mid-century. "Are you there?" was a sensible question, since where *was* that voice? It was in one's head, nowhere else; "voice" no longer denoted "presence." Where are the voices in *The Waste Land*? They are in the poem, that is all we can say; no longer, as in Browning's monologues, does speech locate itself in a place and time. "You who were with me in the ships at Mylae"— are we still in a London street? Eliot's poem cannot bring to mind a peopled stage: a central exchange, perhaps, spectacularly short-circuited. Bookmen who missed such an analogy demanded to know who was speaking to whom and why. The attention Eliot had paid to the telephone derived from what no London critic had, a Harvard training in phenomenology.

As for what people were reading, the custom of *Tit-Bits* readers continued as before; or not quite as before, since they were acquiring the cinema habit. On the eve of the war there'd been four hundred screens in London, many of them hung temporarily for nonce show-ings. Each week some eighty thousand Londoners came. (Five million Americans *a day* were going to the movies.) By 1921 London had 266 cinemas proper: imitation theatres where people went solely for films, places condescended to, once the novelty had worn off, as low-brow haunts indeed. In England, for a surprisingly long time, cinema was dismissed as a working-class recreation. It transmitted best-sellers downward to sturdy folk whom long stints of reading exhausted. As long ago as 1913 a six-reel *East Lynne* had been issued; later *The Sorrows of Satan* was promised but canceled. The King and Queen of England were not seen seeing a film till 1924, and Baden-Powell's handbooks for Boy Scouts never faltered in their scorn of "the picture-palace."

The Everyman's public was disoriented and divided. Its stake in an immutable past made it vulnerable like no other group to all manner of disagreeable post-war novelty, but since money was what brought control over the new toys, its less affluent half suffered more. Former war-correspondents—Philip Gibbs, H. M. Tomlinson—embarked on new careers as novelists, and did well by reassuring Everyman in his thousands that knowing one's way around was still possible. One secret, they intimated, was to disregard highbrows.

The stir, the action, was amid the coteries that competed, after 1919, for control of avant-garde opinion. Their disputes left Everyman wholly bewildered.

* * *

Adults could welcome any link with the times in which they had spent most of their lives, and it's unsurprising that the Georgian Anthologies sold well and kept selling, ever reprinted, reprinted. They could re-assure turners of pages, as they had while war still raged, that civilization in the old sense was within call. "Georgian"! The word had been coined within two years of King George V's accession. Even then a need for identity had been urgent; Queen Victoria's subjects didn't think to call themselves "Victorian" till she'd reigned nearly four decades.

The first of these little collections of what now seems very tame poetry had been assembled in 1912 by Edward (later Sir Edward) Marsh, private secretary to the First Lord of the Admiralty, Mr. Churchill. By the end of 1919 "it was in its thirteenth thousand and still going strong." The second, 1915, sold over nineteen thousand copies, establishing "a record for a book of its kind which may never be surpassed." There was a third, a fourth, a fifth; but by '22 the need had dissipated.

A biography over half the length of Boswell's doesn't help us pin Edward Marsh: no butterfly, a butterfly's shadow, and a *waspish* shadow. At twenty he'd thought it "harder to fall in love with women the more real they are" and he seems never to have managed the feat, though his letters abound in "dear boy." The dearest was Rupert Brooke, a trunkful of whose memorabilia, including the khaki tie Brooke was wearing when he fell terminally ill, the handkerchief from under his pillow, and some copies of a pamphlet called *Sexual Ethics*, turned up in Marsh's attic after he'd died, aged 80, in 1953. In 1918 T. S. Eliot remarked that "the Georgians caress everything they touch." He was right about the impulse, though Brooke seems to have thought of himself as heterosexual.

Fastidious about all minutiae, Marsh was the best proofreader of his time, and put his talent at the service of many. Though he could dismay friends by urging *Sons and Lovers* on them, and would even praise *The Rainbow*, on the whole he stood for no nonsense. Stravinsky's *Le Sacre du Printemps* seemed to him like "hearing a canary, a slate pencil, a motor whistle, and a paper bag all at once," and as for poetry, he believed above all in "perfect form," by which he meant regular meter. "When reciting he would never stress a word to point the meaning, for fear of breaking the smooth *legato* incantation which to him was the essential beauty of metrical verse." When he spoke, likewise, "it was difficult to follow what he was saying. . . . The straining ear caught little more than a flow of rapidly articulated air." The general effect, though, was "agreeable." That's not a bad description of Georgian poetry, which, though it upset Arthur Waugh, bookman, had appeal for thousands, including Marsh's biographer.

The upset of Arthur Waugh pertained to meter, and given the date, 1916, that is interesting. He quoted from a nonentity, Lascelles Abercrombie:

O the fine earth and fine all for nothing!

and being unable to hear

O the fine éarth/ and fine áll for ńothing!

he raged at "incoherent violence" and "deliberate avoidance of a metrical tradition." By now we can say that fingers trained to count thumps were failing to detect something Abercrombie took random pleasure in, a beginner's ear for quantity.

It's wonderful the frenzy any slight metrical novelty could stir a bookman to; wonderful too how innocuous the anthologies after all were. They seemed un-Victorian; that was their wide appeal—un-Victorian, yet vaguely dreamy in a way that did not disconcert. If novels were city artifacts, were not poetry's pleasures those of a country weekend? Many pages seemed in a playful way rather pagan. Pre-war reviewers had taken the first collection pretty seriously; both Edmund Gosse and the *TLS* had detected, with slight misgivings, what Gosse called "a violence, almost a rawness in the approach to life itself," a sure sign that up-to-dateness was being imputed. Even D. H. Lawrence thought these poets were "bursting into a thick blaze of being" after a long nightmare dominated by "the nihilists, the intellectual, hopeless people—Ibsen, Flaubert, Thomas Hardy." So here it was at last, a distinguished thing! Abercrombie was frequently mentioned as its star.

But eventually, for every reader including Waugh, one Georgian would stand out. He was Rupert Brooke, a promising light versifier who'd toyed with thoughts of fish-heaven and a scaly god—

> Immense, of fishy form and mind,
> Squamous, omnipotent, and kind

and also hymned a perfect village, Grantchester:

> . . . In Grantchester their skins are white;
> They bathe by day, they bathe by night; . . .

That would be, one day, the spirit of *Brideshead Revisited* (as in *Le Grand Meaulnes*: the good life, here on earth, somewhere), and it could seem refreshingly un-Tennysonian. Young Brooke had been as handsome as a god, such a sensitive moreover that he could feel, he said, "quite sick and faint with passion at the beauty of a painting by [Augustus] John." James Elroy Flecker, another lover of beauty, called him "our Donne Redivivus." Friends predicted great things. But by the time of the second volume Sub-Lieutenant Brooke had died of sunstroke and septicemia en route to the Dardanelles, which helped earn him a paean from bookman Waugh—

> . . . and now this bright young harbinger of becoming possibilities sleeps by the Aegean Sea:

> A dust whom England bore, shaped, made aware,
>   Gave, once, her flowers to love, her ways to roam,
> A body of England's, breathing English air,
>   Washed by her rivers, blest by suns of home.
>
> And in his grave rest, beyond doubt, the highest
> Expectations of the poetic movement which
> He seemed destined, in the very hour of his death,
> To turn into richer and more profitable channels.

Wait, wait, I've miscopied; reprint that last sentence as prose. . . .

Much more was written in that vein by many. It's impossible to suppress the suspicion that bookman and Everyman alike preferred poets dead. From a dead poet's future you need fear no surprises. And in foreclosing promise, has not his very death been part of his legacy?

Promise foreclosed is a poem in itself. And to have foreseen, in ripely traditional measures, his very death, and mixed it with thoughts of England! That one sonnet of Brooke's got instantly "loved," in the way of certain durable Victorian pictures: Sir Luke Fildes's *The Doctor*, Sir John Millais's child blowing bubbles. That had sold Pears' Soap. Enhanced by a *Times* eulogy from Mr. Churchill, Brooke's sonnet helped with enlistments:* "He did his duty. Will you do yours?"

That was just the kind of thing Shaw had foreseen, a frantic pumping-up of vague purpose. Everyone's behavior is quite understandable. Mr. Churchill, then First Sea Lord, was bluffing his way past the Dardanelles fiasco. Eddie Marsh, orchestrator of testimonials, had giddily loved Rupert, who likely glozed over the nature of the fixation that was getting him a pied-à-terre in London and dinners at the tables of the powerful. (Once, when he caught a chill, he was put to bed at 10 Downing Street.) People like the Dean of Saint Paul's, who extolled the way the dead-soldier sonnet expressed "a pure and elevated patriotism," had forensic obligations—in that case, an Easter sermon, in which the Dean, to his credit, did observe that Brooke's piece fell short of Isaiah's vision. And everyone longed to be given some purposeful feelings about an empty war.

> If I should die, think only this of me:
> That there's some corner of a foreign field
> That is forever England. . . .

That was stuff to give the troops!

After the war, though, it was Everyman who craved it; the Georgian books sold and sold; Brooke's *Collected Poems, with a Memoir by E. Marsh* sold also. Brooke's slim accomplishment suffered, since if you think of him as the author of "If I should die . . ." then his three or four better poems seem aberrant, trivial, whereas if you can fix your attention on "Heaven" and "Grantchester" and "Tiare Tahiti" then it's the war-sonnets that divagate inexplicably. Light-fingered octosyllabics were his métier, as in "Tiare Tahiti":

---

* Henry James, on receiving from Marsh all five of Brooke's "Soldier-Sonnets," wrote a sentence worth preserving: "The circumstances (so to call the unspeakable matter) that have conduced to them, and that, taken together, seem to make a sort of huge brazen lap for their congruous beauty, have caused me to read them with an emotion that somehow precludes the critical measure." In short, just now, March 1915, it's unseemly to hint at jejunity.

> Mamua, when our laughter ends,
> And hearts and bodies, brown as white,
> Are dust about the doors of friends,
> Or scent a-blowing in the night,
> Then, oh! then, the wise agree,
> Comes our immortality.
> Mamua, there waits a land
> Hard for us to understand. . . .

There, shedding contingency, we shall merge with Plato's Great Absolutes, such as "The Good, the Lovely and the True." But putting that in simple language mocks it; for

> . . . there's an end, I think, of kissing,
> When our mouths are one with Mouth.

So let us not wait for that, but instead seize the innocent Tahitian moment:

> . . . Hasten, hand in human hand,
> Down the dark, the flowered way,
> Along the whiteness of the sand,
> And in the water's soft caress,
> Wash the mind of foolishness,
> Mamua, until the day. . . .

Agreeable verse, to be sure, though it evanesces if we bring Marvell near it—

> The grave's a fine and private place,
> But none, I think, do there embrace.
>
> Now, therefore . . .

Light verse works like dinner music, through continual reminiscence of something else: never risking the force of Eliotic allusion, no, just disporting itself in a field already mown. Thus it needn't try for underlying coherence; that's been prepared already. The Coy Mistress is surely what Brooke would have us see his own trifle hanging from, for if Mamua will miss the likeness, we literate people will not. Is Mamua being talked down to a little? Possibly. The poem pats her sleek little head while letting the rest of us know that it knows all about *carpe diem*. Still, how smoothly its quatrains and couplets run. Rupert Brooke was used to being charming for his supper.

However we judge his agreeable qualities, "If I should die . . ." left them invisible. It suggested that he had always tried to be *serious*, to succeed only at the last. Thus poor Waugh, hypnotized by the gaseous sonnet, drew attention to "Tiare Tahiti," in particular to the line "When our mouths are one with Mouth," not to ask whether the wit comes off (not quite) but in order to reprove "inherent ugliness, an ugliness which becomes almost vulgar," the defect of poets who lack a noble theme. Such, Waugh's readers were to understand, was the unregenerate Brooke. "But when the call came to make the supreme sacrifice"—aha, trumpets.

That one minor poet got misrepresented is a trifle, compared with what was happening to the idea of poetry. Serious was what it was understood to be, and lyrical and "natural" and sincere. No rolled trouser-bottoms need expect welcome in its arcanum, no patient etherized upon a table. Any poem was to be just like familiar poetry, a vagueness all sensitive readers have in their heads. But if it was too much like anything in particular—if such a line as "The army of unalterable law" (at the end of Mr. Eliot's "Cousin Nancy") turned out to have been used already (by George Meredith, in "Lucifer in Starlight")—why, out with the impostor! That is plagiary. It was even held, on the authority of Milton himself, that poetry ought to be "simple, sensuous and passionate," though that is not what Milton was saying. (*Paradise Lost*: simple!)

By 1919 the marvelous social machinery that facilitated ingress for a Bennett, a Pound, a Lawrence had gotten unobtrusively dismantled. The age of hostesses and teas was gone. To situate yourself in post-war London you wanted connections or Oxbridge credentials, though chameleon Eliot made do with Harvard ones. That was because the all-important thing now was access, via a coterie, to a printing-press.

For the resumption of the literary life had seen new groups and coteries mobilize, and whereas the 1914 Vorticists had been mobilized against "John Bull," the new groups tended to grimace at one another. Herbert Read, who was on the spot, summarizes the way things stood by 1920: "There were by then three centres of intellectual ferment:

the so-called Bloomsbury Group; the poets associated with Harold Monro and his review *Poetry and Drama*; and the Sitwells, who carried on a campaign against the literary establishment (the Squirearchy as it was sometimes called, for its most prominent member was J. C. Squire)." He also mentions Middleton Murry, who founded *The Adelphi* and collected the disciples of Lawrence. Read himself, though he early on made a pact with the Sitwells, was to give his longest allegiance to Eliot, who by 1925 had gotten Lady Rothermere to finance *The Criterion*.

(She'd been born Mary Share; her husband, the source of her affluence, was Harold Harmsworth, brother of Alfred Harmsworth, the cyclist we last spotted hanging out near *Tit-Bits*. Since that time, Alfred had become Lord Northcliffe, and Harold, Lord Rothermere. Their elevation acknowledged all the money they'd made. It came from *The Times* and kindred enterprises.)

Access to a review, at least to a printing-press: that was the key. *Poetry and Drama*, *The Adelphi*, *The Criterion*; and Bloomsbury had the Hogarth Press, which meant that its books were hand-set in Leonard Woolf's basement: hand-me-down William Morris. Jack Squire, the Squirearch, ruled the *London Mercury*, on the whole an Everyman citadel. And the Sitwells, well, they had money—not money by Rothermere standards, coal-money like Clive Bell's. As long ago as 1916 they'd founded *Wheels*, more or less a "family anthology" that endured for six "cycles" (till 1921), and later they bought *Art and Letters* from Read, who'd co-founded it from the trenches. Edith Sitwell got a sense of existence from editing *Wheels*, Osbert Sitwell ran *Art and Letters*. The most talented of the three, Sacheverell Sitwell, on the whole hung back from his siblings' efforts to establish what Cyril Connolly would call "their own alternative Bloomsbury."

Middleton Murry, a lifelong nurser of causes, was to hold no cause dearer than that of the genius of his wife, Katherine Mansfield, whose "sensitive" short stories were widely exclaimed over, though Malcolm Cowley was shrewd about her limitations: "One situation recurs constantly in her work. There is a woman: neurotic, arty, hateful, and a good, stupid man whom she constantly torments. . . . Another situation, which she repeats rather less frequently, is that of the destruction of a woman's individuality by some stronger member of her family. . . . She has three backgrounds only: continental hotels, New Zealand upper-class society, and a certain artistic set in London." That means, of course, that she was working out a set of personal conflicts. Whether she could have worked them through cannot be known, since she died at 34, in 1923, of consumption. Yet hers, Virginia Woolf confessed to her diary, was "the only writing I have ever been jealous of"; she left her mark on Elizabeth Bowen, Katherine Anne Porter, Eudora Welty; and when Carson McCullers read her book "to pieces," the library at Columbus, Georgia, had to replace it.

Like a feminine Rupert Brooke, she became a cult, extolled for all she never lived to do. As late as 1976 the cult throve on, in what one biographer calls "a soppy edition, complete with soft-focus photographs" of her correspondence with Murry. Earlier, George Orwell for one had been irritated by her formula: "a pointless little sketch about fundamentally uninteresting people, written in short flat sentences and ending on a vague query." The irritation responds to the cult, and Murry, as her editor, her first biographer, her critic, her literary executor and custodian of her manuscripts, spent a third of a century defining that cult. Lawrence wrote him astutely, "She was *not* a great genius. She had a charming gift, and a finely cultivated one. But *not more*. And to try, as you do, to make it more is to do her no true service." Murry, though, was enriching himself from her fame, and he persuaded himself that Katherine would approve. He even published his dream of how she rose from her coffin:

> As I watched, Katherine Mansfield raised herself wearily out of the shallow turfy grave. With her fingertips she took back the hair from her still-closed eyes. She opened them at last, and looked at the garden and the house, and smiled. Then, as though weary, she sank back to sleep again. It was peace; it was good; and what she had seen was also good.

It seemed tasteless to argue against something like that, and you'd never guess that she'd once referred to him as "a little mole hung out on a string to dry." In the new back alleys of publicity, Murry had constituted himself a one-man gang.

The gangs, the gangs. At one point the Sitwells wooed Lawrence away from Murry; long afterward, though, Edith was to describe him as "a plaster gnome" and express particular contempt for *Lady Chatterley's Lover* ("very dirty and completely worthless"). That was because she suspected the Chatterleys' Wragby Hall of depicting the Sitwells' Renishaw, and Clifford Chatterley of being based on Osbert. On both counts she was partly right, though not importantly. Also, for a while the Sitwells were Wyndham Lewis's collective patron, as his great portrait of Edith testifies at the Tate. But he had doubts about their "special brand of rich-man's gilded bolshevism"—they talked pacifist-left but preferred to see revolution make its points elsewhere—and by 1930 he'd pilloried them memorably in the "Lord Osmund's Lenten Party" section of his gargantuan *The Apes of God*. Since he didn't care for Bloomsbury either, he was pretty much isolated by then. For you had to be allied with somebody or something affluent. Partly, inability to stomach that was what had sent Pound to the Continent in 1920. It was an uncongenial world entirely by the standards of what he'd encountered in 1908.

Thus one thing on which all gangs were agreed was the unacceptability of Ford, "the stylist" Pound depicts in *Mauberley*, offering "succulent cooking" beneath a leaky thatch. The onetime editorial genius of *The English Review* had proved the most maladroit of literary politicians, and could barely even get himself reviewed. In 1915 *The Good Soldier*, that metaphor for the smashup of a world, got passed over amid acclaim for Conrad's *Victory*, and so little did the *Parade's End* tetralogy of 1924–28 become a possession of the public imagination that when Evelyn Waugh plagiarized its situations to sustain his own war-trilogy, *Sword of Honour* (1952–61), no one seems to have noticed. True, Waugh's was a different war.

And Bloomsbury . . . But we'd best draw a new breath.

9 : BLOOMSBURY

Someone once characterized "Bloomsbury" as a congeries of men and women all of whom were in love with Duncan Grant. That sally has a certain symbolic truth. Grant was the constant; he outlived them all. And, as one group-biographer gracefully puts it, "Duncan's androgynous affections were all-embracing." His cousin Lytton Strachey fell in love with him early, but Grant found him over-possessive and preferred to be loved, as he was for years, by John Maynard Keynes, who kept it up even after marrying the ballerina Lydia Lopokova. Grant solaced Vanessa (Stephen) Bell when Roger Fry had ceased to be her preferred alternative to her husband, Clive Bell, the aesthete, and that annoyed Bell, who'd gotten used to Fry. And so on. He was a busy minor painter. (And Roger was too, and Vanessa. They were all of them busy.)

All this intimate hospitality was one thing that did bind rare spirits together.* To be of merely one sex was rather ungenerous. They were the New Athenians, living like gods the authentic post-Victorian way and loftily ignoring Mrs. Grundy. They never teased Mrs. Grundy the way Oscar had, and, coming of well-to-do families, they'd the means to build a wall high enough for obstructing her gaze. When Virginia Woolf called them "ascetic and austere," one thing she may have meant was that all bed-hopping stayed, so to speak, within the family. Another bond was Cambridge, where the boys matriculated and the Stephen girls, Vanessa and Virginia, wistfully visited. There a number of them were disciples of G. E. Moore, whose *Principia Ethica*—Newtonian title!—asserted that "by far the most valuable things

---

* It could also lead to some pretty crass presumptions. In Berlin, Keynes saw "a naughty boy, a naughty Jew-boy, covered with ink, pulling a long nose as the world kicks his bottom, a sweet imp, pure and giggling." Naturally, "I had a little flirt with him." That was Albert Einstein.

which we can know or can imagine" are "certain states of consciousness, which may be roughly described as the pleasures of human
intercourse and the enjoyment of beautiful objects." (Clive Bell got
Virginia to read it. Duncan, though, didn't need theory.)

That made a splendid ethic for dwellers in a privileged enclave.
Investing value wholly in states of mind, it didn't require you to *do*
anything whatever. Your friends, your vases: your states of mind amid
those constituted heaven. If such amenities didn't furnish Bernard
Shaw's heaven, that pointed to his incapacity for the answering states
of mind; there's a striking resemblance between G. E. Moore's ethic
and Clive Bell's exaltation of connoisseurship. Shaw, like all re-
formers—in fact like most Eminent Victorians—was Benthamite at
heart: had even fallen victim to what Keynes called "the final *reductio
ad absurdum* of Benthamism known as Marxism." Moore had protected the lot of them from that.

Beatrice Webb, Shaw's fellow-ideologue, called Moore's book "a
metaphysical justification for doing what you like and what other
people disapprove of," and it's hard to argue that it wasn't. Yet, however the sentence about personal intercourse and beautiful objects may
resemble some effusion of Rupert Brooke's, *Principia Ethica* is by no
means a glad paean. It makes, page by page, an Alpinist's difficult
way, that sentence one rare flower from the stoniest peak. Many were
tempted to skim the analytic Table of Contents—virtually a paraphrase
of the book—and zero in on the last chapter, which offered an answer
"far less difficult than the controversies of Ethics might have led us
to suspect," the key to everything being, ah, "states of consciousness."
Looking at the end was a *fin-de-siècle* speciality. Earlier, the last chapter of Pater's *Renaissance*, with its exaltation of moments seized simply
for those moments' sake, had stirred up a fuss that made Pater suppress
the chapter for a while. Both writers, as Robert Skidelsky spells out
for Moore, were exercised by the Victorian tension between public
good and private well-being. The former, God now absent, was even
reducible to having to sit on committees, and it wasn't hard to spell
out private benisons superior to that. You'd not even, Moore showed,
be embracing "Hedonism." Hedonism meant supple compliance with
the moment's appetites; but Moore sought to define an objective Ideal
Good. It was nicely accessible if you weren't a navvy,* and even pretty

* "I must go to tea now to meet some bloody working men who will be I expect as ugly as men
can be"—Keynes to Duncan Grant, 31 July 1908.

boys could figure in it. The community might preach other values, but never mind those.

Special circles at Cambridge guarded an old tradition of o'ersoaring the communal consensus. The Apostles, that secret society of the elite, had its roots, as Skidelsky elsewhere writes, in "undergraduate rebellion against the Establishment, then chiefly represented by the Church of England. But to proclaim openly an attachment to rationalism, agnosticism, and the spirit of free enquiry was to damage one's chances of promotion and preferment. The peculiarly English solution to this dilemma was to create a private space for subversive thinking, protected from intrusion by secrecy and by homosexual attachments, while continuing to enjoy all the advantages which membership of the Establishment provided." That would one day yield charades more lurid than Bloomsbury's: as when dapper Sir Anthony Blunt, Surveyor of the Queen's Pictures, habitually surveyed them with one eye while keeping the other peeled for his Moscow contacts, to whom he'd commended Guy Burgess and Donald MacLean and like transcensions of the bourgeoisified.

"Undergraduate rebellion against . . . the Church of England." But pooh, by 1910 the Church of England was too dead to matter. Church and chapel might be left to the likes of the royal family and the underbred and the anxious. Bloomsbury wasted no time being anti-church; sufficient to be anti-Victorian. Virginia Woolf deplored Arnold Bennett, Victorian, materialist. Lytton Strachey mocked Eminent Victorians; they were, well, Victorian, comic. All of them mocked Mrs. Grundy incarnate, the sixty-inch Queen. So the word "Victorian" accreted numbing force; that's been perhaps Bloomsbury's most pervasive legacy. And they were not Victorians, oh no, not they! They were something new, more outrageous than even Lawrence: a self-appreciating superior class that deferred not even tacitly to any communal usage. One Victorian relic they did cherish, acute class-consciousness. Yes, that had to stay. But the Seven Deadly Sins were dead, beginning with pride, which was simply natural, like envy, not to mention lust. The new list of the Virtues was short, and began with snobbery.

And yet another bond was a common age: except for Fry (born 1866, which made him a year older even than Arnold Bennett), they belonged to the Joyce-Lewis-Pound-Eliot generation, sprung from a magic decade, the 1880's.

One secret of that generation was its timing with respect to the war. A Pound, an Eliot, having been old enough to value the Europe it swept away, could still feel able to reconstitute the means of art in the time that came after it. *The Waste Land* and *Hugh Selwyn Mauberley* are conspicuous instances of binocular vision. A Yeats, by contrast, 53 when the war ended, could make little of its aftermath save in Ireland, and made still less of the new poetry: as late as 1936 he was calling Eliot "satirist rather than poet." And for an Auden (born 1907), the war was a schooldays' environment; the post-war only was what he understood at first hand.

So Bloomsbury was potentially enabled. But save for Maynard Keynes's *The Economic Consequences of the Peace*, Bloomsbury writing implied little direct awareness that the war had happened. What it did show awareness of was literary fashion; and though it registered fashion far less crudely than did poor noisy Edith Sitwell, whose propelling rage was the rage to seem up-to-date, still it's permissible to feel a suspicion that one of the things self-awareness cushioned it from was the world outside the window. Its collective nickname, derived from the London district where the Stephen sisters first settled, with the British Museum near at hand, suggests—wherever its people really lived then and later—an encapsulation in a village, though a village with a fine library. That too is symbolically true. Their locale was never "London," the great London. All of them divined that the Capital in the old sense—the place that drew Goldsmith and Johnson, later James and Bennett, still later Pound and Eliot, the place where (Johnson said) you felt "the full tide of human existence"—had somehow grown obsolete. Pound fled it to Paris and Rapallo, Lawrence to everywhere, and the post-war English poets have not been Londoners, not even by adoption: witness R. S. Thomas in Wales, Tomlinson in rural Gloucestershire, Bunting in Northumbria, Geoffrey Hill in the West Midlands. (And Eliot? But how equivocal was the Possum's London commitment! We'll be coming to that.)

Pound's *Hugh Selwyn Mauberley* (1919–20) registers the obsolescence as only a foreigner could have. Mauberley, the heir to the ages, a Clive Bell impressionable enough to be reduced to silence, has come in at the end of long-dwindling opportunities. The landmarks of his world are "Mr. Nixon" (Bennett) on his yacht, "Brennbaum" (Max) encased in impeccability, "The Lady Valentine" (Ottoline Morrell?) unsure of what the arts she patronizes may be *for*. And "the stylist" (Ford) has been exiled to a cottage with a leaking thatch. "A farewell to London," Pound later called it; he meant not only his personal farewell, but a farewell to its two-centuries' role. If there's nothing to hope for from the Lady Valentine, neither is Johnson's option on parting from Lord Chesterfield open any more:

> . . . Conduct, on the other hand, the soul
> "Which the highest cultures have nourished"
> To Fleet St. where
> Dr. Johnson flourished;
>
> Beside this thoroughfare
> The sale of half-hose has
> Long since superseded the cultivation
> Of Pierian roses.

No, you needed your own village, your own funds, your own printing-press. Maynard Keynes proved a stock-market genius; that helped fund his pal Duncan Grant.

Their pruriencies would not be detaining us save for the claim that they pertain to literature. That implies the corollary claim that literature is authenticated by the writer's inner turmoil. So we need access to that. And, Lord, the plethora of access! Soap opera, it's all been accurately called; Jill Johnston remarks on a catering "to something much beyond the literary concerns that gave birth to the public Bloomsbury," and her last clause may be judged over-generous; the pretense that Bloomsbury pertains to literature at all rests on one gifted vulnerable woman. Though Strachey's catty biographies were once regarded, it's because of Virginia Woolf that we bother still. She is Bloomsbury's sole accredited "creator" and its proffered emblem of creation's cost: novels each one touchy as an eyeball, achieved between bouts of madness; then the terminal madness, and the body in the Ouse. It's a tale to mesmerize non-readers even. Save for her, Bloomsbury where she delved and span would be by now a social curio: as, in handcrafting for her renown a fine catafalque of editions, Bloomsbury's heirs and acolytes show that they know. It's not puritan to deplore the exploitation.

Her legend, so tended, rises free of unread books—not that *Mrs. Dalloway* or *To the Lighthouse* need be daunting—the way Thomas Chatterton's did two centuries ago. Chatterton had been Wordsworth's

> marvellous Boy,
> The sleepless Soul that perished in his pride,

and Keats dedicated *Endymion* to his memory. A suicide at 18, he left behind little that anyone wants to read twice. But ever since Romanticism dawned it has been essential to have such a martyr available: a martyr to—oh, just to brutal exactions: to the world too much with us. That bewept victim was Chatterton at first, then for many years John Keats, "killed by an article." But gradually the Keats theme grew old-fashioned. An age of politics and psychoanalysis demanded a victim who'd undergone evils more abstract: the new Oedipal devils, and stridency and anti-feminism, also if possible Hitler. Virginia Woolf (obiit 1941, Hitler's year of apogee) could not have escaped the part.

Vienna was where such destinies were codified, and her corner of London seems a Viennese suburb. Her brother Adrian became a psychoanalyst; so did Lytton Strachey's brother James, the translator of Freud; and Freud's British publisher after 1924 was The Hogarth Press—i.e., Leonard and Virginia Woolf, writing invoices and boxing books in their basement. If of few lives has so much detail been so tactfully divulged, we need not be surprised either that an air of guided insight has attended the divulging. (We may be surprised, though, that she never consulted an analyst; was she never urged to consult one?)

Indeed, tending the legend of Virginia Woolf may be thought of as a Bloomsbury cottage industry. Quentin Bell, her nephew, wrote her biography. His wife, Anne Olivier Bell, edited the five volumes of her diaries. Nigel Nicolson, son of her flame Vita Sackville-West ("Am I in love with her? But what is love?"), saw to the six volumes of her letters. And her husband, Leonard Woolf, not only supplied the armature narrative in his five-volume autobiography, he also patiently edited her fugitive pieces, four volumes beyond the two she published herself, and repackaged the whole in a multi-tome *Collected Essays*. As this page was written a like service had not been performed for T. S. Eliot, whose *Egoist* essays you must still chase down in *The Egoist*. It all amounts to an assertion she'd not have made, that she was her time's regnant sensibility.

No question, the authority of intimates is reassuring. Had editing the diaries been left to an outsider, the notes that identify X and Y and Z would be sometimes blank and elsewhere imperfectly plausible. Still, a confluence of interest seems worth remarking: a family agreement that genius does credit to the family.

But back to her psyche; Virginia Woolf's vulnerability is one thing well documented. The daughter of Leslie Stephen who created the

DNB, Virginia, yes, had rare talent: talent hardly to be extricated, as it proved, from depression and lifelong guilt. Shunning mirrors, she couldn't powder her nose in public. Her mother's death had been a trauma; so too had been the conduct of her half-brother Gerald Duckworth, who fondled her intimately when she was 6, and of her other half-brother, George Duckworth, "invulnerably dense," who did something similar when she was 12.* And she seems to have been suppressing also a memory of her father flinging her into the roaring sea, naked, when she was tiny. The contents of such a Cagliostro's cabinet might have been assembled, for purposes of demonstration, by Dr. Freud himself. Yet if we wonder how she lasted fifty-nine years to fuss so tensely over so much paper, we are left in no doubt. For three decades' relative stability anyhow we're to thank her husband Leonard. That is widely attested.

"It was the wisest decision of her life," Quentin Bell tells us of her decision to marry Leonard Woolf. Then Leonard Woolf's own account does help us think him the ideal consort for a martyr to nerves. For the length of a five-volume autobiography he's as stalwart as a tent-pole, as earthbound. Whenever all about him are losing their heads, he's so much keeping his as to be listing the pounds Virginia brought in year by year with her pen. That's the gist of what he thinks to tell us about her career.

Her first publications were in what everyone called the *TLS*, where no one had to know who had written them.

The *Times Literary Supplement* was launched in 1902. Later Northcliffe tried periodically to close it down, not liking to publish something that taxed his attention. One time it survived because Bruce Richmond, the editor, simply ignored Northcliffe's order till the Press Lord had forgotten. Now officially the *TLS*, it's still around. Richmond's diaries, after his death, proved to contain chiefly curt notes on Greek authors, so his commitment to reviewers' anonymity goes unventilated. It was only in 1974 that the paper's seventh editor, John Gross, insisted on signed reviews.

Richmond mayn't have felt there was anything to explain; the anonymity he institutionalized is a very old English custom. The attacks on Keats by Croker and Lockhart—the ones that used to be said had hastened his death—those were anonymous. Anonymity prevailed at

---

* But did either molestation happen? Jean O. Love notes that Quentin Bell, the biographer, came to modify some of his statements, and wonders whether Virginia was "only building another portrait"—one of her family-centered fictions.

the century's turn to such an extent that, so Frank Swinnerton tells us, six assailants of a trifle by Conan Doyle all turned out to be one man named Robertson Nicoll, and Andrew Lang was alleged to have placed some twenty raves for his friend Rider Haggard's *King Solomon's Mines*.

Such precedent did not deter Richmond, who imagined, apparently, that his *Supplement* could simulate impersonal Judgment. It was often, as one might have expected, a chance for nonentities to get knives in. But in 1905 being published but unnoticed was just what Virginia Stephen needed, and she didn't abuse its privilege. So began a long career as an "essayist."

Here she is, for instance, soothing readers of a 1909 *TLS* into suitable reverie about a *Life* of Laurence Sterne:

> It is the custom to draw a distinction between a man and his works and to add that, although the world has a claim to read every line of his writing, it must not ask questions about the author. The distinction has arisen, we may believe, because the art of biography has fallen very low, and people of good taste infer that a "life" will merely gratify a base curiosity, or will set up a respectable figure of sawdust. It is therefore a wise precaution to limit one's study of a writer to the study of his works; but, like other precautions, it implies some loss. We sacrifice an aesthetic pleasure, possibly of first-rate value—a life of Johnson, for example—and we raise boundaries where there should be none. . . .

This *and* that; this *but* that; this *and* (although that) *yet* that too: filled out as they are by her gracefully balanced cadences—never a syllable superfluous or wanting—these gesturings with the left hand and the right serve not to mobilize attention but to lull it: to assure us of options only produced to be occupied, of vistas disclosed that we may gape into their vacancies. So custom's schemata are banished, and we're drawn into musings on Sterne, agreeable, *pointilliste*, fantastic. The author of the book she was reviewing—Professor Wilbur Cross—may have wondered that his work got very scant mention. But that was a *TLS* custom, for the book to be merely an occasion. Today the reader of Virginia Woolf may spot an oblique sketch of Bloomsbury-to-be: "Shandy Hall, the home of cranks and eccentrics, nevertheless contrives to make the whole of the outer world appear heavy, and dull and brutal, and teased by innumerable imps." Any devotee of Cross may turn for consolation to Connecticut, where they named a highway after him. And the reader of the *TLS* in 1909? That reader had an agreeable, stylish read. And anonymous Virginia Stephen had the confirmations of print.

Though the Sterne piece is unusually thin, it is not unrepresentative; Virginia Woolf the critic is seldom meaty. That outer world "teased by innumerable imps" exemplifies a frequent mannerism, the disarming metaphor. "As well might one attempt to rationalize the charm of a muddy country road, or of a plain field of roots in winter"—that's the gist of what she once had to say about Hardy's prose style. She's a master of such tropes, and became a master of modulated sentence-lengths within the paragraph, and she has the Everyman habit of reading books with the hope of getting close to their authors, and she leaves us little save the memory of that stylish read. She is not among the great critics. The essays brought in necessary money, and they kept her pen fluent. Nor can she have been unaware that the formulaic "we" and "one" of the *TLS* screened all clues to her gender. By implied convention, its adjudicating mind was male.

By 1912 she was Virginia Woolf, and *The Voyage Out*, 1915, by Virginia Woolf, was unequivocally her own work, a woman's. Marie Corelli was still going strong, *The Sorrows of Satan*'s printings now past sixty, but you'd not mistake Virginia Woolf's prose for hers. No, Woolf's was something feminine, Corelli's simply evangelical.

"Feminine" is one way to name that darting fluid precision that can catch nuances of feeling in a sentence or two: "It was only by scorning all she met that she kept herself from tears," or "To feel anything strongly was to create an abyss between oneself and others who feel strongly perhaps but differently. It was far better to play the piano and forget all the rest." Another way to characterize such sentences is to say that Lawrence might have written them: not that *The Voyage Out* could pass for his. It's orienting to remember that 1915 was also the year of *The Rainbow*, Virginia Woolf making her start just when Lawrence was redefining fiction in ways that suited her scope. "She is completely aware," wrote an astute early reviewer, "that anything like complete understanding between people is rare and transitory. . . . What she cares about is . . . the impulse to create relationships, the lapses back, the substitutions, the sterile recessions." That's also the concern of *Women in Love*, and for writers so preoccupied, "plot" and "character" of the old kind fade into irrelevance.

Which brings us to "Mr. Bennett and Mrs. Brown," a paper Virginia Woolf read to The Heretics, Cambridge, in 1924. That was the context of her famous pronouncement that late in 1910 human character changed. She instanced one's cook; the Victorian cook "lived like a leviathan in the depths, formidable, silent, obscure, inscrutable." (And so, in Leslie Stephen's gone world, cooks should.) But the modern cook was "in and out of the drawing-room, now to borrow the *Daily Herald*, now to ask advice about a hat." For servants not to know their place any longer, that betokened an upheaval of the great deeps. Yet Virginia Woolf can be jaunty about them. What she couldn't be jaunty about was such a man as the "illiterate, underbred" author of *Ulysses*, a Jesuit-trained polymath who had known neither Cambridge nor a Bloomsbury drawing-room. When Harriet Weaver brought his typescript to The Hogarth Press, Virginia wondered, "Why does [Joyce's] filth seek exit from her mouth?"—an unseemly image for a lady to have entertained. Harriet Weaver, "the poor woman" (the affluent daughter of a Victorian physician), had, Virginia Woolf told her diary, the table manners of "a well bred hen." There's no pleasing so rigorous a diarist.

Virginia was a wonder, an imperturbable champion snob, in her diaries (meant for herself) as serenely dislikable a lady as English annals afford. In "Mr. Bennett and Mrs. Brown," merely for the Cambridge Heretics, she's restrained. All she lets herself be bothered by there is that Arnold Bennett is such a . . . materialist. He keeps talking about bricks and valuations, instead of about the fluctuant soul of whatever "Mrs. Brown" he pretends to deal with. The Cambridge Heretics knew what to make of a provincial with a mind for bricks.

Now Virginia Woolf's example is *Hilda Lessways*, and that's a more interesting novel than she'd have us believe. It is the second part of the Clayhanger trilogy, remarkable in offering to tell a whole story over, from the woman's side instead of from the man's. In *Clayhanger* (1910), Edwin, who'd vowed he'd be an architect, found himself instead a job printer in Burslem* of the Potteries: heir to his father's business; gratified, yes, but earnest, restless. He's roused by a woman named Hilda, an unexplained friend of friends, who is clearly roused too by him. But mysteriously—it's her style to not explain anything—she departs for Brighton, whence she's soon writing him,

> DEAREST,—This is my address. I love you. Every bit of me is absolutely yours. Write me.—H.L.

---

* Bennett renamed it "Bursley"; and his "Hanbridge," its neighbor Hanley, was the "Coketown" of Dickens's *Hard Times*.

The next thing, he hears she's been married, to a Mr. Cannon. And years later she re-enters his life, Cannon canceled; and they're betrothed.

Like random lightning, these enigmatic happenings streak through Bennett's calm portrayal of something he remembered well: a youth lived in the last quarter of Victoria's century in one particular corner of provincial England. So firm, so centered is the Bursley milieu and Edwin's process of growing into it that Hilda's flickering and flashing stands for little more definite than the sum of what is never to be known. (If you grew up in Schenectady, you missed Dubuque.) Then in *Hilda Lessways* (1911) he undertook an amazing project: to bring Hilda alive, to make Edwin a mystery for *her*, to replay scene after scene not as he'd experienced it but as she had. Margaret Drabble in her life of Bennett calls the total effect "stupendous," so scrupulously are their two visions differentiated, so utterly is each of them entranced by a romantic misapprehension of the other. Unhappily, the sequel has been read as a mere explanation of what *Clayhanger* left mysterious, so *Clayhanger* gets reprinted but *Hilda Lessways* does not.

(I'll not defend the third part's relevance. War and other interferences delayed it till 1916, by which time *These Twain*, projected as the story of Hilda's and Edwin's marriage, had gotten entangled in the disintegration of Bennett's. So it doesn't round off the trilogy the way he'd planned.)

Hilda grew up in a world defined by property, by freeholds, by modest rents, by boarders and scrubbing-girls. And that irked Virginia Woolf, who found in *Hilda Lessways* an author tiresomely preoccupied with property, crassly indifferent to a woman's feelings. But Hilda's feelings are elided by Hilda herself. She's a creature of pure willful impulses she has no incentive to examine—"My life is marvellous" is what flashes through her head when she learns the "husband" she's pregnant by is a bigamist! So Bennett's unit of attention is the vivid moment in which Hilda makes yet one more eruptive move. These moments startle amid an ordinariness he renders with quotidian calm. Margaret Drabble rightly calls them moments "of pure character." Virginia Woolf doesn't remark them. She demands to be presented with the "real" Hilda.

Like Clive Bell, she was a born crowd-pleaser, provided the crowd was the right one, and she'd gauged her Cambridge audience perfectly. That whimsical date, "December 1910," with its lawyerly qualification, "in or about"! The Heretics knew very early they were in for a

jolly evening. But "Mr. Bennett and Mrs. Brown" has been esteemed
as the manifesto of a new kind of fiction, and what it manifests gets
harder to be sure of the more closely we try to follow. Writers must
begin, we find Virginia Woolf saying, from some common ground
with their readers. For Edwardians, house property was such a common ground, and Bennett made use of that. "Indirect as it seems to
us, the convention worked admirably, and thousands of Hilda Lessways were launched upon the world by this means. For that age and
generation, the convention was a good one." Then what of her earlier
claim that Bennett botched *Hilda Lessways*? If a novel can only work
by its consonance with our unarticulated values, then we literally
cannot read any novel that dates from before our own time, and Virginia Woolf is certainly not claiming that. And what pertinence has
the premise about human character changing in 1910? *Hilda Lessways*, true, is dated 1911, but its people's characters were formed in
Victorian times, and the events it chronicles terminate in 1892. If she
were saying that the methods of Arnold Bennett won't suffice for
portraying someone truly modern, then she might be right, but that
is not what she is saying. No, "Mr. Bennett and Mrs. Brown" will
not serve as a serious criticism of Arnold Bennett; he's no more than
a handy symbol for out-of-dateness, someone they'll laugh at easily in
Cambridge. For The Heretics, as for countless subsequent readers,
the paper was carried by its skittish wittiness—by such paragraphs
as this one:

> The Georgian novelist, therefore, was in an awkward predicament.
> There was Mrs. Brown protesting that she was different, quite different,
> from what people made out, and luring the novelist to her rescue by
> the most fascinating if fleeting glimpse of her charms; there were the
> Edwardians handing out tools appropriate to house-building and house-
> breaking; and there was the British public asseverating that they must
> see the hot-water bottle first. . . .

Amid so ludicrous a supporting cast, those earnest house-breakers
and hot-water-bottle fanatics, her "Georgian novelist" seems positively
scrupulous. Looking more closely, we discover a list of these "Georgians": "Mr. Forster, Mr. Lawrence, Mr. Strachey, Mr. Joyce, and
Mr. Eliot"; we may add Mrs. Woolf, who by 1924 had published
three novels. Lawrence and Joyce, yes indeed, and of course Woolf;
but what Lytton Strachey is doing in that list we cannot tell, nor the

authors of *Howards End* and *The Waste Land*. And when Virginia
Woolf lets us know at first hand what it's like to try to present character
now that Edwardian methods are obsolete—"to try this sentence and
that, referring each word to my vision, matching it as exactly as possible, and knowing that somehow I had to find common ground between us, a convention which would not seem to you too odd, unreal,
and far-fetched to believe in"—she's describing an unending tentativeness that doesn't match at all our impression of the other writers
on her list.

Joyce and Eliot bothered her especially, and The Heretics heard
about their lack of finesse:

> Thus, if you read Mr. Joyce and Mr. Eliot you will be struck by the
> indecency of the one, and the obscurity of the other. Mr. Joyce's in-
> decency in *Ulysses* seems to me the conscious and calculated indecency
> of a desperate man who feels that in order to breathe he must break the
> windows. At moments, when the window is broken, he is magnificent.
> But what a waste of energy! . . . Again, with the obscurity of Mr. Eliot,
> I think that Mr. Eliot has written some of the loveliest single lines in
> modern poetry. But how intolerant he is of the old usages and polite-
> nesses of society—respect for the weak, consideration for the dull! As
> I sun myself upon the intense and ravishing beauty of one of his lines,
> and reflect that I must make a dizzy and dangerous leap to the next,
> and so on from line to line, like an acrobat flying precariously from bar
> to bar, I cry out, I confess, for the old decorums, and envy the indolence
> of my ancestors who, instead of spinning madly through mid-air, dwelt
> quietly in the shade with a book.

The one indecent, the other intolerant, impolite: those indolent ances-
tors who knew what a book should be would not have permitted such
persons into the house. Yet how proud they would be to see their
descendant step down, smiling and unsweating, from the jungle gym
Mr. Eliot has erected! The hero of such an occasion isn't the poet
but the dauntless reader; it's like Clive Bell's *Art*, where the hero is
the connoisseur. Bloomsbury was a breeding-place for such passive
heroes.

She was inviting The Heretics to laugh—you can always laugh—at
the aftermath of 1922, the year R. P. Blackmur would dub "Annus
Mirabilis." That year had seen two non-standard publications: *Ulysses*

(Paris, Shakespeare & Co., 740 pages) and *The Waste Land* (New York, Boni & Liveright, 64 pages). Nine months later The Hogarth Press had issued a British edition of the latter, typeset in the Woolfs' own basement by Virginia herself. She had heard Tom read it in June ("great beauty & force of phrase: symmetry & tensity. What connects it together, I'm not so sure") and a year later had told Tom and his wife it was "a d——d good poem," but by '24 it was a jungle gym. To what she couldn't quite confront she was responding the way she always did, with nervous humor. International Modernism had declared itself, and the status of "English" changed forever, as hardly anyone save Ezra Pound knew. Pound amused himself for a while with a new calendar which terminated the Christian Era at midnight, 29/30 October 1921, when Joyce said he'd completed *Ulysses*, and dated subsequent events not A.D. but P.S.U.—*post scriptum Ulixi*. His own birthday, 30 October, Day 1 P.S.U., he designated the Feast of Zagreus. His humor and hers were differently based.

For Mrs. Woolf was disoriented. She supposed that a couple of writers—an Irishman, an American—had been making rather outré "experiments" from within the insular tradition, after all the only English-language tradition there was.

Part of her mind knew better. When she mentioned intolerance for old politenesses, she was not after all accusing Eliot, a man she'd dined with, of placing muddy feet on some family settee. She was hampered by not facing up to what she did know: that *The Waste Land* presupposed, and hoped to create, a readership unburdened by any illusion that English Poetry in its present state bore the impress of the long ages. When the bookmen talked of respect for tradition, they meant that individual talents should have the modesty to leave it alone. A "poet" who inflicted on us something such as

> When lovely woman stoops to folly and
> Paces about her room again, alone . . .

was indulging in distasteful mockery of a gem enshrined by tradition. And someone who copied onto his page the words "Those are pearls that were his eyes" was plagiarizing, no less, whether to impress the ignorant by sham eloquence or to shock the cognoscenti with his impudence. The cognoscenti made a game of spotting quotations (the *TLS* has since made it a weekly competition), and by jingo they could spot that one—*Tempest* I.ii.399! Cognoscenti of Virginia Woolf's caliber would also have related "Sweet Thames, run softly" to Spenser's *Prothalamion*, and doubtless in some country parsonage lurked the canny wight for whom "A noise of horns and motors" would recall "A noise of horns and hunting" in John Day's *Parliament of Bees* (1641). First prize! A year's subscription to the *TLS*!

But the British pastime of spotting quotations was exactly Eliot's abhorrence: its reduction of poetry to a snobs' game, to a "heap of broken images" that don't *matter*. Functional Greek and Latin had already been killed by an expertise that tut-tutted over false quantities, and a functioning vernacular tradition was going the same way. There was more health in a reader for whom "Those are pearls that were his eyes" did not instantly cite an island's heritage, but assembled words which (though memory may relate them to Shakespeare) could still work eloquent magic in this new setting, uncrushed by obligation to England's Bard. Mr. Eliot on his high stool in Lloyd's Bank might conceivably have written such words himself, so little did they lose in losing quotation marks.

That is one of his themes, that dismemberment of the past. But Virginia Woolf assumed that all readers of "English" were English: were quotation-spotters, asking what held it together (save insolence). Her novels too, which Americans must read the way they read Trollope, with allowances, comport with English assumptions.

> "That is all," she repeated, pausing for a moment at the window of a glove shop where, before the War, you could buy almost perfect gloves. And her old Uncle William used to say a lady is known by her shoes and her gloves. He had turned on his bed one morning in the middle of the War. He had said, "I have had enough."

Transpose that from Bond Street to Fifth Avenue and watch its tacit signals evanesce. More than gloves, those English gloves are values, and the English shop less a mart than a tradition's discreet cenotaph; as for Uncle William's reticence *in articulo mortis*, that implies habits and a code you'd be long in explaining to a literate and sympathetic Chinese. Shorthand like hers is meant for readers in England, where it works like a meeting of eyes within the family. No "modernist" save in sharing certain assumptions with Lawrence, Virginia Woolf in such passages is a classic English novelist of manners.

But *The Waste Land*, published almost simultaneously in London and New York, presupposes neither British values nor American ones.

The shards it collects from the poetry and drama of England it treats as it does the Provençal, the French, the Italian, the Sanskrit: as incidents in a long Indo-European story.

Ulysses in a similar way, published in Paris, does not ask at all for admission to the canon of English fiction, or of Irish either. It presupposes a thorough command of English vocabulary and grammar, and it hopes too that many Shakespearean tags will be recognized (though the loss if they are not isn't catastrophic), but it doesn't require you to have ever read an English novel. A translation of the *Odyssey* is more pertinent.

And radical novelty put Mrs. Woolf off. We've seen her, three decades after 1910, still hedging on the Post-Impressionists, making Roger Fry's triumph consist in having spotted painters who'd one day fetch handsome prices, and we've seen her posit Joyce's "obscenity," Eliot's "obscurity," just the aspects, and only the aspects, that had troubled card-carrying bookmen, and we may wonder at the strength of her claim to be Bloomsbury's antenna. To an Arnold Bennett she could condescend from her safe perch in the upper middle class, but innovation tormented her with jealousy. Here she is, 16 August 1922, reading *Ulysses* itself: ". . . a queasy undergraduate scratching his pimples. And Tom, great Tom, thinks this on a par with War & Peace! An illiterate, underbred book it seems to me, the book of a self-taught working man, & we all know how distressing they are, how egotistic, insistent, raw, striking, & ultimately nauseating. When one can have cooked flesh, why have the raw?" That's pretty desperate; reminiscent too of J. M. Keynes girding himself to meet "ugly" workingmen. And she had a formula for great Tom Eliot's susceptibility: "But I think if you are anaemic, as Tom is, you glory in blood." Being "fairly normal myself," she added, "I am soon ready for the classics again."

She adds that she is even then "laboriously dredging [her] mind for Mrs. Dalloway," and there'd not have been a *Mrs. Dalloway* but for *Ulysses*. The mid-August diary entry, the one that dismisses Joyce's monster, contains her first mention of her new undertaking. She meant to call it *The Hours*, and through its early pages clocks chime as they do in Joyce's. It was published in 1925. In America, where a public for high-toned dither would one day support *The New Yorker* Harold Ross founded that very year, Harcourt, Brace thought it "wonderful," and it certainly was not obscene, even though, like *Ulysses*, it listened in on the minds of people who perambulated city streets in mid-June.

* * *

It is "wonderful" if what you crave is the quelling of linear plot, which there was reason to be bored with by '25. Plot, click click, had come to mean the detective shaking out a crumple of events from some new corner. What a gentleman this sleuth could be! Already Lord Peter Wimsey had made his appearance, an Oxford lady-graduate's daydream, and though on his dreamer, Dorothy L. Sayers (M.A. Oxon '15), the diaries of Virginia Woolf are calmly silent—Miss Sayers's connections were High Church, not Bloomsbury, even after she'd settled in Bloomsbury—still their pretensions merit comparison. The *DNB* assures us with a straight face that the "classical" mystery genre Dorothy Sayers planned to milk for a living was already (1921) "understood to be the favorite reading of intelligent and cultivated persons." She "foresaw the success which might attend upon a more specific appeal to such readers whose approval would establish a reputation; and since the books need not be difficult—except in the teasing sense—a wider public might quickly be educated up to them." So "she mastered the art of giving a pleasant literary flavour to her stories," to such effect that no writer since Wilkie Collins has come nearer than she did to "fusing the attractions of the [detective] kind with the values of serious fiction." The author of this incoherence, J. I. M. Stewart, must be presumed to understand serious values, having written, so *The Oxford Companion to English Literature* assures us, "critical works on Shakespeare, Joyce, Peacock, Kipling, Hardy, and others." As "Michael Innes" he is also responsible for a detective named Appleby. What he's telling us is that the "intelligent and cultivated" public was by 1921 hopelessly fragmented.

Some of it wanted its puzzle-books to have "a pleasant literary flavour." The Oxford graduate obliged, to such effect that she's ever since been offered in proof that crime-fiction can be "literature." The subtitle of the final Wimsey exploit (*Busman's Honeymoon*, 1937) even put literature first—"A love story with detective interruptions"—and the chapters sport literary epigraphs, from Beddoes, John Ford, even Eliot's "Hollow Men," by way of implying that canonized writers have been as much possessed by death as any murder-monger. Yet the Wimsey saga is unreadable and always was, unless you are middlebrow enough to crave literariness in what ought to be *Tit-Bits* narrative, and gullible enough to equate superfluous words with kulchur. Meeters of both criteria not being lacking, Wimseys sold well and sell still, even though Miss Sayers's sense of language lacked the sureness of Edgar Wallace's. When Mrs. Leavis pointed to similarities between Lord Peter and some daydream of Ouida's* she got herself reproved for a "venomous" airing of "personal grievances." Doubtless she envied Dorothy's success!

Virginia Woolf, though—what might the cultivated expect from her? Ah, *sensibility*, the real thing, without epigraphs.

> She had reached the park gates. She stood for a moment, looking at the omnibuses in Piccadilly.
> . . . She felt very young; at the same time unspeakably aged. She sliced like a knife through everything; at the same time was outside, looking on. She had a perpetual sense, as she watched the taxi cabs, of being out, out, far out to sea and alone; she always had the feeling that it was very, very dangerous to live even one day. . . .

Mrs. Dalloway is having one of her moments of disincarnation ("this body, with all its capacities, seemed nothing—nothing at all") and Virginia Woolf specialized in that order of psychic oddness. Mrs. Dalloway's sense of being unreal goes somehow with her being "Mrs. Dalloway"—"this being Mrs. Dalloway, not even Clarissa any more; this being Mrs. Richard Dalloway." Though that's not dwelt on— Mrs. Woolf seldom dwells on themes, but alights on them for the duration of a moth's flutter—it can stir passions she may not have dreamed of. For imagine merely being "Mrs. Leonard Woolf!"—like being merely Mrs. Humphrey Ward.

Another thing *Mrs. Dalloway* contains is a 'tec story with clues but no detective. The body of Septimus Smith impaled on the fence-spikes is as bloody a spectacle as ever Wimsey confronted; and, why did Septimus take that fatal plunge? Since we'll not be put through the vulgarity of hearing a sleuth "explain," we'll either mumble "hysteria" or else trust a sleuth from outside the text, someone such as Mitchell Leaska, who unravels "a highly evasive kind of associational magic" involving, for instance, bananas, a coal-scuttle, a screen, all touching

---

* Ouida (1839–1908), and not Marie Corelli, whose nonsense after all issued from fervid conviction—e.g., about the immoral French. But Ouida dreamed of men who were miracles of languid virtuosity, and so did Dorothy Sayers. Bulwer-Lytton thought Ouida's *Folle-Farine* "a triumph of modern English fiction," and the Modern Language Association commenced in 1974 to accord Miss Sayers a special section at its annual meetings.

on a dead man toward whom Septimus, we must deduce, had entertained homosexual feelings that curdled his feeling for women. The doctors who fail him at the eleventh hour are named Bradshaw and Holmes, potent names in the universe of Conan Doyle. The Bradshaw of Mrs. Woolf, though, is no oracle, and the Holmes is an oaf. It's a modest little joke and seems to go unnoticed, even by Leaska. Something about the texture of *Mrs. Dalloway* inhibits alertness to whimsy.

What we're to do with *Mrs. Dalloway*, writes Mr. Leaska, is discipline ourselves to glimpse "the shadow play of consciousness and motive so abysmal with ambiguity and possibility as to make critical commentary seem to reside in some ablative region on the far side of language." That points to a certain lack of ease in the performance, which makes, it's to be feared, for unjoyous rereading. *The Waves*, *The Years*, they can't even be read, though Peter Conrad has wittily remarked on resemblances between the opening of *The Waves* (1931) and the Post-Impressionist fuss of 1910:

> "I see a ring," said Bernard, "hanging above me. It quivers and hangs in a loop of light."
>
> "I see a slab of pale yellow," said Susan, "spreading away until it meets a purple stripe."
>
> "I hear a sound," said Rhoda, "cheep, chirp; cheep, chirp; going up and down."
>
> "I see a globe," said Neville, "hanging down in a drop against the enormous flanks of some hill."

—what sensitives, Bernard and Susan and Rhoda and Neville, not to mention Jinny and Louis! (Virginia Woolf liked that Greek-chorus effect; see the opening of "Time Passes," Part II of *To the Lighthouse*.) Poor dim Clarissa Dalloway belongs in a different universe, the mere world of limousines and access to the Prime Minister (who turns up at Clarissa's party). No, *The Waves*, we know from the start, is a Bloomsbury self-congratulation, unreal from end to end, voice after voice finely straining for fineness of perception.

> "And time," said Bernard, "lets fall its drop. The drop that has formed on the roof of the soul falls. On the roof of my mind time, forming, lets fall its drop. Last week, as I stood shaving, the drop fell. I, standing with my razor in my hand, became suddenly aware of the merely habitual nature of my action (this is the drop forming) and congratulated my hands, ironically, for keeping at it. Shave, shave, shave, I said. Go on

shaving. The drop fell. All through the day's work, at intervals, my mind went to an empty place, saying 'What is lost? What is over?' And 'Over and done with,' I muttered, 'over and done with,' solacing myself with words. . . ."

Lord! And her one rereadable novel is *To the Lighthouse*, which, as David Daiches remarked long ago, works by removing the Ramsay entourage to "a remote and misty isle" where clocks and city directories and like obduracies can't puncture the "semi-transparent envelope" of her predilection. "Life," she wrote in a 1919 essay called "Modern Fiction," "is not a series of gig lamps symmetrically arranged; life is a luminous halo, a semi-transparent envelope surrounding us from the beginning of consciousness to the end." A gig is a two-wheeled carriage, still a living memory then; and how we're to imagine gig lamps "symmetrically arranged," as an aid to understanding what life is not, is something to be puzzled out; the phrase seems a characteristically nervous stab. Imagine, perhaps, walking at dusk past a row of waiting cabs, their lights obedient to perspective's geometry, now ranged ahead, now out of sight behind us; then imagine instead how it is to be surrounded by a private radiance moving as we move.

To be conscious, to be alive, is to see by that radiance, and one day it will go out. What it would be like to see it go out was something she wondered for decades. On page 226 of *Mrs. Dalloway* Septimus Warren Smith hurls himself from a window; it was once to have been Mrs. Dalloway who took such a plunge. Her hold on life remained slack through to the last draft, but Virginia Woolf's final choice was to let her die by proxy.

Mrs. Ramsay in *To the Lighthouse* (1927) has her own hollow moments, when

her mind . . . remorselessly beat the measure of life, made one think of the destruction of the island and its engulfment in the sea, and warned her whose day had slipped past in one quick doing after another that it was all ephemeral as a rainbow—this sound which had been obscured and concealed under the other sounds suddenly thundered hollow in her ears and made her look up with an impulse of terror.

When mortality does claim Mrs. Ramsay it is offstage, during the ten-year interlude "Time Passes." Of what happened we know only that it was sudden. Two other deaths are a little more particularized: daughter Prue, in childbirth; son Andrew, in the war. Thus the family undergoes attrition, like all families, the summer house in Scotland decays, like all houses. That nothing goes ever quite as anyone would want was the ceaseless burden of the book's long first part; most notably, the children and their father never did make their trip to the lighthouse. Because of weather? In a book where everything *portends*, weather can manifest the grain of the universe.

It manifests the grain of Mr. Ramsay, who throws plates through the window and storms out lines like "What's the use of going now?" Mr. Ramsay seems not to be one of Virginia Woolf's triumphs; when "Instantly, with the force of some primeval gust (for really he could not restrain himself any longer), there issued from him such a groan that any other woman in the whole world would have done something, said something, all except myself, thought Lily," we try in vain to imagine what he did and succeed in imagining only Lily Briscoe's consternation. He's an emblem of Tyrannic Nagging, and an instance of Virginia Woolf's difficulties at the boundary between emblem and act, between the semi-transparent envelope and what you'd see or hear: what she could sidle toward only by caricaturing Bennett's "materialism." That plate Ramsay whizzes through the window! How explosively male! And something he was saying at dinner, "about the square root of one thousand two hundred and fifty-three. That was the number, it seemed, on his watch." There's no way to imagine that really happening, Ramsay making an extempore pronouncement about the square root of a number that happens to have no rational square root.[*] And how was 1,253 "on his watch"? No, our author can't really be bothered to imagine. It's not helpful to know that she was laying, to her own satisfaction, the ghost of Sir Leslie Stephen. Did Sir Leslie rave about the roots of watch-dial numbers?

"What did it all mean?" Mrs. Ramsay wonders. "To this day she had no notion. A square root? What was that?" It is part of "this admirable fabric of the masculine intelligence ... upholding the world" like iron girders. That's Virginia Woolf's own dismissal, we may want to guess: square roots, typifying such things as (she'll let us think) men talk their feelingless talk about. (One remembers Leonard Woolf's "system" for financial records: see the formidable table on page 142 of *Downhill All the Way*.) And that is a radical defect of

[*] 35.3977400408557 . . . , and so on to no last term.

imagination, that unwillingness to conjure real plausibility. In *The Waves* she tried to do without it altogether; when she doesn't go that far she hopes we'll believe that *anything* could happen: that men especially might say or do just anything. (Arnold Bennett knew differently.)

To the Lighthouse, where such faults matter least, culminates and closes with Lily Briscoe finishing her picture:

> With a sudden intensity, as if she saw it clear for a second, she drew a line there, in the centre. It was done; it was finished. Yes, she thought, laying down her brush in extreme fatigue, I have had my vision.

It will never be much of a picture, Lily has more than once bleakly realized ("Yet it would be hung in the attics, she thought; it would be rolled up and flung under a sofa").

The book sold 3,873 copies the year it was published, by the scrupulous Leonard's accounting, and he adds that by 1964 Britons had bought a total of 113,829 copies, Americans 139,644. Averaged over thirty-seven years, those are not sales as Dorothy Sayers measured sales. On the other hand, *To the Lighthouse* is a genuine highbrow novel; Mrs. Leavis herself said so. Leonard Woolf strongly objected to that description; the way Virginia had validated Fry's Cézanne, he appealed to the ledger. He adduced sales four decades after publication; how could a book still being bought in such quantities be "ununderstandable by ordinary people?" He perhaps gave too little weight to the likelihood that most of the American sale anyhow—some twenty thousand in 1965—reflected classroom procurements. It's Dorothy Sayers who's still sold in airports, while in seminars at girls' colleges, I'm told, students recognize Mr. Ramsay especially. He reminds them, so their term papers say, of their fathers.

10 : FRIGHTFUL TOIL

"Honest criticism and sensitive appreciation are directed not upon the poet but upon the poetry": so T. S. Eliot wrote in 1919, having stood in a cave in France gazing upon bulls and bison depicted with intentions we cannot guess at by hands and minds long perished into anonymity, the anonymity of "that vanished mind of which our mind is a continuation." Thrust as they are mysteriously into our time, they cannot tempt us to dream back to theirs, or presume to share the impulse of their painters. So they leave us confronting nothing but themselves. Eliot judged that a bracing paradigm. "History can be servitude," as he'd write a quarter-century later. It was liberating to have art freed for once from its own history.

By contrast, our feeling that we've *inherited* Shakespeare interferes with our reading him. "Who, for instance," Eliot once asked, "has a first-hand opinion of Shakespeare?" He had no doubt that there was much to be learned from "a serious study of that semi-mythical figure." Learning it would oblige readers, especially English ones, to forgo all fancied kinship with Sweet Will and confront the astonishing plays.

And a modern poem with a name signed to it might be, Eliot guessed, as impersonal as a cave-drawing or as *Coriolanus*: might evoke by its alchemy of language "that inexhaustible and terrible nebula of emotion which surrounds all our exact and practical passions."

The cave-paintings were not "published." So far as we in our century are concerned, they were simply left behind. And to publish, since the 1700's, has not been equivalent to leaving something behind. No, it's been to make claims on a system of attention with limited capacity though much power to bestow rewards. This system can certify a poet for esteem; can even judge whether he merits room in the curriculum, a useful mill where literature is ground. The system's guardians attend to the poet, not the poem. Has he wiped his boots? In Keats they had a Cockney upstart to sneer at. When *The Waste Land* appeared in 1922 they leaped at once to decry a presuming cerebralist.

Someone in the *Times Literary Supplement* found the author "parodying without taste or skill," and "walking very near the limits of coherency," but hoped that he would one day recover control. That review was at least a get-well card, but most weren't. F. L. Lucas, the bookman's bookman, exposed a charlatan: "The parodies are cheap, and the imitations inferior." Eliot's notes had adduced the folklore-scholar Jessie Weston's *From Ritual to Romance*, but Lucas gave her scholarship short shrift. Miss Weston, he asserted, was "clearly a theosophist, and Mr. Eliot's poem might be a theosophical tract." It was all "fantastic mumbo-jumbo," an "unhappy composition" that "should have been left to sink itself." J. C. Squire, himself a poet,* surmised that it was "a faithful transcript, after Mr. Joyce's obscurer manner, of the poet's wandering thoughts when in a state of erudite depression"; he added that "a grunt would serve equally well." And America's Louis Untermeyer, then as later the assiduous chameleon, echoed British authority. He called it "a piece of literary carpentry, scholarly joiner's work; a flotsam and jetsam of desiccated culture . . . a pompous parade of erudition."

Desmond Maxwell, whose florilegium of such remarks is useful, reminds us that nobody in those early years thought *The Waste Land* a poem at all. It was "a series of slightly related separate poems," in Alec Brown's phrase, and it was "tacked together." The show of unity, enforced by an overall title, an epigraph, a dedication, and (once the notes had been added) by lines continuously numbered, may have helped to goad all that contempt. Untermeyer's barbs—"carpentry," "joiner's work"—seem aimed at some shakiness in the joinery. A cohering oneness was missed.

A way to get a cohering oneness is to write your entire poem in the same meter, an expedient Eliot had eschewed. Another is to tell a story, like Homer, and in *The Waste Land* no story was to be found.

---

* . . . Deep in the sky and my heart there wakes
A thought I cannot reach. . . .
                    —J. C. Squire, "At Night" (1913)

("Deep feeling, eloquence and wit"—Robert Lynd.)

It was therefore a pretentious botch, one moreover based on "litera-ture," not on "life." Not that anyone cared about the poem, one way or another. The point was to expose the botcher, and Virginia Woolf on Eliot's intolerant obscurity seems positively kind and likely meant to be.

How this supremely important poem got written is worth a little attention. It was impelled, like *Paradise Lost*, by the poet's desire to undertake something weighty; in December 1919 he mentions a long poem he has had on his mind "for a long time," giving no sign yet of knowing what's to go into it. The following September (1920) he's still wishing he had a little time to think about it. Then by 9 May 1921 something has happened: the poem is "partly on paper."

What had finally set him going was a book the *TLS* sent him for review, Mark Van Doren's *The Poetry of John Dryden*, where he read how for two decades after the Restoration, John Dryden's London resembled the Rome of Ovid. "With civil war just past and a com-monwealth overthrown, with court and city beginning to realize their power, with peace prevailing and cynicism in fashionable morals ram-pant, with a foreign culture seeking the favor of patrons and wits, the new city did for a while bear a strange resemblance to the old Empire."

A war just past, a rampant cynicism, wits gone wild after continental novelty: we may guess how that could have sounded, in 1921, like contemporary London.

> London, the swarming life you kill and breed,
> Huddled between the concrete and the sky,
> Responsive to the momentary need,
> Vibrates unconscious to its formal destiny. . . .

This stanza, meant to be focal in the long poem, did not survive Eliot's final editing. An uncommon stanza in rhyming *a b a b*, it is recog-nizable to most modern ears because Gray used it in his *Elegy*. Mark Van Doren has something to say about its history, and about Dryden's fascination with its "leisurely authority." Most pertinently, it is the stanza of his *Annus Mirabilis* (1667), of which Eliot seems to have been calculating an echo.

Annus Mirabilis (as Van Doren notes) was dedicated "To the Me-tropolis of Great Britain, the Most Renown'd and Late Flourishing

City of London." Dryden commenced his Preface with the supposition that he might be "the first who ever presented a work of this nature to the metropolis of any nation," a boldness justified by his awareness that no other city ever deserved such praise. Other cities, he says, have won their fame "by cheaper trials than an expensive tho' necessary war, a consuming pestilence, and a more consuming fire." His last twelve stanzas prophesy London's illimitable future:

298

... The silver Thames, her own domestic flood,
Shall bear her vessels like a sweeping train;
And often wind (as of his mistress proud)
With longing eyes to meet her face again.

299

The wealthy Tagus, and the wealthier Rhine,
The glory of their towns no more shall boast;
And Seine, that would with Belgian rivers join,
Shall find her luster stain'd, and traffic lost.

300

The vent'rous merchant, who designed more far,
And touches on this hospitable shore,
Charm'd with the splendor of this northern star,
Shall here unlade him, and depart no more. . . .

Such was the prospect before London in 1666. By 1921, having undergone yet one more "expensive tho' necessary war," and one more "consuming pestilence," which figures in demographic history as the great influenza epidemic, it was playing host to such ambivalently vent'rous merchants as Mr. Eugenides, "unshaven, with a pocket full of currants," and seemed ripe for a Fire Sermon if not for a fire.

Unreal City [wrote Eliot]
Under the brown fog of a winter noon
Mr. Eugenides, the Smyrna merchant . . .

and he followed this with the apostrophe to London that commences in the stanza of *Annus Mirabilis*, the "heroic stanza," alternately rhymed, which Dryden was to call "more noble, and of greater dignity, both for the sound and the number, than any other verse in use amongst us."

It specified how the City was Unreal, its whole life leveled down to the plane of sensation. To this, to the likes of Mr. Eugenides, to a life of "phantasmal gnomes" and "pavement toys," had the London of Dryden's magniloquent prophecy come; and Eliot appended seventeen more *Annus Mirabilis* stanzas, presenting in Dryden's form though not his diction the movements of the typist and the youth with the spotted face who enact an unreal automation of Love itself.

> . . . She turns and looks a moment in the glass,
> Hardly aware of her departed lover;
> Her brain allows one half-formed thought to pass:
> 'Well now that's done: and I'm glad it's over.'

That long passage, Tiresias' vision, was all in the "heroic stanza" once, and the fine laconic gravity of its final state was achieved by ruthless deletion that cut through quatrains and amalgamated their details. By then the poem's coordinates had so shifted that a tacit allusion to Dryden no longer mattered. But when Eliot started writing his long poem with what is now Part III, he'd intuited an urban poem, a London poem, and a poem of firm statements and strong lines, traceable to the decorums of Dryden's urban satire.

> The time is now propitious, as he guesses,
> The meal is ended, she is bored and tired,
> Endeavours to engage her in caresses
> Which still are unreproved, if undesired.

Such a quatrain proclaims its Restoration ancestry: straightforward syntax, with a high proportion of principal to dependent clauses; Latin precision—"propitious," "endeavours"—lending overtones of wit to native monosyllables; and the neat closing antithesis, "unreproved, if undesired," establishing a viewpoint which is not that of the innocent eye but that of the Lockean judgment, making distinctions.

Such verse, so sparse, so centered on its affirmations, cannot justify itself by its wit or local accuracy, only by a certain authority which is part of what Eliot meant by "impersonality," which may correspond to what is called "sincerity" in the poet, but of which his sincerity is by no means the guarantee. Of verses composed by these canons of statement, Dr. Johnson once remarked that the difficulty was not to make them but to know when you had made good ones. Johnson often helped other poets who were in that difficulty. We learn from Boswell of lines he supplied for Goldsmith, and if we had the manuscript we might find in it lines he deleted, the way to improve imperfect Augustan verse being to take things out. Sense tends to collect itself into metrical units, and build by accumulation; structure is paratactic; omissions don't show. And as former writers had taken verses to Johnson, Eliot, when he had written all that he could of his poem, took the drafts to Ezra Pound, by then removed to Paris, and Pound cut and cut.

Eliot's nerves were bad; it grew increasingly clear that the marriage he'd made in 1916 was unlucky. Suffice it to say that Vivienne was terribly unstable. After the Dryden catalysis of May 1921 he took rest-cures. In October he went to Margate, where nothing connects with nothing; in mid-November to Lausanne ("In this decayed hole among the mountains"), taking with him what he'd written, the "Augustan" pages that underlie what is now Part III of *The Waste Land*, longer than now because it then included a lackluster pastiche of Pope. By 13 December, in Lausanne, he was "working on a poem." That meant, transcribing other bits he'd brought with him, and fitting them into Parts I, II, and IV according to a schema apparently sponsored by his admiration for what he'd read of *Ulysses* in *The Egoist* and *The Little Review*.

What he took to be the method of *Ulysses* entailed a parallel between modern and ancient that might lift into art what he thought of as a "panorama of anarchy and futility." Eras and cultures resemble one another, and from their resemblances we collect a normative sense of what it can mean to live in a civilization. The English Augustans had been encouraged by points of correspondence between their London and the Rome of Augustus. Eliot's parallel was between Augustan London and modern, and it did not hearten. It signified a relapse into habit. History, Eliot had written in 1919, "gives when our attention is distracted." By this he appears to mean something like what Wyndham Lewis meant in the 1917 "Inferior Religions," an essay Eliot admired: that to fall into the rhythms of an archetype, into "the habit-world or system of a successful personality," is to be guilty of inattention. "A comic type is the failure of a considerable energy," Lewis had written, "an imitation and standardizing of self." Such beings are "illusions hugged and lived in, little dead totems." That elucidates such an image as "pavement toys," and such a passage as the one about how things are in Hampstead, which Eliot typed in Lausanne and may have composed just after he got there, the urban satirist's impulse still upon him:

> The inhabitants of Hampstead have silk hats
> On Sunday afternoon go out to tea,
> On Saturday have tennis on the lawn, and tea
> On Monday to the City, and then tea.
> They know what they are to feel and what to think,
> They know it with their morning printer's ink. . . .

And it illuminates his use of historical parallels. In *Annus Mirabilis* Dryden, meaning to enhance the recent war with the Dutch, compares it to the Second Punic War. In *The Waste Land* Eliot introduces an ex-sailor who has fought in some analogue of the First Punic War— "You who were with me in the ships at Mylae!"—by way of suggesting that the same dreary wars recur as the wheel revolves. His point seems not to be, not what used to be often alleged, that the present is tediously inferior to the past: rather, that the present is inferior to its own best potential insofar as it courts resemblance to the past. Tradition, with the whole past of Europe in its bones, ought to be engaged on something new.

An epigraph from "Heart of Darkness," later canceled, had enforced this theme of paralyzing reenactment: "Did he live his life again in every detail of desire, temptation and surrender during that supreme moment of complete knowledge?" For if history gives when our attention is distracted, so does personal circumstance, and if London had become a jumbled quotation of former cities, he himself too, in his unfortunate marriage, had become something like a quotation: a character in an over-familiar play which sometimes seemed to be *The Duchess of Malfi* and sometimes a poor French farce. Once, when he read *The Waste Land* in a London salon, the Young Man Carbuncular himself was there; were these, the young man wanted to know in ecstasy, patting his pimples, *carbuncles*?

His plan for controlling all this, prompted by *Ulysses*, was apparently to work out a parallel with the *Aeneid*: the hero crossing seas to pursue his destiny, detained by one woman and prophesied to by another, and encountering visions of the past and the future. Madame Sosostris was Eliot's Cumaean Sibyl; the woman at the dressing-table was his Dido, later to draw her long black hair out tight and go mad; the city to which he comes, both founded and yet to be founded, was the London whose future John Dryden had foreseen through the past of Aeneas' Rome. Virgil's Sixth Book, in which Aeneas visits the underworld, had of course been Dante's point of departure earlier, and Eliot's long "Death by Water" section, which Pound was to reduce to a mere ten lines, exploited Virgil and Dante together in making Gloucester (Massachusetts) fishermen repeat the last voyage of Ulysses and get wrecked by an iceberg.

Yes, yes, work, work; and then one night in Lausanne he had an experience he was never to come to terms with. He began to write verse in rapid longhand, as though to dictation.

> After the torchlight red on sweaty faces
> After the frosty silence in the gardens
> After the agony in stony places . . .

. . . page after page, the whole of Part V, "What the Thunder Said," to be marked by Pound, "OK from here on I think," and to survive into the final poem nearly unretouched. Tom Eliot distrusted "inspiration" and "the inner voice"; that shouldn't have happened. It happened.

Some of its materials had been on his mind for many years. The opening, and the apocalyptic passage with the bats and the whisper-music and the towers upside down in air, reproduce and improve scraps of verse expert eyes have since dated "1914 or even earlier." For at least seven years, it seems, an urban apocalypse had haunted his imagination, the first versions tied to such images of walking through a city as we find in his 1910 "Rhapsody on a Windy Night." This vein of material now took possession of the poem. So did the very weather of 1921—a year, as it happens, of "unprecedented heat and drought." In a burning sterile dryness that seemed like a curse laid on Europe, the familiar commentators' motifs pushed their way to the poem's surface: the Chapel, the Quester, the Grail, the Fisher King. Later, the notes would encourage us to fit them to what revision had left of the earlier sections. Luckily, one enigmatic passage in Part I, with a "heap of broken images" and a red rock, would make the first pages seem to have foreseen the last. And almost the last thing to be arrived at was the poem's overall title. More than any other element, it does seem to hold things together, forcing headlong energies inward as if toward a center.

Insofar as his proto–*Waste Land* had a plan, the *Aeneid* would seem to have underwritten that plan. Unlike Joyce, Eliot was not a writer whom plans enabled; even regular verse forms, like the *Annus Mirabilis* quatrain into which he'd cast the narrative of the typist and the Young Man Carbuncular, tempted him to fill out a scheme with weak and passive lines, and a plan on a larger scale led to whole weak and passive pages. That was a difficulty he never solved in his plays, and it would have wrecked *The Waste Land* had not Pound persuaded him that once the dead sections were excised and the wobbly ones energized, what was left made an emotional unity.

But when Pound wasn't in the same room his conviction seems to have faltered. No sooner had he returned to London from their famous séance than he was proposing to use his 1919 "Gerontion" as a preface. That was the first sign that his nerve was failing. To prefix "Gerontion" would have been to supply an excuse for the poem's discontinuity: it would all have become "thoughts of a dry brain in a dry season," acquiring thereby a psychological unity that could be argued for, as well as an emotional unity you could either assent to or miss altogether. The famous note about Tiresias is a copout of the same order. "Tiresias, although a mere spectator and not indeed a 'character,' is yet the most important personage in the poem, uniting all the rest. . . . What Tiresias *sees*, in fact, is the substance of the poem." Here Tiresias is but a later name for Gerontion, and the thousands of readers who've been grateful for that note—F. R. Leavis in 1930 was one of the first—seem not to have wanted to alloy their gratitude with doubts about the centrality of a character who puts in his one appearance with the poem more than half over.

So that note was a second symptom of faltering conviction. A third was "The Function of Criticism," an essay of two years later in which we see Eliot at pains to persuade himself that "the larger part of the labour of an author in creating his work is critical labour; the labour of sifting, combining, constructing, expunging, correcting, testing." He even called it "this frightful toil." We may say "persuade himself," knowing as we do what the essay's first readers could not have known: that Eliot had had the unnerving experience of seeing his long poem come together at the behest of an evening's automatic writing. "What the Thunder Said" trampled all the careful plans under; and if Pound was his Great Taskmaster, the frightful toil of reworking what Pound left of the rest of the poem had been exacted by the need to pull it all up to the level of "What the Thunder Said."

The frightful toil is easy to underestimate. In undertaking it, Eliot revealed his heroic dimension. Anyone else, handed back his magnum opus blue-penciled to half its length, its schema wrecked, only that irruption from nowhere left unaltered—anyone else would have burned it all in despair. Eliot summoned all his powers. He kept lines Pound had cut; he rephrased others; he made bridge-passages of seamless quality. What he mailed back to Paris, nineteen double-spaced typed pages, ran (said Pound) "from 'April' . . . to 'shantih' without a break. That is 19 pages, and let us say the longest poem in the English langwidge." Pound would seem to have shared Poe's doubts about long poems.

But what *was* it? Something Eliot was always a little uncomfortable with: an elusive unity he'd never foreseen, embodied in five irregular parts whose separate rationale no one could explicate. By 1935 he had written "Burnt Norton," to go at the end of his *Collected Poems*. He had brewed that up in his old way, out of fragments, in fact fragments that wouldn't fit into his play of the same period, *Murder in the Cathedral*. But he'd also done something the exigencies of subduing *The Waste Land* hadn't permitted: had calmly fitted its elements into a controlled five-part whole, quite as if he knew what he was about; and the five parts corresponded neatly to the five parts of *The Waste Land*, giving that poem, in retrospect, a form.

Pound had suggested a few years earlier that "the sonnet" originated when someone got stuck trying to make a canzone. If so, then the form of the sonnet came into being when someone else followed the pattern. A "form" is something done twice. Only when there were *two* sonnets could you speak of "the sonnet." And one thing Eliot was doing in "Burnt Norton" was creating a form for *The Waste Land* by doing it again. Only when the thing had been done twice could it cease to be just what was left over when the cutting had stopped. So the new poem's first part talks not of "April" but of "time," and wanders not into the Hofgarten but into an English garden, which proves haunted. Even "the heart of light" turns up in both poems at the same place. Part II is in two sections, "poetic" and "prosaic," as in the earlier poem the high ritual of the woman in the room had been juxtaposed with the demotic of the woman in the pub. Part III recalls us to a "here" which is London, and states plainly its theme of disaffection and desiccation. Part IV is a brief, irregular, but formal lyric, with death in it, and it comes where the death of Phlebas the Phoenician had come. And Part V is about Words, not Sanskrit roots this time but Words in general, also remembering the mystic Word of Saint John. In the penultimate line of "Burnt Norton" we find a word not present in *The Waste Land*, the word "waste":

> Ridiculous the waste sad time
> Stretching before and after.

Having written "Burnt Norton," Eliot could feel at last that he'd *written* the earlier poem, not simply abandoned it: and that, however desperately, he'd achieved something formal in abandoning it at just the stage he had.

It is just as well that the drafts from which we've reconstructed this story were inaccessible in the heyday of the bookmen. Nothing could better have confirmed their glib suspicion that the poet never knew "what he wanted to say" and remained unsure that he'd "said it." For their spirit does not die, and it's notable, ever since the drafts were published in 1971, how much has been made of a single unlucky phrase. It seems that Theodore Spencer, in a lecture at Harvard, once repeated words he attributed to Eliot, and Eliot's brother, in the audience, wrote them down. Then Valerie Eliot, thinking them oracular or perhaps usefully counter-oracular, gave them the prominence of an epigraph. Thus it came about that at third hand we could hear what was allegedly the voice of the poet, calling *The Waste Land* "only the relief of a personal and wholly insignificant grouse against life; . . . just a piece of rhythmical grumbling": a way of putting it, not wholly satisfactory.

It has the merit, if you like things kept simple, of trivializing the poem into a symptom. J. C. Squire, with his "wandering thoughts when in a state of erudite depression," had catered to a like appetite. And a whole new school of exegesis has been catalyzed, with the poem tacitly retitled as "Dyspeptic Tom's Rhythmical Grumble." Now, what was the substance of his grouse against life? No sooner asked than answered. Since his death, at least three biographers have moved Vivienne Eliot to the center of the poem: the Hyacinth Girl, the woman

whose nerves are bad.* The current Eliot, presented with sophisti-
cation in books by A. D. Moody and Ronald Bush, with blunt naïveté
in Peter Ackroyd's biography, made poetry, in Moody's careful words,
"out of what the man lived through." This is a possibility for which
we lack, at present, a critical vocabulary: hence Ackroyd's vulgarity,
Moody's and Bush's tentativeness.

But the evidence for the "frightful toil" abides. What he was toiling
at has the importance of a scientific discovery, entailing as it did
something analogous to Einstein's emergence from the "common sense"
of Newton.† From a poem answerable to a plan, *The Waste Land*
became a kind of poem new in English, a poem cohesive only within
the system of forces its own rhythms and emblems generate. And the
language acquired new resources for refracting public experience, neither addressed to events in the manner of Yeats—

> . . . a drunken soldiery
> Can leave a mother, murdered at her door,
> To crawl in her own blood, and go scot-free . . .

—nor withdrawn into issueless Coleridgean privacy—

> A grief without a pang, void, dark, and drear,
> A stifled, drowsy, unimpassioned grief,
> Which finds no natural outlet, no relief,
> In word, or sigh, or tear—

—but capable, with its "memory and desire," its "hooded hordes" and
its "taxi throbbing waiting," of touching the world into which the
century's doings had transported everyone. Far from having "something to say," it performs one of poetry's ancient offices, offering us
words we might say, assuring us that what we avert our gaze from is
not after all inaccessible to our language.

In Paris he and Pound had worked on the poem page by page,
piecemeal, not trying to salvage an unsalvageable structure but to
reclaim the authentic parts from the contrived. It was fortunate that

---

* Better leave the poem its incoherence, then, to certify those intolerable pressures. It is even
argued that Pound's hands should have stayed off, that what he salvaged was an inauthentic
poem we've been making do with all these years, that the true poem is the artless anguished
cry, lame lines, false starts, and all.
† There are even scientific parallels for the episode of automatic writing, most famously the way
the ring-structure of the benzene molecule was revealed to Friedrich Keukulé in a dream.

contrivance had been guided by neo-classic formalities, making the verse out of separate weighty lines whose sense and force could survive the deletion of their neighbors.

That the poem at last ran from "April" to "shantih" without a break was true if your criterion for absence of breaks was Symbolist, not neo-classical. Working over the text as they did, shaking out ashes from amid the glowing coals, leaving the luminous bits to discover affinities, they recapitulated the history of Symbolism, a poetic to systematize the affinity of details neo-classic canons had guided. Eliot in his *TLS* review had paid Dryden an unexpected compliment, that in being prizeworthy for what he'd made of his material he resembled Mallarmé. It was something akin to Mallarmé, finally, that his own effort to assimilate Dryden came to resemble: the ornate *Herodiade*, or the strange visions (*"Une dentelle s'abolit . . ."*) of unpeopled rooms where detail strains toward detail and we cannot feel sure what the rhetoric portends.

Something akin: yet the difference is profound. For "pure poetry" Mallarmé had paid a fearful cost, eviscerating poem after poem of everything denotative, leaving torsions of absence to intensify a void. Eliot's taxi, though, is a taxi (four-cylinder, the rhythm tells us); his "falling towers" resemble French church spires he may have seen falling in wartime newsreels; his "hooded hordes" evoke armies' winter gear; a note reminds us how Saint Mary Woolnoth's "dead sound on the final stroke of nine" could be verified on the spot. And if "each man fixed his eyes before his feet" makes a London crowd resemble a detail from Dante, it's also an American's observation of how Londoners behave on a busy pavement, the New York custom being to look straight ahead. In *The Waste Land* it's the world we share that's reclaimed by poetry; and if Eliot achieved this without "knowing what he wanted to say," so much the better. A poet who knows what it is he "wants to say" may be sure it's been said already.

11 : A KNOT OF CRITICS

Science, oh dear, science; the thought of it rather vexed Roger Fry. "Allowing that the motives of science are emotional, many of its processes are purely intellectual, that is to say, mechanical." (Intellectual, mechanical: odd equation. Fry was likely reflecting on a narrow escape of his own; it was science he'd long ago gone up to Cambridge to study.) *Art* of course is different: "At no point in the process of art can we drop feeling." And when someone in *The Athenaeum* "boldly" called the scientist's satisfactions aesthetic—"It is in its aesthetic value that the justification of the scientific theory is to be found, and with it the justification of the scientific method"—Roger Fry promptly wove a cat's-cradle of unprecedented emptiness: what about a scientific theory that disregarded facts? Would it not have "equal value for science with one which agreed with facts?" On 6 June 1919, in *The Athenaeum*, Roger Fry could see "no purely aesthetic reason why it should not."

Readers of *The Athenaeum* promptly heard from someone who could. "There must be some incompetence about a view of art or of science which allows no clearer exposition [than Fry's] of the relations between them," said a letter in the issue for 27 July. "The notion of truth is the decisive notion, not only for the scientific value of theory, but for its aesthetic value as well." Like Newton's laws, works of art offer access to "propositions," though not propositions you could otherwise formulate. "When the work of art is great the proposition is such that in no other way could we apprehend it, and our access to it is so complete that it appears perfectly self-evident and inevitable. It is this kind of knowledge, and not any more or less accidental pleasure which it may afford, which is properly called aesthetic satisfaction."

In the best tradition of British Letters to the Editor, that was staunch and could be thought cranky. Not only might an aesthetic inhere in algebra (though only in *correct* algebra); art like science offered access to substantialities. The nine carefully written paragraphs were signed "Ivor Richards," and they marked the first appearance in print of the man, then 26, whose bewildering vigor would guide articulate thought about poetry in England for the next decade and more.

As early as his *Athenaeum* letter, I. A. Richards has no patience for languid rites of connoisseurship. He will not have the work of art sit aloof, serene, like Clive Bell's Persian bowl, an unravished bride that leaves plain folk indifferent though from time to time a Bloomsbury "appreciator" works himself into ecstasies in its presence. No, when he enumerates "the points of most fundamental difference" between his account and Fry's, Richards starts with "my substitution of the complete experience called 'contemplating a work of art' for the 'work of art' in the narrower sense." We are not to "split this whole into 'work of art' and resultant pleasure or emotion."

Also Richards wanted as many people as possible to *have* that experience. That entailed a thirty-year agenda for literary critics, from Empson and the *Scrutiny* group to the New Criticism in America. Discussing a poem would entail a slow-motion scan of the intricate way a skilled reader came to terms with it, in order to instruct the less skilled. For without the reader there was literally no poem: no "work of art" at all, just marks on a page. The poem *was* the "complete experience" of reading it. To be content with calling Shakespeare a national possession, and examine students on the Tragic Flaw in *Othello*, was to collaborate in keeping him safely dead. How far such collaboration had progressed was alarming.

That was just what F. R. Leavis meant in 1948 when he brushed aside notions of "a 'taste' that can be set over against intelligence"— "taste" being a name for the mysterious gift fortune had seemingly bestowed on such as Clive Bell; for, "unappreciated, the poem isn't 'there,' " and "appreciation"—a shorthand for what Richards had called "the complete experience called 'contemplating a work of art' "—in no way resembles a knowing sip at a wine. For (Leavis persisted) "You cannot take over the appreciation of a poem," the way shoppers can copy lists of the better vintages, or the way literati take over, from curricula and later from book reviews, their glibness about what is agreed to matter. It is not enough to have received England's literary heritage. The heritage will perish unless people learn how to read.

Tradition "cannot be inherited," Eliot had written, "and if you want it you must obtain it by great labour." He'd had poets in mind; Richards and Leavis were now saying the same of readers. What did people *do* when they read? That was now a central question. Soon Richards would have dismaying data to show.

Now examine some book dates:

    1920: *The Sacred Wood*, by T. S. Eliot
    1922: *The Criterion*, vol. I, no. 1 (ran till 1939)

Next:

    1923: *The Meaning of Meaning*
    1924: *Principles of Literary Criticism*
    1926: *Science and Poetry*
    1929: *Practical Criticism*

—all by I. A. Richards, the first title in collaboration with C. K. Ogden.

    1930: *Seven Types of Ambiguity*, by William Empson
    1932: *New Bearings in English Poetry*, by F. R. Leavis
           Fiction and the Reading Public, by Q. D. Leavis
           Selected Essays, by T. S. Eliot
           Scrutiny, vol. I, no. 1 (ran till 1953)
    1935: *Some Versions of Pastoral*, by William Empson
    1936: *Revaluation*, by F. R. Leavis . . .

A long, tight sequence. And now a few birthdates:

    1888: T. S. Eliot, everyone's example
    1889: C. K. Ogden (collaborator with I. A. Richards)
    1893: I. A. Richards
    1895: F. R. Leavis (attended Richards's lectures, c. 1925)
    1906: Q. D. Leavis (pupil of I. A. Richards)
    1906: William Empson (pupil of I. A. Richards)

—a twenty-year span, two intellectual generations; so closely knit, however, by both interaction and preoccupation that quarrels and mannerisms, outcroppings of jargon, quiverings of fanaticism, seem but incidents in what Leavis, quoting Eliot, grandly called "The Common Pursuit." The enterprise was unlike anything in previous English experience: at once empiric, academic, amateur, pedagogic, aesthetic, evangelic, scientific, insular, international, generous, crankish, anti-scientific, and devoted to poetry and to tradition. It involved, when you include the contributors to *Scrutiny*, several hundred active participants. And year in, year out, for nearly twenty years some of the most compelling writing done in England, as well as much of the most rebarbative, was writing written about the reading of writing. Bookmen had recourse to the word "narrow."

Having been a serious student of Pierce and Bradley, Eliot was almost wearily aware of complexities lurking in the meaning of "meaning"; he could think of language not as a message-bearer but as "a network of tentacular roots reaching down to the deepest terrors and desires." That eluded not only the wit of Philip Beaufoy, but the wit of bookmen content to be coyly mystified whenever words stirred feeling. Since they took note of language only when it annoyed them, the bookmen were apt to ascribe poetic power to something hidden in the soul of the poet. A. E. Housman, he was a True Poet; Rupert Brooke had been a True Poet; Imagists, one could be sure, were not True Poets. True Poets were responsible for Stirring Stuff.

Invoke, though, as Eliot once dryly prescribed, Comparison and Analysis—examine in short with some scrupulousness the commerce between your own sensibility and this piece of writing, that one, another one—and you were soon convinced about the network of tentacular roots. Words could never *not* stir intricate responses;* one thing really mysterious was how they could sometimes seem not to: how Plain Prose was possible at all. One explanation was what Ford had long since complained of, the prevalent Beaufoyese, that dialect of hansoms hailed, avenues explored, measures taken, which sheer familiarity had rendered unnoticeable, like the noise of mid-city traffic.

* As Dorothy Sayers knew in her years of concocting copy for Benson's Advertising Agency. "My Goodness! My Guinness!" was a contribution of hers to the dialect of the tribe.

By elimination of that, very plain words could be freed to release their power:

> My external sensations are no less private to myself than are my thoughts or my feelings. In either case my experience falls within a closed circle, a circle closed on the outside; and, with all its elements alike, every sphere is opaque to the others which surround it. . . .
>
> —F. H. Bradley

or,

> Cover her face. Mine eyes dazzle. She died young.
>
> —John Webster

or,

> The winter evening settles down
> With smell of steak in passageways.
> Six o'clock.
> The burnt-out ends of smoky days . . .
>
> —T. S. Eliot

When Leavis was making the point that good prose achieved its plainness not by absence but by exclusion, "exclusion felt as a pressure," it was Eliot's prose he adduced:

> Exclusion implies a firm and subtle grasp; Mr. Eliot is a major poet, and Mr. Eliot's prose is among the most finely and purely prosaic ever written; it is the efficient instrument of a fine critical intelligence.

For you couldn't miss Eliot's *intentness*, as he went about showing how a Marvell or a Bishop King in verse, a Joyce or a Conrad in prose, could conjure by simple words "that inexhaustible and terrible nebula of emotion which surrounds all our exact and practical passions and mingles with them." Bookmen, though aware of "emotion" here and there, were uneasy save with emotions they were used to getting from books: "lads" and "comrades" and "oak," iambic certainties.

Eliot liked terms with a scientific ring—"comparison," "analysis," "catalyst"—because they implied what he thought needed implying, austere discipline of attention as in the Harvard curriculum he had known. Beyond that, Eliot claimed no laboratory certainties. I. A. Richards, though, was the British amateur incarnate. Like Thomas Hobbes encountering Euclid backwards, he'd been led from a Kipling story to Swinburne's name to an anthology where the "Battle Chorus" from *Erectheus* choked him with tears (he was in his early teens, and laid up with TB); then knowing (from Swinburne) the answer to a schoolmaster's question, "What were the sacred flowers of Athens?," was what got him to Cambridge, where he read History and met C. K. Ogden, classicist ("a little, white-faced, large-glittering-spectacled undergraduate, four years older than me"), who talked him into Moral Sciences (and sold him two books). Note that the direction of his life was changed when Swinburne, of all poets, offered *information*. Poetry had been efficacious; we'd best not underrate the force of such a paradigm.

In Moral Sciences he got enthralled by Bloomsbury's sage, G. E. Moore; what held him, though, wasn't intercourse with beautiful objects, but Moore's incessant "What do we mean?" ("Moore was vocally convinced that few people could possibly *mean* what they *said*. I was silently persuaded that they could not possibly *say* what they *meant*.") Next, a new bout of TB,* and a return to Cambridge for "a medical qualification in order to become a psychoanalyst." Which led to physiology and psychology ("out of G. F. Stout, out of the James Ward article in the Encyclopedia Britannica, and William James's two volumes, *The Principles of Psychology* . . . Those and Sherrington's *Integrative Action of the Nervous System* to put the physiology in it").

What a mishmash, threaded by passion! Swinburne, G. E. Moore (remembered mostly for saying "What do we mean?"), obsolete psychology, the nervous system . . . And Ogden, with whom he wrote *The Meaning of Meaning*: a labile omniscience: the opportunist who'd demanded cash for those books: the man whose condition for giving the Jeremy Bentham Centennial Lecture in 1935 was that the underclothes on Jeremy Bentham's mummy should be changed (they were): a man who once held an option to purchase Stonehenge (for which, Richards reflected, he no doubt saw a use) . . . Beings like Ogden and Richards are barely conceivable in academic America, where credentials are normally static. (The physicist Richard Feynman does come close.)

---

* Despite all his medical problems, Richards lived to be a hale 86.

Luckily, Richards had never "read"—i.e., "majored in"—English. Also luckily, when he needed cash at the start of the '20's, the Cambridge English school, just forming then, didn't care. They authorized him to collect 16s. from anyone who came six times to hear him lecture on Principles of Literary Criticism. There would not have been wide agreement that there *were* such principles. The stint lasted some eight years, and two major books came out of it.

Principles of Literary Criticism (1924) has not worn well, its appeals to neurology having lost their dazzle. But Richards needed to be able to say that better poems achieved a more complex ordering of—*something*: and he chose neural impulses. Order those optimally, and you are both calmed and alerted, which is what Art does. That led to perhaps the book's single most bizarre detail, the diagram that suggests a map of dendrites and synapses and is actually (John Holloway has suggested) an impression of Eliot's "tentacular roots," reaching down to squiggles where lurk the terrors and desires. It looked, in '24, "scientific." But *Practical Criticism* (1929) is the book that has mattered. Still yeasty after nearly six decades, it has deflected many thousand readers from, in D. W. Harding's words, "their otherwise almost inevitable progress towards the point when they regard 'the time when they read poetry' with slightly more wistful feelings than they have for 'the time when they played Red Indians.'"

The idea was brilliant. For several terms, beginning in '25, Richards passed out to classes of about sixty students sheets of unsigned poems, four or five, to be mulled over for a week and commented on. Perhaps two-thirds of the respondents were undergraduates; the rest included graduate teachers, up to the caliber of William Empson and F. R. Leavis, both present at various times. (Once Eliot himself appeared, but he may not have done the assignment.) The following week Richards would lecture on their written comments. No such body of evidence on what went on in educated readers' minds had been collected before.

From the first half of *Practical Criticism*, a guided tour of the "protocols," we can see how by the mid-1920's it would have been unwise to award poetic laurels by secret ballot. The most approved poem was the one that began

> Between the erect and solemn trees
> I will go down upon my knees. . . .

("One is able to understand what the author means"; "The thoughts behind this approach perfection.") The runner-up, just one percentage point behind, opened as follows:

> There was rapture of spring in the morning
> When we told our love in the wood.
> For you were the spring in my heart, dear lad,
> And I vowed that my life was good.

("A fine poem written with deep emotional feeling.") That was liked by 53 percent of the respondents. But a mere 30 percent had good words for Donne's tremendous sonnet,

> At the round earth's imagined corners blow
> Your trumpets, angels, and arise, arise
> From death, you numberless infinities
> Of souls, and to your scattered bodies go. . . .

("The numerous pronouns and adverbs mix up the thought"; "The long strings of monosyllables are ugly"; "Not even by cruel forcing and beating the table with my fingers can I find the customary five iambic feet.") And on D. H. Lawrence's "Piano," a discovery of Richard's, a poem *about* insidious sentiment, the wrath of fully 66 percent descended: "Silly, maudlin, sentimental twaddle . . . nothing short of nauseating"; "Too feeble to be anything so definite as nauseating." Most did not even discover that the poem contains *two* pianos, a grand and an upright. It was surprising, poem after poem, how little luck respondents had in what Richards called "construing"—just following syntactic guides through a bare sense. In the fifteen years between his schooldays and theirs, that skill may have been fading along with Latin.

One thing very engaging about the first half of the book is Richards's genial aplomb as he sorts out the comments, never soliciting the knowing snicker. It's clear how his auditors could feel they were helping with a scientific inquiry, not being trapped into acts of self-exposure. And it's exhilarating still to watch the co-author of *The Meaning of Meaning* make a useful word out of such a rubber stiletto as "insincerity." This Richards defines as "the flaw that insinuates itself when a writer cannot distinguish his own genuine promptings from those he would merely like to have, or those which he hopes will make a good poem. Such failures on his part to achieve complete imaginative integrity may show themselves in exaggeration, in strained expression, in false simplicity, or perhaps in the manner of his indebtedness to other poetry." That is scrupulous and definitive, and helpful in coming to terms with a Rupert Brooke, who mayn't have really quite known what he felt at all.

In the second half he augments our critical vocabulary by patiently deconstructing and reconstituting such words as "sentimentality" and "doctrine." Then there's "Stock Response," a really useful coinage (it's what happened when the word "king" came unstuck from the phrase "king of all our hearts" and prompted someone to complain about "patriotic verse"). And "Technical Presuppositions," as that "rhymes *must* be perfect, that lines *must* not run over, that sonnets *must* have a definite division": those wrought much havoc, attributable, Richards thought, to "accidents of teaching, bad inductive inferences, . . . expectations we slip into without reflection." One of them was "the common theory that the value of poetry is in the value of its subject":

"Ah, this is a description of the experience of lying and looking at clouds!" He picks out something he can call the subject. Usually he has little difficulty deciding about the value of this subject. He can then argue, "It is good to lie and look at clouds; this poem conveys the experience of lying and looking at clouds; therefore this poem is good." Or conversely: "Lying and looking at clouds is a commonplace and trivial activity; this poem represents such an activity; therefore, this poem is commonplace and trivial."

That explicates much of the fuss about *Ulysses*.

With its classified and scrupulously numbered "protocols," *Practical Criticism* looked "scientific" enough not to get dismissed as just literary opinion. It was readable enough, on the other hand, to attract the people who needed it most, young teachers. It is salutary in declining to offer a "method"—instead, ways to make intuitive procedures explicit—and has probably done untold good, in particular to the pupils of its readers.

And it illuminated something alarming: the actual state of literary responsiveness, in the second generation (since 1870) of mass literacy. Richards's subjects were not drawn from the *Tit-Bits* public; they were "products of the most expensive kind of education"—most of them "undergraduates reading English with a view to an Honours degree." And they beat out rhythms on the table with their fingers, and could be put off by the word "king." Truly, "Far more than we like to admit, we take a hint for our response from the poet's reputation." And where do we ascertain the poet's reputation? If a post-curricular poet, why, from, oh, the *TLS*, where reviewers have gone before us and ventured a first-hand response. And how do reviewers for the *TLS* read? Well, many of them were once "undergraduates reading English with a view to an Honours degree."

Possible causes group themselves into two families.

(1) Great literature has inherent worth

Look, then, for what's damaged the ability to read it:

—taste formed on best-sellers and trash;
—urban sameness, and the decay of community;
—distractions (films, wireless);
—the Education Act of 1870, implying that literacy is a mechanical skill;
—the death of Latin and Greek;
—the dust now gathering on Bibles.

(2) "Greatness" is a value socially imposed

So look for social changes:

—the young feel free to like what they *really* like;
—the war broke up old hierarchies of "taste";
—simpler is after all better;
—the "canon" was nothing but a list of Great Names, as Richards acknowledged in suppressing the names of his poets;
—why read anyway? It's a penance.

The second option, with its Marxist ring, has been prominent since the 1970's, and nowadays British literary discussion is proud to display stigmata of the class struggle. But in the late 1920's the inherent worth of "the best that has been thought and said" still went by and large unchallenged. To restore the lost art of reading, that was the mission.

William Empson, at Cambridge since 1925, switched in 1928 from mathematics to English, where I. A. Richards tutored him in the first part of the Tripos. "At about his third visit," Richards remembered, "he brought up the games of interpretation which Laura Riding and Robert Graves had been playing with the unpunctuated form of 'The expense of spirit in a waste of shame.' Taking the sonnet as a conjuror takes his hat, he produced an endless swarm of lively rabbits from it and ended, 'You could do that with any poetry, couldn't you?' This was a Godsend to a Director of Studies, so I said, 'You'd better go off and do it, hadn't you?' A week later he said he was still slapping away at it on his typewriter. Would I mind if he just went on with that? Not a bit. The following week there he was with a thick wad of very illegible typescript under his arm—the central 30,000 words or so of the book."

The book was of course *Seven Types of Ambiguity*, published late in 1930. Its spirit is well illustrated by its very first example, "Bare ruined choirs, where late the sweet birds sang," where (wrote Empson, emptying his cornucopia)

> . . . the comparison holds for many reasons; because ruined monastery choirs are places in which to sing, because they involve sitting in a row, are carved into knots and so forth, because they used to be surrounded by a sheltering building crystallised out of the likeness of a forest, and coloured with stained glass and painting like flowers and leaves, because they are now abandoned by all but the grey walls coloured like the skies of winter, because the cold and Narcissistic charm suggested by choir-boys suits well with Shakespeare's feeling for the object of the Sonnets, and for various sociological and historical reasons (the protestant destruction of monasteries; fear of puritanism) which it would be hard now to trace out in their proportions; these reasons, and many more relating the simile to its place in the Sonnet, must all combine to give the line its beauty, and there is a sort of ambiguity in not knowing which of them to hold most clearly in mind.

"Crystallised out of the likeness of a forest": that phrase for a Gothic cathedral bespeaks a poet. But Empson's bent for mathematics is present too; a science that works always within the compass of predeclared definitions gave him his slant on the special oddity of human language, where no one can ever feel sure how much a word includes. (Look back at my word "compass": is it somehow mathematical? I can add that I knowingly fetched "predeclared" from the computer languages, in confidence that it would not trouble anyone unversed in them. But did geometry prompt my "bent" and "slant"? Not that I know of.) Readers may find cohesions of which writers were never conscious. As Empson put it in 1947, "Whenever a receiver of poetry is seriously moved by an apparently simple line, what are moving in him are traces of a great part of his past experience and of the structure of his past judgments." That is wise, and exact.

Since *Seven Types* was meant to offer "the general assurance which comes of a belief that all sorts of poetry may be conceived as explicable," it presupposed readers whose "past experience" and "past judgments" were enough like its author's to make the discussions cohere. If you didn't already find "Bare ruined choirs . . ." a fine line, a dissection of its appeals would never help you and could even lead to "a shocking amount of nonsense," so when he taught English literature in Japan and China, where words like "bare" and "choir" would be dictionary items rather than foci of association, Empson would warn his students off his own book.

So we come to the besetting difficulty with all criticism that observes what goes on in our heads as we read: it can only make sense by presupposing some consensus on what does go on. So much can go on in such a diversity of heads; and if, as Richards and Leavis said, the poem isn't "there" save in being read, by what canon may we say whose reading matters? In "A Woman Homer Sung," a poem Empson omitted to discuss, W. B. Yeats writes,

> . . . Whereon I wrote and wrought,
> And now, being grey
> I dream that I have brought
> To such a pitch my thought
> That coming time can say,
> 'He shadowed in a glass
> What thing her body was.'

There "pitch" is ambiguous in the Empsonian way. What had we best think of? Musical pitch? My own inclination is toward the *OED*'s division IV, "Highest point, height, etc.," and especially

18   The height to which a falcon or other bird of prey soars before swooping down on its prey; rarely *gen.* the height to which any bird rises in the air. Often in phr. *to fly a pitch.* [Examples from Shakespeare et al.]

That does go with Yeats's predilection for all manner of birds, though you'd not concretize to the extent of making this poem's "thought" a full-feathered falcon. But what of a reader who cannot rid his mind of the black stuff they put on roofs? And is eloquent, Empsonianly so, in making black pitch fit in? (We'll omit the details. But I've heard it argued.) What, in short, of the question of *whose* reading?

What happens in your mind when you meet a word is shaped by your prior experiences with it, and someone who's not read Shakespeare very much is more likely to be drawn toward the pitch that defiles than someone who has. "How high a pitch his resolution soars!"; "It is of such a spacious lofty pitch"; "And what a pitch she flew above the rest!"; "And enterprises of great pitch and moment":* such instances, though not consciously remembered, are apt to guide response to the phrase of Yeats. (And the phrase, "The pitch that defiles," though it's not in the Bible, does have a Biblical ring; "defile" and its inflections occur in the King James Version dozens of times. Since Shakespeare and the King James translators lived in the same community of usage, it's unsurprising too that "pitch" and "defile" are also joined by Shakespeare, three times at least.)

How you read, in short, depends on what you're used to reading. It's helpful to invoke Stanley Fish's powerful metaphor of "interpretive communities," and to suggest that critical activity began to seem so urgent in England around 1930 because *social* fragmentation was being perceived. There were readers, it was now distressingly clear, whose experience included little or no Shakespeare, little or no Scripture. That was distressing only in part because *Hamlet* and Holy Writ are good for one, though such a presupposition is never easy to exclude. Worse, members of two different English-speaking communities could no longer even read the same newspaper, because, making out the same words, they'd glean different messages. And as for reading Yeats, or Eliot . . . ! (Eliot once had to point a commentator toward the New Testament base of "A Song for Simeon.")

---

* The Quartos say "pitch," and so does the *Riverside Shakespeare* (1973), on which the *Harvard Concordance* is based. If you remember "pith," you're remembering a text that followed the First Folio.

We have seen how at least three different reading publics congealed at about the beginning of the century, expecting different satisfactions altogether; also how the smallest of them, the avant-garde public, was further riven as editors and Bloomsbury battled for control. There in particular, social loyalties were apt to complicate allegiances. And now the universities were being heard from, and Cambridge especially: not Cambridge the meeting-place that had spawned Bloomsbury, but Cambridge of the lecture-halls and tutorials, with a new complication, that of pedagogic *authority*. (Students, Fish remarks, "always know what they are expected to believe.")

So, looking up from his sheafs of "protocols," Richards claimed the teacher's privilege of adducing "immaturity": lack of general experience, lack of reading.

> "Making up our minds about a poem" is the most delicate of all possible undertakings. We have to gather millions of fleeting semi-dependent impulses into a momentary structure of fabulous complexity, whose core or germ only is given us in the words.

Clearly, the wider your experience the better you can bring off a feat of that kind. And Richards had his myth of the ordered neural impulses to imply that while we don't know (yet) how to quantify it, something exists that's potentially quantifiable, to earn the black-pitch reader a lower index than his falcon-pitch interlocutor. And if behind that hedonistic calculus you detect, mummified but undead, old Jeremy Bentham, yes, you are right. The best poem is the one that promotes the greatest good of the greatest number of neurons.

Richards may not have guessed how much he was assuming. Was there, it is pertinent to ask, a single book that everyone in a 1920's Cambridge classroom had read? Or could be expected to read? A generation earlier one could have said the Bible; for a generation before that, add *Pilgrim's Progress*. (And never mind today.)*

And we've seen Empson simply positing a reader whose enjoyments are much like his own. That resembles the assumption Virginia Woolf sensibly made about readers of her novels.

* * *

* "That is very fine; is that Brooke?" asked a member of King's College, Cambridge, 1975, on hearing Milton quoted. (Anecdote from Professor Albert Cook, who unluckily doesn't remember what Milton it was.)

But Frank Raymond Leavis (1895–1978), of Cambridge yeoman stock but never unaware of a Jewish marriage*—Leavis, "a thwarted genius," in the phrase of one man who knew him—declined to suppose that, save by the most rigorous tutelage, anyone could presume to an authentic English way of responding to anything. Inauthentic ways included the kind they taught you at Oxford, where the "Greats" (classics) curriculum unfitted men to read their own language (they were glib with the whole terminology of "value," and thought the best living poet was A. E. Housman). Meanwhile, "English" students at Cambridge, savagely incapable as the Richards protocols had shown, tumbled through Literary History and out into the world with unreduced incapacity. And the dons—what writers did the dons really admire? They admired P. G. Wodehouse, and Ernest Bramah (you've not heard of him? never mind); and as for *olde* authors, they inclined toward Charles Lamb, say on roast pig ("A Dissertation upon Roast Pig"!—delicious title!). Lamb was a select author whom Everyman's Library offered in optional red leather binding. All that enraged Leavis. It ought to sober anybody.

In 1930 he published *Mass Civilization and Minority Culture*, ten thousand words that began by regretting the loss of Matthew Arnold's advantages. Arnold could speak of "the will of God" and "our true selves," but if you spoke of "culture" today people asked what you meant. Well, you meant what was no longer there once it had to be explained: the unspoken consensus on which the machine and Lord Northcliffe's papers had impacted, and the films had impacted too, and Edgar Rice Burroughs, who was selling a million copies a year of books contrived, he himself said, to be read "with a minimum of mental effort"; not to mention the fellow who might have had Dorothy Sayers in mind when he pronounced that competent advertising copy

> . . . cannot be written except by men who have read lovingly, who have a sense of the romance of words, and of the picturesque and dramatic phrase; who have versatility and judgment enough to know how to write plainly and pungently, or with a certain affectation.

---

* The saddest Leavis story I've heard has him demanding to know if he'd been removed from some Cambridge post or other out of anti-Semitism. On hearing it patiently explained that the appointment was by definition non-renewable, he wondered aloud, "What shall I tell Queenie?" It's appalling to think of so powerful a mind so entangled.

My Guinness!

"An accurate taste in poetry," Wordsworth had written, "can only be produced by severe thought, and long continued intercourse with the best models of composition." Leavis, 131 years later, could only believe that Wordsworth's cultivated reader "was a very much more competent reader than his modern representative. Not only does the modern dissipate himself upon so much more reading of all kinds: the task of acquiring discrimination is much more difficult."

Here we get an early glimpse of an icon in Leavisian mythology, the enabled pre-industrial reader. Now Wordsworth, as Leavis knew very well, was little better received in his own time than T. S. Eliot was being received in Leavis's. Eliot himself would remark that the people who called Wordsworth silly were really finding him difficult, and it's an odd reflection that the author of *Lyrical Ballads*, of all people, was perhaps England's first "difficult" poet: a poet who demanded to be met on unfamiliar ground. (Donne hadn't demanded that, nor had even Cleveland.) As for "long-continued intercourse with the best models of composition," that is exactly what Oxford told its Greats students they were getting, and Cambridge its English ones. Much depends on what you mean by "intercourse" and by "best."

So Leavis was simplifying (though it's hard to know what else he could have done), and tacitly preparing himself an agenda. *New Bearings in English Poetry* (1932) was a first attack on the current notions of "best." It dismissed the claims of Alfred Noyes to be a poet, greatly qualified those of Walter de la Mare (distinguished, but "as remote as Poe" from the present) and of Thomas Hardy ("his rank as a major poet rests upon a dozen poems"), segregated Yeats as both late-Victorian and Irish, and proposed that "a decisive re-ordering" had been effected, for the few who could read, by three poets chiefly: Gerard Manley Hopkins, T. S. Eliot, and the Pound of *Mauberley* (for the *Cantos*, alas, were "little more than a game," and Leavis nowhere mentions the *Propertius*).

New Bearings exemplified two Leavisian qualities: a ruthless narrowing of the field of attention, and (when he was intent on what he respected) a command of particulars so cited and characterized that it was hard to disagree except in detail, if you understood what he was saying at all. *Revaluation* (1936), his best book and a miracle of condensation, took Eliot at his word about new work rearranging the Ideal Order, and restructured poetic history since the seventeenth century to foreground writers who could still interest us as living ones did. In the process Spenser disappeared, Milton became a learned and mischief-making aberration, Dryden faded in the incandescence of Pope, and Shelley ("in some ways a very intelligent man") depended, for his effects, "upon a suspension, in the reader, of the critical intelligence." But, critical intelligence suspended or no, whole academic careers are founded on Spenser, on Milton, on Shelley, and by 1936 F. R. Leavis was being thoroughly disliked.

How that came about, in the corridors of academic power, it would take not a C. P. Snow but a fabulist of James's stature to do justice to. He'd been a stretcher-bearer in the war; he returned "severely shell-shocked and scarcely able to talk, and for the rest of his life he suffered from insomnia." Then, in 1921, moments before sitting for the Cambridge examinations in which he resolutely earned a First, he saw his father, who'd just been wishing him well, killed by a motorcar. In wars and machines the twentieth century had lethally declared itself. What it had done to him it had done to England, and in hating it he hated too such careers as its facilities abetted. By '32 men who found him uncomfortable were trying to get him a Chair in South Africa or Australia. One day he found his study reassigned, his books heaped in a corridor. "Just being paranoid," goes an American saying, "doesn't mean you're not being persecuted." The most Cambridge ever did for Leavis was a Readership, three years before he retired.

So the snarling tone of the late books is comprehensible. By 1975 he'd so entrenched himself in so lost an England that even T. S. Eliot was, "however much more subtle, a fellow-countryman of Pound, and shared the American blankness, the inability to recognize the evidence—the fact—of the kind of human world that has vanished." He'd long since made a totem of "life," by which he meant "Lawrence," a Lawrence he never offered to read as exactly as he'd once read poetry. His realm grew joyless. Reading late Leavis, you would never guess that he'd lived through the most fructive eruption of "English" since the Renaissance. Each approval meant a dozen balancing disapprovals, and by the end there was little to point to save Lawrence and ashes.

Empson, in his late years "nutty as a fruitcake"—I'll not name my source for that judgment—came to hate whatever had been touched by Christianity, the God of which, he said (ignoring Dante), was "the wickedest thing yet invented by the black heart of man."* Leavis hated America, machinery, all affront to "the living principle." Richards, an enthusiast to the end, did not tire of promoting his old friend Ogden's invention, Basic English, the set of 850 words by which all the rest can be defined, so that at the cost of long-windedness you can use only those and say anything, replacing each big word by its definition. He thought Basic might save humanity. (We now call something else BASIC, and its readers observe strict definitions, and are machines.) *Scrutiny* ceased publication in 1953. And Eliot? Eliot in *The Criterion* disappointed Leavis and must still disappoint the alert. He'd promoted, alas, a new subset of bookmen: bookmen who were also churchmen, also didn't wince at a mention of *The Waste Land*, though its exigencies never seemed to touch their understanding of anything else. A sad outcome on the whole, to so brave a beginning. The twenties seems a decade of brave beginnings. Yes, some readers did get salvaged. But in the thirties, forties, fifties, sixties, despite so much guidance, most English readers still could not feel sure who their living writers were. In the eighties they still can't.

---

* Elsewhere in *Milton's God* (1961) he seems to connect Christianity with a lethal craving for tobacco. The publisher's blurb mentioned Empson's "characteristic delicate personal flavor." It is surely the maddest critical book of the century.

12 : A DISHONEST DECADE

And so to the "thirties." Aldous Huxley had come and not gone, and now there was Auden: Auden, perpetually "promising," "promising" till the day he died. Still, it was a grim decade. "A low dishonest decade" he called it, didn't he? It opened in fiscal doldrums and closed with the island yet again at war.

It was also the decade of *Murder in the Cathedral* and of Eliot's 1935 collection that closed with "Burnt Norton" ("Ridiculous the waste sad time"); of Pound's "usura" Canto; of *Work in Progress* becoming *Finnegans Wake*; of the aging wheezing Ford in chronic exile (Michigan, Provence); of the Spanish Civil War and Wyndham Lewis's novel about absentee warriors, *The Revenge for Love*. And it was the decade of Auden, Wystan Hugh Auden (1907–73), whose promise Eliot spotted as the decade opened. *Poems* (1930, Faber and Faber) "was well received and established him as the most talented voice of his generation." Yes. "In 1956 he was elected professor of poetry at Oxford." He has seven columns of entries in the *Oxford Dictionary of Quotations*.

He and Aldous Huxley had much in common; they'd "gotten up" any subject you could name, and really to keep up with them you had to be reading a deal of magazines and Pelicans.

His world from the first was secretive: of the missed rendezvous, of the spy.

> Your letter comes, speaking as you,
> Speaking of much but not to come.

. . .

He, the trained spy, had walked into the trap
For a bogus guide, seduced by the old tricks.

    . . . They would shoot, of course. . . .

In his middle work, solitaries who might once have been spies survey
a bleakness that is what all has come to. Herman Melville:

For now he was awake and knew
No one is ever spared except in dreams. . . .

Voltaire:

Cajoling, scheming, cleverest of them all,
He'd led the other children in a holy war
Against the infamous grown-ups, and, like a child, been sly
And humble when there was occasion for
The two-faced answer or the plain protective lie. . . .

Yeats:

The provinces of his body revolted,
The squares of his mind were empty,
Silence invaded the suburbs. . . .

In his sixties, a big seamed ruin, he made bleak epigrams—

Some beasts are dumb,
some voluble, but only
one species can stammer.

—and big spy-novel gestures:

. . . but someone in the small hours,
for the money or love, is
always awake and at work.
Here young radicals plotting
to blow up a building, there
a frowning poet rifling
his memory's printer's-pie
to form some placent sentence,
and overhead wanderers

> whirling hither and thither
> in bellies of overbig
> mosquitoes made of metal.

That's from about 1972; "printer's-pie" is a mess of unsorted letters—all that poets have to work with, we're to understand—and the "wanderers" (Greek *planetes*) are artificial satellites with antennae like mosquito-legs, which helps tell you how to value both the poets and the politically impassioned. All is mechanically alert and bogus.

Such was Auden's vision. He was also "difficult" in a way ingenuity couldn't fail to explicate—

> Sir, no man's enemy, forgiving all
> But will his negative inversion, be prodigal . . .

—where the trick is to recognize the Elizabethan "will his" of which "will's" is our contraction, making "will his negative inversion" mean "absence of will," the sole thing "Sir" won't forgive. So you trotted around Robin Hood's barn to find what you were hoping for, an easy cliché. Early Auden was the Cleveland of up-to-date poetry, when he wasn't being the Graham Greene of literature.

Yes, Cleveland, to Eliot's Donne. John Cleveland (1613–1658, and twenty-five editions by 1700) was clever at saying familiar things in a hard way, scratching such itches as the future would one day relieve with the daily crossword. Cleveland's way of rising to an occasion is to defamiliarize it by tricks of encoding. Thus Edward King has gone under the sea (1638), taking, so the poem has stipulated, all learning with him. Cleveland continues,

> . . . Water and fire
> Both elements our ruin do conspire.
> And that dissolves us which doth us compound,
> One Vatican was burnt, another drown'd. . . .

Of the four elements that account for our bodies two are dangerous, and one of them—water—has claimed King. But what is fire doing here, and what about the Vatican, which was never "burnt"? Well, take it as antonomasia for "library": then reflect that the Library of Alexandria, a "Vatican" by that special usage, was set aflame by Mohammedans in A.D. 640, to all literate people's regret. So fire is learning's emblematic foe, and having, almost exactly a millennium later, suffered a second such loss with the drowning of King, we pair water with fire and call its victim a second Vatican. Once decoded, "On the Memory of Mr. Edward King" proves an *easy* poem.* Its reader need only learn nimbleness at decoding. And so must Auden's, confronting, for example,

> . . . a rebellious wing that wills
> To better its obedient double quite
> As daring in the lap of any lake . . .

(An easy one. The "obedient double" is the wing's reflection in lake water. And "rebellious," via Shelley, makes the wing a synecdoche for poetic soaring.) Yet he's nearly always entertaining, brisk, and bright, and not muffled, however encoded. Nor were needful clues inaccessible. Central attitudes, first of all, were widely shared, from idle sort-of-communist headshaking over middle-class idleness to crime-fiction hints that something pretty ominous was going on somewhere.

> Seekers after happiness, all who follow
> The convolutions of your simple wish,
> It is later than you think. . . .

That was a public-school note; like Rupert Brooke before them, most of the thirties poets had been public-school boys, and they didn't take their responsibilities lightly. Charles Madge addressed a potent shade:

> Lenin, would you were living at this hour:
> England has need of you . . .

and Spender, enraptured by Russian films, hymned pylons, which marched across the green landscape, bringing power to the masses.

"The combination of revolution and privileged self-interest" was, as C. H. Sisson notes, not only Oxford thirties leftism but "the old Whig formula": nothing unfamiliar there. Bits of jargon helped keep it from seeming old, and the clue to those was never hard to come by either. For the thirties' Auden a smattering of popular psychoanalysis

---

* For the same commemorative book Milton wrote *Lycidas*, which they made room for at the end.

helped; for later, of, oh, *The Scientific American*. And each time you penetrated a new Auden poem you'd earned entrée, as it were, to the secret club where the Boys of the Long Summer, notably Wystan, kept up their wonderful talk.

Yet other ways of writing verse were feasible. Examine the clarity of this, from the April 1936 *Criterion*.

> Faridun watched the road
> and the army missed the young king.
> When the time came for his homecoming
> they were getting a welcome ready,
> wine, music and dancers.
> They had fetched the drums and led the elephants
> out of the stable,
> hung the whole land with garlands.
> . . . A cloud of dust on the road,
> presently a fast camel,
> a rider in mourning, keening,
> a gold box on his lap,
> in the box a piece of brocade,
> in the brocade . . . !
> Came to Faridun,
> pale, crying, sighing of woe,
> they could not make out what he said,
> prised the lid off the box,
> snatched the cloth, there was Iraj's head.
> Faridun fell from his horse like a dead man. . . .

By no means encoded, that aims for supernal explicitness.

Never, ever, is anything *perfectly* clear; the arrow falls short of the moon, and Basil Bunting was to exclude those lines from all his collections. But they mark a direction opposite to the normal "thirties" direction, which presupposed a reader alert for instant themes from the *Daily Express*. They're ascribed to " 'Faridun's Sons,' by Firdusi": Abul Kasim Mansur Firdusi, c. 950–1020, from a glance at a French version of whose *Shanameh* Arnold in 1853 got "Sohrab and Rustum." Tantalized, circa 1931, by the same version in a mutilated copy he'd picked up on the Genoa quays—even the title page was missing, and how did the story come out?—Bunting forced himself to learn Persian. And Arnold hadn't even finished reading the French.

Not that Matthew Arnold was lazy; but a quick scan sufficed to precipitate what he was ready to write, a poem about himself and his famous father. Code again: English people, disguised by names Arnold could fetch from a French transliteration of Persian. We can't stress too much how poetry by then had come to be a rite of naming one thing while intending another: a way of saying *something else*, without your even necessarily knowing what it was you were saying. Not so Bunting, who knew what he wanted to present: the ceremony prepared for the young King's return, and the shock when what returns is his severed head. "Faridun fell from his horse like a dead man. . . ." Bunting was interested, you see, in the story.

In '33 Pound got Faber to publish twelve Bunting poems in his *Active Anthology*; that was to be, for decades, about the extent of his publication in England. The selection included the "Villon," which had previously appeared (1930) in *Poetry* (Chicago) and in a fugitive collection, *Redimiculum Matellarum* ("A Chaplet of Chamber-Pots," privately printed, Milan). Even this third time around it seems not to have registered, and Bunting had no British publisher till 1965. Yet "Remember, imbeciles and wits"—when you read that out, make a cool pause after "Remember"; then let us hear the "and" with a rising inflection—

> . . . Remember, imbeciles and wits,
> sots and ascetics, fair and foul,
> young girls with little tender tits
> that DEATH is written over all.
>
> Worn hides that scarcely clothe the soul
> they are so rotten, old and thin,
> or firm and soft and warm and full—
> fellmonger Death gets every skin.
>
> All that is piteous, all that's fair,
> all that is fat and scant of breath,
> Elisha's baldness, Helen's hair,
> is Death's collateral:
>
> Three score and ten years after sight
> of this pay me your pulse and breath
> value received. And who dare cite,
> as we forgive our debtors, Death?

Abelard and Eloise,
Henry the Fowler, Charlemagne,
Genée, Lopokova, all these
die, die in pain.

And General Grant and General Lee,
Patti and Florence Nightingale,
like Tyro and Antiope
drift among ghosts in Hell,

know nothing, are nothing, save a fume
driving across a mind
preoccupied with this: our doom
is, to be sifted by the wind,

heaped up, smoothed down like silly sands.
We are less permanent than thought.
The Emperor with the Golden Hands

is still a word, a tint, a tone,
insubstantial-glorious,
when we ourselves are dead and gone
and the green grass growing over us. . . .

No denying it, readers exist who will find those stanzas less accessible than anything of Auden's, and how account for that? Candor, for one thing, can unsettle: "all these / die, die in pain": we're used to an ironizing of something softer. Then that litany of names—"Elisha's baldness"? In 2 Kings ii:23 little boys jeered at it, whereupon she-bears ate forty-two of them. But such outré Biblical details as a Dryden could rely on aren't current today. "The Emperor with the Golden Hands"? From Villon's *Grant Testament*, line 393, *"L'emperieres au poing dorez"*: Byzantine emperors, annotators tell us, whose icons flaunt gilded gauntlets. (A phrase like Villon's is absolute and will outlast our mortality, a notion Shakespeare wouldn't have found enigmatic.) Lopokova? A ballerina, still a public name when the stanzas were published (Maynard Keynes espoused her). And Patti? Genée? . . . but we're not making progress. For allusiveness isn't the difficulty. The difficulty may be described as social. This poem (of which I've cited only a fragment) confirms us in no serviceable postures: helps us in no way with the daily news. If we're not responsive to a fine performance—notably to a near-impossibility, Villon mimed in English—it is obdurate, empty.

Thus its mention of "Elisha's baldness" carries no wink to confirm us in feeling superior to a quaintly barbaric tale. Contrast "Victor," a 1937 ballad of Auden's, where a naïf named Victor

> Climbed into bed, took his Bible and read
> Of what happened to Jezebel. . . .

What happened to Jezebel (2 Kings ix:33–35) was that horses trampled on what was left of her and dogs ate most of what was left of that, and serve the hussy right. That is clarifying for Bible-reading Victor, and when his Anna proves faithless he dispatches her with a carving-knife. He is just the sort of vacuous provincial—a bank clerk—who'd comply with promptings from a lurid, outmoded book. *We'd* not have been so suggestible, that's understood.

Now "Victor," seemingly simple and straightforward, would have bewildered Samuel Johnson wholly, so airily does it presuppose our agreement that relating Scripture to life is a non-problem. Not only would Johnson not have thought that evident, he'd have scorned any implication that a literate reader could.

And that's some of Auden's secret: he lived without embarrassment in the space where undergraduate callowness merges with unschooled self-esteem, and whoever else lived there he could dazzle with syntactic agility while violating no trust in shared attitudes. We've seen Virginia Woolf presuming in the same way, and accurately, that the Cambridge Heretics will endorse each wink and nod of the caricature she's calling "Arnold Bennett." In that strategy Byron was a forerunner of both, and Auden in the *Letter to Lord Byron* he published at 30 lets Byron serve as the very paradigm of what such writing needs to complete it, an ideal sympathetic reader whom the rest of us can look to for cues.

> According to his powers, each may give;
> Only on varied diet can we live.
> The pious fable and the dirty story
> Share in the total literary glory.

If Lord Byron is assenting—as he must be: only assent could license such familiarity—then who among us will venture to do less?

So to be educated (to "share a common culture") is to know the correct response to every drop of a name: Byron (worldly), Wordsworth (dull), Lawrence (prophetic), Eliot (sage), Jeans and Eddington (cosmic). . . . Not to have been educated along those lines could be advantageous. Basil Bunting has described his encounter with Scripture. By no means a "believer," he knew the strange book well, thanks to a Quaker boarding-school in Yorkshire where

> Every morning you had to get a large lump of the Bible by heart before breakfast. At breakfast the Bible was read to you. At tea time, after tea, the Bible was read to you again. And on Sundays there were *very* large lumps of the Bible, besides Scripture lessons in between. And with that, and some other accidents, I came to be far better acquainted with the Bible than any of my juniors that I have come across.

One thing he came to appreciate, he said, was "the extraordinary narrative skill of some chapters of the book of Kings. I remember the early chapters of the second book of Kings in particular"—just where, as it happens, we find the story of Jezebel, also of bald Elisha and the forty-two boys and the bears. The narrative skill—that's the sort of thing he'd notice. And in *Villon* "Elisha's baldness" comes through as a recorded neutral fact, recalled offhand, no attitude prescribed.

No attitude prescribed: and that's unsettling. Beneath those amusing difficulties of Auden lies a welcome commonality of attitudes. We know how to take everything; the very point of a poem is to assure us we know how to take whatever it may mention. "Irony" was the thirties' strategy. Irony says, here's your stance. Don't credit the more blatant headlines. Fix on this poignant detail (the sleuth and Freud teach you how). Learn to cascade the cards from hand to hand. "Read *The New Yorker*, trust in God, and take short views."

> Remember, imbeciles and wits . . .

Not even that is a view short enough.

What had happened, by a kind of public conspiracy, was the coalescence of Everyman's and *Tit-Bits*: a formula by the way for *The New Yorker*, where Auden was speedily made welcome. What is often described, not inaccurately, as his "juvenility," his lifelong cheeky prep-school cleverness, points to a radical uncertainty about the seriousness of anything. "Isherwood noted how as a young man his character changed with his hat." When Professor Joseph Warren Beach noted

Isherwood noting that, he made the charge seem unanswerable, and it seems so still.

Everyman's and *Tit-Bits*: and the best of *Tit-Bits* was what Leopold Bloom retained from it, information, as that white cats need not be deaf, that black absorbs heat. The best of Everyman's needs no laboring: Shakespeare, Spenser, Fielding, Dickens, accessible. The worst of both is obvious: of Everyman's, the hint that Tradition is a closed system to which gentility pays its homage in shillings; of *Tit-Bits*, the premise that attention need not be collected so long as there is some cohering assurance, Newnes's, Northcliffe's, Sidney Webb's, Professor Joad's.* It was the worst of each that was achieving symbiosis, flaccid literariness fused with a habit of distraction. Nor moreover was the third public absent, the public for the new, a body still as ill-defined as it had been in the nineties. The part of it that was young, and university-centered, took naturally to a poet who gave manifest evidence of 'tec-reading and cinema-going. A bard could not be more of his time than that. (Did the author of "Ash Wednesday" go to the cinema? You couldn't tell, though the author of "Burnt Norton" did show signs of familiarity with the tubes.)

Nothing in particular to be blamed. The book was simply receding: supplanted as time-killer by cinema, wireless, and motor, as informer by the mass-circulation press, as locus of values by media punditry. Alert reading, reading that compares and judges, had become, within a generation, as Richards and Leavis saw, a specialist's skill. (And how prissy are such words as "compare" and "judge"! That they'd become needful was itself a portent. Had there not been a time when the bare word "reading" subsumed them? An age, pre-Northcliffe, pre-Newnes, when all reading was "alert"? Perhaps not; but criticism needs its myths. Something anyhow had surely altered, some elusive crucial digit in the ratio between print and mind.)

Meanwhile, journalists hunted the highbrow relentlessly. In the twenties, what with the fuss about *Ulysses*, the milder fuss about *The Waste Land*, and the way the antics of the Sitwells seemed to make reliable copy on any slow day, Everyman had gotten it firmly into his head that highbrows resembled the Post-Impressionists of yore and the

---

* Who remembers C. E. M. Joad? He passed for Everyman's Philosopher. His career was destroyed when they caught him trying to save a few coppers by evading a transport turnstile.

Russian anarchists of prehistory in being carriers of a deadly virus. Had Milton been a highbrow? Perish the thought. Milton was in Everyman's Library!

So "Beachcomber" in the *Daily Express*, "Timothy Shy" in the *News-Chronicle*, let the populace suppose that Sitwellesque antics were what letters had come to since . . . oh, perhaps the death of Rabelais. These two merit singling out as having passed, in private life, for erudite men. "Beachcomber" was J. B. Morton, an Oxford-educated Francophile; "Shy" was Dominic Bevan Wyndham Lewis,* author of a life of Villon. Day after day, in the papers, they were hilarious, and you shared the hilarity by sharing disdain for anything that seemed to transcend common sense.

They were middlebrow Catholic intellectuals who'd drawn courage and stratagems from Belloc (by the thirties a lonely man, long widowed, long strident, long settled into habits of overwork). Like him Catholic but not Irish, like him remote from the quiet social ritual of England's Old Catholic families, unlike him, however, in having undergone conversion—a formal act of separation from English easy-goingness—they found a facile role in condemning modernity *en bloc*. Not influential, no, they were symptomatic, drawing pay from the press to jeer at whatever the press itself publicized: motor-cars, the law courts, suburban cliché, Mayfair fashion, frazzle-haired poets, painters who displaced noses, psychiatrists, pundits, and people whose hope for salvation had been placed in diets, in morning dumbbells, in ways to keep worn hides "fit": inferior religions.

Alienation from the whole century could be made to seem a Catholic English layman's moral duty. One man who developed such a role into a cranky life-style also manifested literary genius of an unmistakable if minor order. Evelyn Arthur St. John Waugh, born into a bookman's household in 1903, would die in 1966 a choleric bogus country-squire, with to his credit much admirable prose and one powerful mythic projection of the national plight.

" 'So now the whole round table is dissolved,' quoted Rossetti sadly as the train steamed out of the station": there, in its exact concise offer of absurdity, a master's hand might have been precognized. Waugh,

---

* The *real* Wyndham Lewis was plagued for years by booksellers' and librarians' inability to distinguish. As for D.B.W.L., he took to hyphenating his "Wyndham-Lewis," thus hinting at some imposture on the part of the Vorticist.

23, is winding up a little booklet he called *P.R.B.: An Essay on the Pre-Raphaelite Brotherhood, 1847–1854.*

His scene is economically staged. Millais and Rossetti are bidding Holman Hunt farewell, and Millais has just come hurrying from the station buffet with a large bag of sandwiches and buns. At that moment Rossetti is moved to quote "sadly" from *Le Morte d'Arthur.* And we see how in a few inconspicuous sentences Waugh could fix as complex a thing as the Pre-Raphaelite ethos. He has caught its high priest in the very act, turning with dignity toward "aesthetic" solace inside a Temple of the Age of Steam.

"So now the whole round table is dissolved," quoted Rossetti sadly as the train steamed out of the station.

From as small a thing as the placing of the verb "steamed," nudged into prominence by alliteration with "station," that sentence derives luminous incongruence. Lytton Strachey would have let us hear a titter; Max we'd have seen buttoning ostentatiously the weskit of an opalescent prose. But Waugh's is a new kind of comic writing. It eschews the rhetorical nudge. In phrasing as stark as Archimedes' lever, it imparts the elements of the incident's happening.

It did happen. So did this, in Paris:

He was a man of middle age and, to judge by his bowler hat and frock coat, of the official class, and his umbrella had caught alight. I do not know how this can have happened. I passed him in a taxi-cab, and saw him in the centre of a small crowd, grasping it still by the handle and holding it at arm's length so that the flames should not scorch him. It was a dry day and the umbrella burnt flamboyantly. I followed the scene as long as I could from the little window in the back of the car, and saw him finally drop the handle and push it, with his foot, into the gutter. It lay there smoking, and the crowd peered at it curiously before moving off.

Save for the etymological triumph in "flamboyantly" (from *flambeau*, a torch), not a word there ventures to glitter. Waugh judged, rightly, that a scene worth the describing had best be described as if for the police. At no time in his life does he lapse into a Beaufoy dialect, or display signs of struggle to emerge from one. That transparent Latinate exactness seems innate: many little words, never making a clutter.

Innate? It can't have been. His father was bookman Arthur, sometime *Yellow Book* contributor, latterly scourge of drunken helots. His elder brother, Alec, for that matter, came to quick notoriety at 19 with *The Loom of Youth*, which suggested, not without relish, that the famed public schools teemed with pederasty. Though Evelyn made a somewhat slower start, by 1934, at 31, he'd achieved not only a style and a comic vision but the parable and the emblem of the England he knew. Adventurers who hack their way to him through his late reputation—scowler at the twentieth century, author of *Brideshead*—may be surprised to find four lines of *The Waste Land* quoted on the title page of *A Handful of Dust*. More surprising still, the book's thumb riffles Eliot's deck. It has its Madame Sosostris—

> Mrs. Rattery sat intent over her game, moving little groups of cards adroitly backwards and forwards about the table like shuttles across a loom; under her fingers order grew out of chaos; she established sequence and precedence; the symbols before her became coherent, interrelated.

—its woman whose nerves are bad tonight, yes, bad—

> "Want to be left alone?"
> "So tired . . . and I've just drunk a lot of that stuff of Polly's."
> "I see . . . well, good night."
> "Good night . . . don't mind, do you? . . . so tired."

—its Death by Water, its quest over stony ground and loose red pebbles; finally its Tiresias, an illiterate at the jungle's heart who guards a cache of Christendom's treasures—

> There was a heap of bundles there, tied up with rag, palm leaf and raw hide.
> "It has been hard to keep out the worms and ants. Two are practically destroyed. But there is an oil the Indians make that is useful."
> He unwrapped the nearest parcel and handed down a calf-bound book. It was an early American edition of *Bleak House*.
> "It does not matter which we take first."

No, it does not.

Evelyn Waugh was writing narrative prose, and such details, unlike their Eliotic counterparts, won't fluoresce when isolated. Their force is contextual and cumulative, and Waugh, with three novels behind him, had a sure sense of what he could do with pace and sequence. There his art does converge with Eliot's, even to occasional choric scenes a few lines long—anonymous speakers assuring one another how the land has come to lie. And it's striking how sardonically exact, in this book, is Waugh's scale of spuriousness and degeneracy. "Formerly one of the notable houses of the county" (says the county Guide Book), Hetton Abbey "was entirely rebuilt in 1864 in the Gothic style and is now devoid of interest." That means interest as defined for the touring-snob; fit readers will find intense interest in the long description that ensues. It presents a Hetton careering between shabby modernisms—"a vast gasolier of brass and wrought iron, wired now and fitted with twenty electric bulbs"—and crumbling Pre-Raphaelite braveries—

> . . . the bedrooms with their brass bedsteads, each with a frieze of Gothic text, each named from Malory, Yseult, Elaine, Mordred and Merlin, Gawaine and Bedivere, Lancelot, Perceval, Tristram, Galahad, his own dressing-room, Morgan le Fay, and Brenda's Guinevere, where the bed stood on a dais, the walls were hung with tapestry, the fireplace was like a tomb of the thirteenth century, from whose bay window one could count, on days of exceptional clearness, the spires of six churches. . . .

Devoid of interest!

The year Hetton was perpetrated, 1864, is the year of the last Dickens novel, *Our Mutual Friend*. Forty-two years later its copyright expired, and J. M. Dent could put Dickens's oeuvre into Everyman's Library. And what is it that Tiresias-Todd in 1934 unwraps in the jungle from his rags and palm leaves but an ant-eaten Everyman's Library, more or less? (Less.) And Tony Last, not the last of the Lasts but the last sentient Last, having fled the Hetton Abbey he's loved lifelong because a woman soured it, next having quested for a tropic Eldorado ("petals of almond and apple blossom, . . . gilded cupolas and spires of alabaster"—a transfigured Hetton): well, Tony will pay out his decentered life, amid bouts of fever, in reading to his illiterate captor, over and over, the novels of Dickens. ("Let us read *Little Dorrit* again. There are passages in that book I can never hear without the temptation to weep.")

That resembles *A Modest Proposal* in its mythic power. No one who has read it has forgotten it, and many remember it who have never read it. It is a nightmare rescription of the Good Life as bravely conceived by Ernest Rhys, one shilling the volume to make Everyman "his own critic and Doctor of Letters." For the Hidden City which does not exist—in fact, a savannah where Todd rules sullen Indians with his shotgun—is indistinguishable in most respects save comfort from fake-Gothic Hetton; nor is Hetton clearly preferable to London, nor London a place of anything save rapacity, triviality, dust and ashes, where you might as well be rereading *Little Dorrit* as doing anything else. A myriad died, Pound had written, "for a few thousand battered books," and it has come down to that—no, to a few hundred; no, to the output of one Victorian novelist minus the excisions of the ants, from repeated hearings of which old Mr. Todd has learned this much, that the novelist believed in God, though Mr. Todd is unsure.

"So now the whole round table is dissolved," Tony Last might have quoted sadly had he had the wit. And Lawrence's savage paradise is dissolved, as is George Herbert's rural one. George Herbert's 1934 surrogate is the Reverend Tendril, reading sermons composed long ago for a garrison chapel in India. "Instead of the placid ox and ass of Bethlehem, we have for companions the ravening tiger and the exotic camel, the furtive jackal and the ponderous elephant": no one cares that it all makes no sense, and Squire Tony's religious observance amounts to this, that he "inhaled the agreeable, slightly musty atmosphere and performed the familiar motions of sitting, standing and leaning forward." So much for rural pieties. And London? London is busy Mrs. Beaver, and Bratt's Club, and a dive called The Old Hundredth,* and that's all.

Heart of Darkness, thinned and lightened? Yes. And freed of rhetorical excess, and made into a popular novel for the mid-thirties. Not a great novel, no. Waugh's deficiency goes without saying: his people, as their names proclaim, are cartoons. Not all Waugh's scintillant economy can conceal his lack of interest in little John Andrew Last, whose death (kicked in the head by a horse) is designed as the shattering-point of the novel, but whose life Waugh can only draw with monstrous-brat templates like those he'll be using for the waifs in *Put*

---

* The Old Hundredth: familiar nickname for the hymn that begins "O God our help in ages past."

Out More Flags. Likewise Tony Last is the Empty Wimp, John Beaver the Limp Parasite, Brenda Last the Restless Wife. A low dishonest decade? A cartoon decade.

By '36 even the monarchy had come to this: that the death of King George V (which eclipsed, as a press event, the near-simultaneous death of Kipling) was hastened, so we learned a half-century later, by lethal injections. What the royal physician Lord Dawson had in mind was fitting an historic moment to the deadlines of *The Times*—which, his syringe once flushed, he put on standby alert—"rather than the less appropriate evening journals." A Lord Dawson invented by Waugh we'd denounce as tasteless, but Waugh's wimps and press lords and addlebrains are on the whole listless by the measure of reality's routine confections.

Todd, though. True, there's little of Todd, a few pages, but Todd—Tony Last's undying Mr. Kurtz—Todd does have, and alone has, a monstrous (passive) energy. For Todd *cares*. "May I trouble you to read that passage again? It is one I particularly enjoy." No one else, anywhere in *A Handful of Dust*, says anything like that. Todd is an *enjoyer* (and so is Waugh). The book's force, Waugh's too, flows through Todd, whom we meet only minutes before the end. He's an arresting and alarming creation.

And the force of Wyndham Lewis's 1928 *Childermass* flows through a Todd-like "Bailiff" who likes to see a few corpses strewn about because they make the rest seem almost alive. Polichinelle, Mr. Punch, the lava-like corrosiveness of Grand Guignol: when anarchic negative totems resembling those control what we can remember of book after book, we may be sure that something is wrong. Imagination's polarities have shifted ominously. Eliot's Sweeney of 1925 was a portent:

> And perhaps you're alive
> And perhaps you're dead
> Hoo ha ha
> Hoo ha ha
> Hoo
> Hoo
> Hoo

Wyndham Lewis, with a richer mind than Waugh's, became also possessed with negation. The "false bottoms" of *The Revenge for Love*, the algebraic suicide that ends *The Vulgar Streak*—such images testify not merely to an international crisis but to a national one. For from within England it seemed no longer possible to conceive of anything any more save ashes. Once Marvell out of the depths of the Civil War had conceived The Garden. Now a garden had died.

Northcliffe did his part to augment the literary heritage. To the Samuel Johnson Museum in Gough Square, the house where the six
amanuenses, five of them Scottish, had helped the great Cham grind
out the great Dictionary, the great Press Lord donated a great gray
stone from the Great Wall of China, detached by who knows what
imperiousness, to validate the Cham's sepulchral trope in *Rasselas*
about one stone to no purpose laid upon another. You can visit it, a
pale massy footnote, protected from the curious by glass.

World War II did not damage it, no. Yet London near Gough Square
saw much destruction. As I once heard the stone's custodian explain,
the Germans had mistakenly supposed that to blitz the heart of London—the "City" ("O City City")—would be to transfix with an arrow
the heart of England. The pedantic Teutons thought that "London"
meant *London*. In fact there was little life there: at night, vacant offices.
She remembered chiefly a bicycle blown to a rooftop, wheels like huge
ogling eyes.

So the inanimate got knocked about. Though a fearful loss of life had
been expected, and cardboard coffins stockpiled by the million in the
last sleepwalking months of the phony peace, yet by its predecessor's
standards the new war's rate of human attrition was light. To say as
much is not to devalue a single death. Still, that grim emergency hoard
was never drawn on. The normal supply of normal coffins sufficed.

The war had come with machine-like inevitability, and in England
as on the Continent it was a machine-war: Stukas, Spitfires, piston-
powered Hurricanes, gyroscopic bombsights, proximity fuses, land-
ing-craft, diesel tanks, radar; above all, keeping the besieged islanders
fed, the age-old British speciality, ocean shipping. "Convoy" was a
word on every tongue. Tube stations deep underground gave thousands nighttime shelter from TNT bombs; in Henry Moore's *Shelter*

Sketchbook forms cumber the platforms, anonymous as mummies. (Moore's huge sculptures also exalt an archaic indifference: bone, pelvis, arm's curve, gigantic presence looming. No fervency of mind.) And at Bletchley, in secrecy, the computer was being gestated, in its first incarnations as gadgetry to break German code. Such a war was only possible thanks to something that had commenced long before, and in England: the implacable mechanization of human toil. The spinning jenny, Yeats's second Eve taken from the side of Locke, was filling the world with her versatile progeny.

And the Information War no longer depended on Fleet Street's obsolescing technology. Wireless could now diffuse into every parlor Mr. Churchill's authentic growls. One thing the war did was enhance the authority of the BBC, for which all manner of people—George Orwell, Dylan Thomas—wrote scripts round the clock. When all was over, Dylan Thomas had somehow triumphed. It was he who emerged from the war the unchallenged Bard.

In firebombed London, Eliot had been writing "East Coker" and "The Dry Salvages," then "Little Gidding," where he meets the shade of Yeats, and had published them in *The New English Weekly*, a some-time Social Credit journal. Poetry-watchers were still getting used to the fact that Yeats had died (28 January 1939). Meanwhile, a generation born in the epoch of World War I was maturing amid the privations of World War II, and some of its spokesmen weren't having any of what they called "classicism." They ascribed it to Auden (Auden! History was spinning!). A few of them (Henry Treece, G. S. Fraser, George Barker, Vernon Watkins; and who are they?) claimed "a large accepting attitude to life" and could cite Dylan Thomas as an instance of that. They called themselves, collectively, the New Apocalypse, and Thomas might have been lowered from heaven for their comfort.

There was a tendency to muddle him with D. H. Lawrence, and that clarified nothing, Lawrence's vision having been resolutely rooted in history whereas Thomas's took no account at all of the public world and what had been happening to it. The machine-world, which out-raged Lawrence, he seemed not to notice, perhaps one reason he got his first popularity in a machine-London hostile machines were smash-ing up.

> Now as I was young and easy under the apple boughs
> About the lilting house and happy as the grass was green,

> The night above the dingle starry,
>   Time let me hail and climb
> Golden in the heydays of his eyes,
> And honoured among wagons I was prince of the apple towns,
> And once below a time I lordly had the trees and leaves
>   Trail with daisies and barley
> Down the rivers of the windfall light.

"Fern Hill" 's apple boughs, green grass, daisies, barley haven't at all what the Brangwen farm had for Lawrence, the particularity of a datable and threatened landscape. Emblems of youth's unthinking gaiety, by the sixth stanza they are taken away by "time," and that means not railways and coal but merely conceding that we must all grow up,

> And wake to the farm forever fled from the childless land.

But my bliss was in never guessing such a thing could happen:

> Oh as I was young and easy in the mercy of his means,
>   Time held me green and dying
> Though I sang in my chains like the sea.

(The library copy from which I take those lines is battered and thumbed as most books of poetry aren't, and someone has written across the top of the page, "Go ahead, find a better poem, go ahead. Impossible." That testifies to passions now quelled. For a dozen years the book has seldom been wanted.)

It's not as if Dylan Thomas had grown lusty in the green Welsh world among apples; he grew up in urban Anglicized Swansea, son of a secondary-school Eng. Lit. teacher who read to him. His own list of writers he imitated includes "Sir Thomas Browne, de Quincey, Henry Newbolt, the Ballads, Blake, Baroness Orczy, Marlowe, Chums, the Imagists, the Bible, Poe, Keats, Lawrence, Anon; and Shakespeare."* So in "Fern Hill" the green, the boughs, the barley are fetched from literature—from *Georgian* literature, come to think of it—and fetched into such a palace of naïve Art as Brooke might have erected had Cambridge and Eddie Marsh and then patriotic afflatus

---

* *Chums* was a boys' paper. Baroness Orczy wrote *The Scarlet Pimpernel*. You've heard of the rest.

not bested him. Part of the novelty of Dylan Thomas was the absence of any of the stigmata that had seemed to validate so many poets: the public school, the Oxbridge voice and curriculum, the enlightened bisexual chumminess, the accepted duty of scoutmastering folk less privileged. "Fern Hill" was once held to represent the peak of his powers. Four decades later it reads like self-popularization; indeed, by that stage he was working out "major" poems with the aid of Roget's *Thesaurus*. What he could fitfully do we hear in something he published in his twenties—

> Especially when the October wind
> With frosty fingers punishes my hair,
> Caught by the crabbing sun I walk on fire
> And cast a shadow crab upon the land,
> By the sea's side, hearing the noise of birds,
> Hearing the raven cough in winter sticks,
> My busy heart who shudders as she talks
> Sheds the syllabic blood and drains her words . . .

—the start of a poem that tells how he makes poetry—

> . . . Some let me make you of the vowelled beeches,
> Some of the oaken voices, from the roots
> Of many a thorny shire tell you the notes,
> Some let me make you of the water's speeches. . . .

Even so early he has mannerisms, notably that postponing way of starting off with a "when"-clause, but what he's after in this poem he somehow catches, the inextricability of words and mind and things and natural sounds, so that to experience anything at all is for him to word it in a tumbling passion. "Hear the voice of the Bard": yes, he brought that off, a few times. It's precarious, and hardly an ample poetic.

Hooted at by Evelyn Waugh as Parsnip and Pimpernell, Auden and Isherwood had removed themselves to the U.S., where Auden's first busywork was the elegy to Yeats, notable for its breathtaking condescension, "You were silly like us." (Yeats was never silly like *that*.)

Their absence cleared the way for the New Apocalypse. That in turn stimulated The Movement (I'll forbear copying its list of names), which stood for something lower-keyed, less disheveled. Poets were grouping in response to counter-groups, as though thinking they'd be read chiefly by other poets. Apart from the freakish popularity of Thomas, that was coming to be true. (What did Everyman read? Everyman read novels. And after the war the great Library itself commenced to disintegrate. There's little of Dent's dream now save in pious name. The *Tit-Bits* public? It would soon have the telly. The enlightened public? Split seven ways as usual, and part of it dreaming that the *TLS* guarded its interests.)

The Movement could claim one fine critical intelligence, that of Donald Davie (b. 1922); his *Purity of Diction in English Verse* (1952) gets past the handbook definition, "choice of words" (for are not all words chosen?), to show us how a diction is a subset from which the words we read are being chosen. That's a stunning clarification. Thus, while Shakespeare allows us to feel that any conceivable word, and some inconceivable, may turn up at any moment, yet Pope, however long we read him, lets us know there are some words, whether four-lettered or polysyllabic, that we will *never* encounter. Pope is using a diction, and picking his words from that. Unlisted, undefined, diction makes itself felt. Constraining resources, it enhances tension. It's like Cézanne's palette, which will flaunt no crimson, Mondrian's eschewal of curves, Bach's choice of key, which tacitly declares that if there are some sounds we are not to hear we may hope for intense exploitation of the rest. The occasion of this clarifying was Dylan Thomas, whose readiness to be bumped here or there by the word next thought of (or located in Roget) needed distinguishing from a Shakespeare's hovering intentness (all language accessible). That was when "Elizabethan" was an accolade being thrown rather mindlessly in Thomas's direction. Nostalgia for a fancied largeness of the age of Good Queen Bess seems laid on like the gas in the British psyche.

"Diction": Davie was bold in even promoting the word. Wordsworth had turned "diction" into a term of abuse, objecting to the diction of Pope's tinny successors. Yet diction had been the Augustans' prime discovery, and Wordsworth, their successor, accordingly too had a diction, called by him "the real language of men." He wrote,

And never lifted up a single stone;

he would not write "incarnadine." And when Eliot made "Polyphilo-progenitive" the entire first line of a poem, he was declaring a diction which would stretch toward "sapient" and "sutlers" but not toward "flapper" or "funny." Davie's "diction" was perhaps criticism's first new useful term since Eliot anatomized "wit" and Richards "sincerity."

Diction; and we are somewhere back near Ford and his exorcism of Original Beaufoy. In 1945 Philip Larkin (b. 1922), the most original poet The Movement could claim, published *The North Ship*, in 1955 *The Less Deceived*, in 1964 *The Whitsun Weddings*, in 1974 *High Windows*: very slim volumes all four, and just those four in four different decades, and all of them very careful about the language they admit. Larkin (A.B. Oxon '43) became University Librarian at Hull; to no more unglamorous a post could an Oxbridge man aspire. Imagine Rupert Brooke librarian of Hull! It's an easy jest that across the pages of Larkin you can hear an urgent "Shhhh."

The North Ship proved a false start, centered as it was on diction forged by Yeats. Its Larkin is "a sack of meal upon two sticks" ("A tattered coat upon a stick," wrote Yeats), sonorously hailing

> The beast most innocent
> That is so fabulous it never sleeps

—a "snow-white unicorn," no less. But no one has ever successfully followed Yeats, and anyway Philip Larkin didn't belong in any sort of mythological universe. He lived in an England of unabashed bleakness, and in the next decade he found ways to write about it:

> This empty street, this sky to blandness scoured,
> This air, a little indistinct with autumn
> Like a reflection, constitute the present—
> A time traditionally soured,
> A time unrecommended by event.

So far, in just a half-century, had imagination's center shifted from LeGallienne's "golden lilies of the Strand." And note the sourness of "traditionally": "tradition" means easy custom, which would have it that brightness lies in the future or the past. But no (the next stanza affirms blankly), this *is* the future childhood anticipated; yes, this is it, the empowered grown-up world. One day, moreover, it will be the past, and will still be vacant; and therefore goodbye, Wordsworth. For we shall look back not on some revelation of daffodils but on *this*, perceiving only

> fat neglected chances
> That we insensately forbore to fleece.

Here diction flirts with the colloquial "fat chance," and that sharper's word "fleece" foresees us some day lamenting our failure to have seized crass opportunity by its scruff. (He's being ironic? Oh? And how do you know? That's a Larkin trick, to affect the vulgar idiom and let us guess if it's really affectation. If the trope gives pleasure, then do we not concede that it's our secret idiom too?)

So sordor is purged of the Eliotic romance that itself once seemed daringly sordid—the

> Streets that follow like a tedious argument
> Of insidious intent,

the

> . . . dead sound on the final stroke of nine,

the

> White bodies naked on the low damp ground
> And bones cast in a little low dry garret,
> Rattled by the rat's foot only, year to year.

Larkin's scrupulous drearness can make such effects seem positively luscious.

The edition of *The Less Deceived* I have open is the fifth, 1962. Five printings in seven years (though likely small ones) suggests readers ready to endorse its drear view of things, even in "modern poetry" unsanctioned by the Faber & Faber imprint. (The Marvell Press? What was that?) Then in 1964, the year before Eliot died, Philip Larkin became a Faber poet. In *The Whitsun Weddings*, from a "three-quarters-empty train," he reported sighting

> . . . Canals with floatings of industrial froth;
> A hothouse flashed uniquely; hedges dipped
> And rose: and now and then a smell of grass
> Displaced the reek of buttoned carriage-cloth
> Until the next town, new and nondescript,
> Approached with acres of dismantled cars.

Not, to hear him tell it, a sad and improper descent, from hedges and grass to acres of dismantled cars; no, simply what's there, the weather of today's English soul. "For good or ill," says Donald Davie, "the effective unofficial laureate of post-1945 England," Larkin measures nothing against anything else. "Canals and smashed cars," continues Davie, "come along with hedges and cattle simply because they come along like that in any railway journey through England, as we all know." They do, they do; and this late in the century, protest, or even disgruntlement, would be merely romantic. There is no rejoicing, no, things are as they are.

Contrast a 1914 train, as remembered by a 1924 writer, Ford Madox Ford:

> The two young men—they were of the English public official class—sat in the perfectly appointed railway carriage. The leather straps to the windows were of virgin newness; the mirrors beneath the luggage racks immaculate as if they had reflected very little; the bulging upholstery in its luxuriant, regulated curves was scarlet and yellow in an intricate, minute dragon pattern, the design of a geometrician in Cologne. The compartment smelt faintly, hygienically of admirable varnish; the train ran as smoothly—Tietjens remembered thinking—as British gilt-edged securities. It travelled fast; yet had it swayed or jolted over the rail joints . . . Macmaster, Tietjens felt certain, would have written to the company. Perhaps he would even have written to the *Times*.
>
> Their class administered the world. . . . If they saw policemen misbehave, railway porters lack civility, an insufficiency of street lamps, defects in public services or in foreign countries, they saw to it, either with nonchalant Balliol voices, or with letters to the *Times*, asking in regretful indignation: "Has the British This or That come to *this!*" . . .

A mere four decades have reduced so much to Larkin's "reek of buttoned carriage-cloth." (Yes, "reek." Have you traveled on a British railway? Gagged on its unthinkable food? Damp sandwiches, cardboard "cheddar." Farewell, Fordie; better off dead. A man I knew remembered your gourmandise.)

But natives haven't the luxury of protest, something Larkin, native, never forgot; and though in his last book, *High Windows*, there's exasperation—

> . . . First slum in Europe: a role
> It won't be so hard to win,
> With a cast of crooks and tarts . . .

—it's the exasperation merely of unwritten Letters to the Editor. He can also be gnomic, like Gray or Tennyson:

> Man hands on misery to man.
>   It deepens like a coastal shelf.
> Get out as early as you can,
>   And don't have any kids yourself.

Bloomsbury was virtually extinct, that was something, and in the postwar decades anarchic energies were there to draw applause. Yes, yes, Amis; yes, yes, John Osborne; later yes, yes, *Private Eye*. No longer did it seem plausible to complain of a still-Victorian Britain smothered by gentility, or of a literary establishment staffed by Cambridge Apostles. But for all the cocking of snooks, for all indication of cogs here and there freeing up, for all the flashy promise of the 1951 Festival of Britain—centenary homage to Prince Albert's Great Exhibition, its Crystal Palace a geodesic Dome of Discovery—the new freedoms released nothing remotely "Elizabethan." Dylan Thomas's self-destruction by alcohol connoted rather negation than tip-toe transcendency. By the time of Thomas's death in 1953, Philip Larkin was preparing a new kind of poet's role. It merits study: not the Bard nor yet an Eliotic invisibility, but a skeptical slouch, hands in pockets, ventriloquizing, "Books are a load of crap."

That phrase comes from a persona for one poem, yes, but it does elide with the public Larkin, who asked an interviewer, "Who's Jorge Luis Borges?," and wished a writer had identified Francis Parkman ("one of his American friends, perhaps"*), and as for reading, he

---

* Wouldn't you take that, in a librarian, for willed ignorance?

didn't, he said, read much: "Novels I've read before. Detective stories: Gladys Mitchell, Michael Innes, Dick Francis . . . Nothing difficult."

"Nothing difficult," no; also "I think if you're in good health, and have enough money, and nothing is bothering you in the foreseeable future, that's as much as you can hope for." Ah. "I think foreign languages irrelevant": indeed, "I don't see how one can ever know a foreign language well enough to make reading poems in it worthwhile." For one thing, "If that glass thing over there is a window, then it isn't a *Fenster* or *fenêtre* or whatever." Lord. So life was meant to be just plain-bloke simple, and what he'd have wished to hope for was a world unpestered by his emblematic Three P's: Picasso, Pound, and Parker (Charlie)—pictures you couldn't see, poems you couldn't read, jazz you couldn't dig. (Jazz did mean a lot to Larkin.)

> It seems to me undeniable that up to this century literature used language in the way we all use it, painting represented what anyone with normal vision sees, and music was an affair of nice noises rather than nasty ones. The innovation of "modernism" in the arts consisted of doing the opposite. I don't know why, I'm not a historian.

"I don't know why"—he never knew the why of anything; getting at "why" was highbrow. And Joyce was "a textbook case of declension from talent to absurdity."

From England's unofficial post-war laureate such plain-guy platitudes are pretty dismaying. "It seems to me that up to this century literature used language in the way we all used it." Well, *Paradise Lost* is a ready counter-example. Though it drew on a story thoroughly familiar to whoever in 1667 could pretend to read, many said they'd welcome help. So in 1668, at the printer's request, Milton supplied for the second edition a lengthy prose summary, later broken up and distributed through the volume. For Milton had assumed, and so had Dante, that what was *expected* of a poet was a work of learning, something to occupy readers all their lives—indeed, like the *Aeneid*, to absorb a community of readers, active during many generations and assisting one another with commentaries. (Shakespeare, needless to say, had different aims, but he hadn't thought of his playscripts' being preserved.) In supplying the prose "arguments" Milton was doing what Joyce had done when he prompted Stuart Gilbert in 1930: helping willing readers get started. Joyce was never in higher company than when he jested that he made no demands on a reader save a lifetime's attention.

The resistant book was a norm for many centuries. The strange newcomer was not twentieth-century "modernism"; that reverted, in new circumstances, to an old tradition, still just sufficiently alive in universities to furnish the nucleus of a readership. What was relatively new was the "easy" book, and notably the novel, a book for people who'd acquired the skills of reading though one couldn't say what in particular they'd read. When the easy book made its appearance in Pope's century, it addressed itself by convention to women, since middle-class girls, however fluent readers, had acquired their literacy in the mother-tongue instead of commencing, like schoolboys, with Latin and Caesar and Virgil. Some acquaintance with Holy Writ you could likely assume, but what on earth else?

Soon consumers of easy fiction wanted easy poetry, like Adelaide Proctor's, and if by the 1890's poetry was seeming vacuous, that was in part because it was proving difficult to make one easy poem seem different from another. (Compare, in their different ages, two minor poets. How various is the work of "witty" Marvell! But the sixty-three poems in *A Shropshire Lad* can be hard to tell apart.)

If easy books have come to seem normal, it's from their sheer quantity. They are read but once, and the appetite is insatiable; perfect artifacts, then, for a consumer-driven economy. Hence the steam presses and the typesetting-machines of late-Victorian mass production. (The brick and the book were among the first mass-produced commodities; a similarity of shape has been remarked on.)

In Philip Larkin we behold perhaps the first British man of letters of notable gifts for whom easy books, and only easy books, were the human mind's natural secretions. As a portent he's been worth dwelling on. Not that the best of his poems are negligible, with such leveled exactness does their idiom twitch in the leveled, diminished world the war had left: the world of Wyndham Lewis's *Rotting Hill*, of shared poverty, blunt scissors, blunt minds, numb hopes.

Officially [the loaf] was one day old, but when he applied the bread-saw it was like sawing brick. He sawed off four slices and grilled them two at a time. The kettle had been refilled and was acquiring a little heat. He threw the remainder of his butter-ration into the repast, added a few pinches of alleged Darjeeling to the pseudo-Ceylon in the teapot: placed on the tray the two dishes of cereal, a teaspoonful of sugar for each. Sugar was always a bad shortage with him. He took down a jar marked "Strawberry Jam," recognized by housewives as mainly pectin and/or carrot pulp, given appropriate local colour of course and flavour to match. . . .

The privations of 1949, so repellent to Lewis, were of course eventually palliated. But mere anarchy too was starting to run amok: "skinheads" in "bovver boots" (shoes for maiming with) made their picturesque entry into civic folklore. In '62 Anthony Burgess published *A Clockwork Orange*, a book no one, to its author's chagrin, seems willing to forget.

So we cracked into him lovely, grinning all over our litsos, but he still went on singing. Then we tripped him so he laid down flat and heavy and a bucketload of beer-vomit came whooshing out. That was disgusting so we gave him the boot, one go each, and then it was blood, not song nor vomit, that came out of his filthy old rot. Then we went on our way.

The best-seller, Lewis once remarked, is unable to lie. It plays back with the highest fidelity, if not what is real, what its public accepts as real: at one time "Vera, it is sweet to die in your service," and at a later time, "So we cracked into him lovely." The acceptance of Burgess's myth marked a public concession that street violence, for years a shocking fact, was unlikely to go away.

For what of an urban reality you can prove with your eyes and ears? If you'll settle for a mindlessness less lurid than that of Burgess's Alex, it's never far to seek. The last time I visited the Trafalgar Square post office, the handset from each of some twenty public telephones had been neatly snipped off and jettisoned. And the last time I stood in a London cinema queue, its torpor got tickled by a sidewalk fight between four toughs from a Volkswagen and six from a Citroën. A big shopwindow flexed with the impact of caroming bodies. Shirts got ripped, noses bloodied, in broad daylight. The queuers remained politely impassive. Yes, the British This or That had come to *that*. (British plate-glass technology, though: that did prove faultless.) Then there was the glimpse of two City men, bowlers and weskits and all, being borne upward on a steep tube-station escalator. The one above, turned round to face the one below, was banging him about the head fiercely with an attaché-case. And they say Lewis exaggerates.

* * *

Long gone was the King James Bible's hold on the public imagination; gone too its long hold on the public idiom. No longer was a furious driver called what jest had called him since Dryden's time, a Jehu. Nor was it only small change of that order that had vanished from circulation; works of literature were also mutating as their phrases fell on new ears. In Victoria's age especially, rhetoric had routinely drawn authority from the King James idiom—"Fourscore and seven years ago our fathers brought forth . . ." Yes, yes, an orator's set-piece, American at that; but what about Yeats's "Innisfree"?

> I will arise and go now, and go to Innisfree. . . .

How, if at all, does that line arouse a mind in which Biblical echoes are not obscurely stirred? "I will arise and go to my father, and will say unto him . . ." (Luke xv:18). And if post-war workaday prose was sounding less like Philip Beaufoy's, that may be ascribable less to improved public taste than to utter Biblical nescience. During the long Victorian crisis of faith, high-minded writers from Matthew Arnold down had sought to rescue for literature a book that was losing credibility as history and doctrine. Now its literary status was declining as well.

In 1939 the Right Reverend Monsignor Ronald A. Knox undertook to retranslate the Bible single-handed. He meant his version for the use of Roman Catholics, for whom the King James had never been an Authorized Version anyhow (they made do with a much worse one, Challoner's revision of the Douay). But to meddle with any extant version at all was to stir up a mare's nest. Knox offered clarity, on the assumption that literary merit derived from that, but what church-goers of all denominations really wanted was the lull of familiar phrasing, never mind if it was sometimes nearly nonsensical. In the years of controversy that ensued, Knox would time and again cite instances of sheer chaos.

> And ye shall go out at the breaches, every cow at that which is before her; and ye shall cast them into the palace, saith the Lord.

So Amos iv:3, where it's pointless to wonder what King James's translators can have been thinking of.

Leave the city walls you must, the Lord says, one by this breach, one by that, and be cast away in Armon.

So Knox, inverting syntax to fence off journalese, but taking pains to keep diction transparent. He's at his best in folk-like narrative:

One day, when the heavenly powers stood waiting upon the Lord's presence, and among them, man's Enemy, the Lord asked him, where he had been? Roaming about the earth, said he, to and fro about the earth. . . . [Job i:6–7]

That's a rakish and sinister Satan, a discovery if you've been used to the King James phrasing, in which man's Enemy (and everyone else) is made to sound like a chanter of cathedral antiphons:

Then Satan answered the Lord, and said, From going to and fro in the earth, and from walking up and down in it.

You'd not guess from such a cadence that Satan was *dangerous*.

Upon Monsignor Knox's head there burst successively the wrath of readers he'd deprived of remembered bits, and the wrath of scholars, especially Old Testament scholars, who charged that time and again he'd not sought their advice but cut exegetical knots very cavalierly. He was all his life a devoted puzzle-solver—completing *Times* crosswords without recourse to a pencil was an occasional recreation—and he thought too that it was possible to be blinded by scholarship, not a thought that brings favor from scholars. One of his more ingenious gambits had been to wrest sense from Saint Paul's letter to the Corinthians by reconstructing what it was an answer to, the Corinthians' letter to Saint Paul. The issues are now forgotten, and so, it is to be feared, is the Knox translation, committee artifacts having ousted it from favor. The curious, though, should look up his Book of Jonas, a folk-tale about a prophet subject to tantrums, with its brilliantly ironic ending: Jonas a testy pukka sahib in his garden complaining to a Lord who's not spared his ivy-plant, and the Lord slyly responding, "And may I not spare Nineve?"

Nor has any power spared the 1611 English Bible. The ending of its spell over secular literature has left casual writing to devise new common idioms—often, new ways to be vulgar—and left studied writing to seek out new models of authority: in educated speech, in synthetic "classless" speech, even in poetic practice overseas.

Or in curial homemade language such as David Jones was compelled to devise for his *Anathemata*, the public idiom by '52 having drifted so far from Victorian moorings that a theme once so comfortably Tennysonian as Christian meditation on "the matter of Britain" was no longer thinkable save in austere encoding.

Or in the ritual tongue of Geoffrey Hill's *Mercian Hymns* . . .

But it's time to announce explicitly the post-war news, that save by factitious cooption—by the sheer illusory power of lists like Faber's and Chatto's—there's no longer an English Literature. Talent has not been lacking, not at all; but, a center absent, talent collects for itself the materials of some unique cosmos. As never before, good poets are dispersed round the land; as never before, each commands a personal readership, including with good luck a perceptive critic (thus Hill stirs the intent eloquence of Christopher Ricks); as never before, no talk, however extensive, about any of them need cause you to mention another. You *think* of them quite separately, and that is a symptom. Larkin was perhaps the last poet whom "everyone" had heard of, and the "Movement" he was connected with soon didn't contain him. Nothing ever contained, or can account for, so disparate a quartet as Hill, Jones, Charles Tomlinson, Basil Bunting: nothing save a common devotion, in utterly disparate idioms, to the past of England. That's a symptom too, that need to reclaim—affirm—a past. Pasts are homemade now; David Jones's (Catholic, Celtic) isn't Bunting's (pagan, Northumbrian), nor has either much in common with the resolutely nonconformist past of Donald Davie. *Tit-Bits* and Northcliffe, maybe, abolished even the illusion of a communal past. "Are all white-eyed cats deaf?—No"—and if not they never were, and all is always Now.

So the centers drift apart, beyond range of synoptic viewing. Faced with choice, I choose to dwell on two I've known, Tomlinson and Bunting. I don't know if they ever met. That's a symptom too.

In 1955 the Fantasy Press in Eynsham, Oxfordshire, published a little book of poems called *The Necklace*. Its author, Charles Tomlinson, was previously unheard of save for one pamphlet, and his book seemed publishable chiefly thanks to a foreword by Donald Davie, Tomlinson's sometime Cambridge tutor and in '55 a credentialed "Movement" man. Davie began, "These poems require no introduction," which was ideally true. He then went on to supply more introductory words than are to be found in the poems he was introducing. That reflects what he was well aware of, their dissenting conception of what a poem was. Readers expected to hear a poet talk, at least to overhear him muse; they'd take his measure by getting a sense of *him*. Against habits like theirs the little book shut like a clamshell. Its very title (from Wallace Stevens's line "The necklace is a carving not a kiss") rejected the ruminatory presence, affirmed the thing *made*.

In theory, Larkin's fans should not have dissented; but theory of less than scholastic precision is tricky. Larkin said that "to write a poem was to construct a verbal device that would preserve an experience indefinitely by reproducing it in whoever read the poem," and "construct a verbal device" does seem to be talking craftsman's language. But qualifiers lie hidden. For one thing, Larkin's practice posits "experiences" of a quotidian order, like those glimpses he'd caught from the train to London. For another, when he came to construct the verbal device he seemed quite content to trust instinct and chance ("Usually the idea of a poem comes with a line or two of it, and they determine the rest"). What tended to emerge was Larkin, or a persona, situated within the experience and musing about it.

For Tomlinson that was meager. Remembering a Chinese scroll might be a more significant experience than riding the train. Also there was much to learn about the fine joinery of devices; craftsman's lore forgotten in England had, for instance, been preserved and refined in America, whereas in The Movement's Little-Englandism he detected "that suffocation which has affected so much English art ever since the death of Byron." Finally, the poem's words need not entail some presence to murmur them. As his earliest instantiation of such insights, *The Necklace* leaned on transatlantic example and might have been brushed aside as derivative by anyone with a sure knowledge of what it derived from:

> Warm flute on the cold snow
> Lays amber in sound
>
> .   .   .
>
> The sage beneath the waterfall
> Numbers the blessings of a flute;

> Water lets down
> Exploding silk.
>
>   .   .   .
>
> Pine-scent
> In snow-clearness
> Is not more exactly counterpoised
> Than the creak of trodden snow
> Against a flute.

Easy now, yes, to say how that remembers "Thirteen Ways of Looking at a Blackbird" (it's even called "Nine Variations on a Chinese Winter Setting"): less easy, perhaps, to see how sharply a willingness to learn from Wallace Stevens broke with British custom. And one significant detail owes nothing to Stevens. The lines "Pine-scent / In snow-clearness" quote exactly the title of a Chinese picture Tomlinson saw at 18. ("If I had possessed Miss Moore's scrupulousness it would have been printed in quotation marks.") To let a phrase be a found object was an American maneuver, one more way to cancel what words so readily conjure, an insistent talking presence like a tour-guide's. (Browning's English conscience had not been satisfied till The Old Yellow Book was processed into words of his own. But Pound lifted Jefferson's correspondence bodily.) Once a poet has admitted verbatim quotation, with or without quotation marks, he's shed the obligation to stamp each word with himself. Language, wherever minted, is minted language.

The liberation of Tomlinson, a boy out of the provinces, had commenced with his quick mind's lighting on odd chances. At grammar school, having bought a Selected Pound for a half-crown, he'd naïvely applied classroom scansion to

> For three years, out of key with his time,
> He strove to resuscitate the dead art
> Of poetry; to maintain "the sublime"
> In the old sense. Wrong from the start—

and decided, since it couldn't be done, that "perhaps some type of syncopation was at work." Then he'd been arrested by

> . . . is almost afraid that I
>   will commit that indiscretion

and (miraculously) spotted "the stress and pausing on 'I' before the line break." Canto II "closed on the word 'And. . . .' That was also something to think about." Later, in Marianne Moore, he found himself admiring not the lady's quirky presence but "the rhyming of light against heavy beat."

What those enlightening recollections show us is a schoolboy bringing to poetry—hardly knowing how—the kind of perception British schoolboys used to bring to trains and wireless kits: an analytic fascination with how something works. The mind that made the first spinning-jenny had paid like attention to an intricate imagined dance (and altered England forever). Analytic attention to process is the British genius. But somehow, some time after Marvell and Pope and Landor, the islanders became persuaded that *literary* perception was of a different order: moreover, that they themselves were literary by birthright. (They do tend to be impeccable syntacticians.) Thus Literature was something you achieved by sheer native sincerity. Of how a poem came Larkin had this to say: "It happens, or happened, and if it's something to be grateful for, you're grateful."

(How odd are communal self-misapprehensions! The English think they're literary; they are technologists. Though Americans think they're technologists, technology scares them; cherishing the disembodied abstract, they find fulfillment in the themes of law. And Ireland, said to be dreamland, breeds logicians, fierce ones.)

Astute eyes might have spotted in *The Necklace* a poet working in ways new in modern England, and learning from writers—foreign writers at that—who didn't necessarily learn from one another. But astute eyes were lacking. Sages, flutes, amber: pretty *precious* stuff to be peddling amid skinheadery. Chinese pastiche?—stale; if you want that, go to Waley. As for the Stevens connection, in '55 Stevens had never so much as been published in England. So there was nobody (save Davie) to protest when every publisher in England rejected Tomlinson's next collection as reflexively as they'd have declined an electric eel. *Seeing Is Believing* at length appeared in New York (McDowell, Obolensky, 1958). That book contains no hint of pastiche.

THE ATLANTIC

Launched into an opposing wind, hangs
  Grappled beneath the onrush,
And there, lifts, curling in spume,

> Unlocks, drops from that hold
> Over and shoreward. The beach receives it,
>   A whitening line, collapsing
> Powdering-off down its broken length. . . .

Continuing the first line from the title is a device traceable to Marianne Moore's "The Fish" (another water-poem); but the powerful metrical mimesis is not derived from her or from Stevens but from—from what? At a guess, from potentialities sensed in *Beowulf*. That is one way to use academic learning.

Tomlinson read English Literature at Cambridge, 1945–48 (and French, and German; and of course he had Latin). And he sees no need to hide his education, though he doesn't use it to pester with allusions. That is "foreign" once again. American poets had begun to show the classroom's stamp in Pound's and Eliot's generation, and the tradition persists (Olson, Zukofsky, Davenport). It wasn't till Tomlinson's and Davie's generation that a like phenomenon began to be discernible in England. True, Tennyson was at Cambridge, but we don't take account of what he learned there, save that Arthur Hallam was praiseworthy, and one thing Sam Johnson learned at Oxford was to get out of it.

Always, a Tomlinson poem, in what he would later discover was the norm of the American "Objectivists," is an undertaking: a something as much itself as a clock or a painting, even when it wears the look of responding or reporting. Near the center of *Seeing Is Believing* we find a "Farewell to Van Gogh":

> The quiet deepens. You will not persuade
>   One leaf of the accomplished, steady, darkening
> Chestnut-tower to displace itself
>   With more of violence than the air supplies
> When, gathering dusk, the pond brims evenly
>   And we must be content with stillness.
>
> Unhastening, daylight withdraws from us its shapes
>   Into their central calm. Stone by stone
> Your rhetoric is dispersed until the earth
>   Becomes once more the earth, the leaves
> A sharp partition against cooling blue.
>
> Farewell, and for your instructive frenzy
>   Gratitude. The world does not end tonight

>And the fruit that we shall pick tomorrow
>   Await us, weighing the unstripped bough.

Six lines, five lines, four lines, the stanzas diminish with the day. Evening shadows will lengthen at their own pace, and no urgency of Van Gogh's will hasten them. "The world does not end tonight": a valuable lesson, in the heyday of Dylan Thomas. And "Stone by stone / Your rhetoric is dispersed": no English poet admires more the obduracy of stone.

Stone is itself: resistant: the other: that which whim cannot subdue, appropriate, transmute. A poem collected in 1963, "The Picture of J.T. in a Prospect of Stone," wishes for a child "the constancy of stone" and continues,

>—But stone
>   is hard.
>   —Say, rather
>it resists
>   the slow corrosives
>   and the flight
>of time
>   and yet it takes
>   the play, the fluency
>from light.

"Takes" means partly "subtracts" but mostly "receives," and the poem, remembering in its title Marvell's "Picture of Little T.C. in a Prospect of Flowers," remembers too how it has been three centuries since a poet could write

>See with what simplicity
>This nymph begins her golden days!

and not sentimentalize some Alice. Marvell ends with an oblique hint at infant mortality— "Lest Flora . . . / Nip in the blossom all our hopes and thee." Tomlinson, in a time less easily floral, has the child emerge

>from between
>   the stone lips
>of a sheep-stile
>   that divides

                    village graves
              and village green

and reverts to this moment as his poem ends:

                    but let her play
              her innocence away
                    emerging
                       as she does
              between
                    her doom (unknown)
                    her unmown green.

There "unmown" too is a word with Marvell's stamp; the poem comes from a 1963* volume in which Tomlinson, his apprenticeship behind him, is resuming the British side of his heritage. That means, drawing on resources unavailable to American poets, for whom single words cannot have such power to evoke exact areas of reference. Though Pound has potent single words, the occasions they remember come not so much from available tradition as from the parts of it his own fifty years' poem has already appropriated. *The Cantos* were forced to create a tradition for themselves. An English poet hasn't that responsibility.

Still, Tomlinson's tradition does not all come ready-made; in Pound's way, he will let us see him extend it. If the title and some of the diction of "The Picture of J.T." remember post–Civil War England, the poem gets its lineation from the three-ply stanza William Carlos Williams, then still living, had invented in "The Descent":

              . . . For what we cannot accomplish, what
        is denied to love,
              what we have lost in the anticipation—
                    a descent follows
        endless and indestructible

"J.T."—his own child, the poet specifies; scholars must guess who the Marvell child may have been—lives in an Anglo-American century, and though her "village green" ("unmown") can only be English, idioms have altered. So also, since 1945, have dooms. "Her doom

---

* By then Oxford University Press had become, to its credit, his publisher.

(unknown)" is a phrase with special torque amid our various and specific knowledges of death.

Much of *A Peopled Landscape* was written after a first visit to the United States. It sees its English matter with new eyes, for reconstituting with new techniques. One thing the title says is that much American landscape—notably in the Southwest that drew Tomlinson—is distinctively unpeopled. So what does it mean in England, where people are abundant, to locate them in their landscape? It means, for instance, the strange harmonious assault of "Walking to Bells," where immemorial English churchyard sounds (Tennyson's "mellow lin-lan-lone") are distanced by the subtle conceit of a breaking wave:

> The spray of sound
> (Its echo rides
> As bodied as metal
> Whose echoes'
> Echo it is)
> Stunned, released
> Where the house-walls
> Stand or cease
> Blows, or does not
> Into the unfilled space
> Accordingly; which
> Space whose Adam wits
> Slept on till now,
> Kindles from cold
> To hold the entire
> Undoubling wave
> Distinct in its jewelled collapse,
> And the undertone
> Sterner and broader than such facile beads
> Gainsays
> Not one from the toppling hoard its tensed back heaves.

Here people are walking, here are house-walls, and here at no great distance is always the sea. (No place in England is more than a hundred miles from salt water.) Poe's "Tintinnabulation of the bells bells bells" was placeless, contextless: an early American showing-off. In Tomlinson's poem a single long sentence with interruptions remembers Milton; "accordingly" remembers the chord in its own etymology; since sound does come in "waves," "undertone" can decorously recall "undertow"; and the short ("American") lines attain rest in a crowded iambic pentameter that resolves all the cumulation of sound in re- membering four centuries of British mastery.

Not that it's done without cost. Save for the hint "Adam" conveys, one dominant past voice is absent from this harmony. Though surely church-bells, the bells in this poem are purely acoustic, and if they sound any summons to worship (surely, for someone?) the poem ig- nores it. A "style," a way of writing, is defined and bounded by what it is forced to omit, and to linger on what this remarkable poet achieved was to grow aware too of what is perforce absent. Amid his strong pieties of place, the religious was absent, and that of course is a mark of the first century since Anglo-Saxon times in which it's been possible to grow up in England, and reconstitute a heritage, and simply ignore what for so long mattered most. Also absent was the whole order of experience Larkin registers, shopgirls, advertisements, junked cars, litter, factories. But major poets (think of Yeats) do not get stuck, and by 1974 (*The Way In*) Tomlinson had the Larkin material under control—

> . . . Flat-dwellers came and went, in the divided houses,
> Mothers unwedded who couldn't pay their rent.
> A race of gardeners died, and a generation
> Hacked down the walls to park their cars
> Where the flowers once were. It was there it showed,
> The feeble-minded style of a neighbourhood
> Gone gaudily mad in panted corrugations,
> Botches of sad carpentry. The street front has scarcely changed.
> No one has recorded the place.
> Perhaps we shall become sociology. We have escaped
> Gladstone's century. We might have been novels.

That records a revisit to Stoke-on-Trent, his boyhood ambience and (approximately) Arnold Bennett's. It's no longer correct to say, what was true of the earlier poems, that scrupulousness borders on anxiety: that each poem celebrates some precarious equilibration. "Beethoven Attends the C Minor Seminar" is unprecarious. (It's about "Ludmilla Quatsch, the queen of the sleevenote," being silenced by Beethoven's ghost.) "The Littleton Whale" is unprecarious too. So is everything since the mid-'70's. And for the note of transcendence, try the Eden/ Arden poems. *The Way In* was a breaking out, unpublicized. He is

England's chief living poet. Publishers decline, unread, books about his achievement; he's "minor." Write about Larkin; write about Ted Hughes!

Across from his Gloucestershire cottage, the last time I visited, a white horse trotted, identified as Lady Betjeman's. Sir John Betjeman, connoisseur of Victoriana and of Henry James's morning clothes (which he owned), was by that time Poet Laureate. His lady's bland horse was an emblem of bathos. Engulfed by public bathos, you contrive risks.

> . . . In the dark
> Height, geese yelp like a pack
> Hunting through space.

Nature contrives them too. And London is far.

Yes, London is no longer the center of poetry. It's still the center of opinion, and the difference does create strains. The Hack's Progress, or, How to Make It in London with Poetry, is a ready scenario for pointed gossip. By one version, you spend your first two years at Oxford getting known and published in the Oxford little mags. (Getting what published? Well, you know, some *poems*: little sensitive ways to say Lo, Lo or Shrug, Shrug.) In your third year you get your own little mag together, with as many names as you can bag, and launch it with a publisher's cocktail party in London. No second issue ever need appear. You are now ensconced on the carousel where the action is: round and round and round, you-review-me-I-review-you, and together we'll all see just who gets reviewed. This account, an ideal composite, is not alleged to fit anyone in particular; an especially hilarious variant is the story of X, who, alas, did it all and it didn't work. He ended up lecturing in the Farthest East, one version of the doom Waugh invented for Tony Last.

But Editing, Anthologizing, Reviewing, being a Poetry Book Society selector: whatever the entrée, those are cardinal activities; when you've made your way into all of them you're *made*. The machinery, for those both knowledgeable and lucky, runs more reliably than at any time in the past; the maneuverings of the old bookmen or of Middleton Murry now look positively rustic. Costs being high (book-printing is farmed out to Singapore or East Germany), few publishers maintain poetry lists at all, and what gets selected for review, or for publication in the weekly journals, is consequently of much significance. Tie together publishing and reviewing and you have a lot of the action sewn up. Life goes on elsewhere—in Gloucestershire or Northumberland—but it doesn't get much notice in the metropolis.

The weekly journals on their personality-hunts have found interesting copy in literary editors. Two examples:

(1) Craig RAINE (b. 1944, educ. Exeter Coll. Oxford, college lecturer eight years) has been since 1981 Poetry Editor at Faber & Faber. That, as everyone hastens to point out, is T. S. Eliot's old post, and to hear Craig Raine tell it, his is an onerous role. ("Who does he think he is? T. S. Eliot?"—thus cry the rejected unto unjust heaven.) At Faber they sell, so Mr. Raine has divulged, "almost £2 millions of poetry books every year," thanks chiefly to that splendid backlist (Eliot, Auden, Lowell, Stevens, Ted Hughes, Larkin, Heaney . . .), and it's up to Raine to "add to this National Trust." As of 1985 he had found just seven new poets, counting himself. Of these, Mr. Oliver Reynolds made him most proud. "A discovery like Oliver Reynolds is what makes my job worthwhile." By that he means his job at Faber & Faber. But his proper job, he thinks, is writing poetry: hence "a constant, nagging desire to resign." Presiding over this nest of sinking bards is not, he will have us know, any kind of sinecure.

(2) Andrew MOTION (b. 1952, educ. University Coll. Oxford, College lecturer four years) edited *Poetry Review* before becoming Poetry Editor at Chatto & Windus, where C. Day Lewis preceded him. "With his consumptive frame and shock of blond hair his looks are unquestionably sensitive," wrote an unsycophantic reporter. "He talks sensitively in a voice of deep, and exquisite politeness. He writes extremely sensitive poems all about love and loss and sad childhoods." It seemed odd to the reporter that a man this sensitive had "done remarkably well in the rough and tumble of modern publishing." Indeed, a new book of his had somehow "already won the John Llewellyn Rhys Prize for 1984 even though it's not officially out till next week." And when arch-rival Faber tried to fly poets around the country in search of audiences, only to have the scheme collapse because Seamus Heaney refused to get into the helicopter, tactician Motion deftly sent some Chatto poets, including himself, around the country by train. Score one.

The reporter made bold to challenge Mr. Motion "on his involve-ment with the so-called Martian Mafia,* that group of poets, novelists, publishers and editors which includes most of his Oxford friends and without whose permission nothing seems to move in British literature at the moment. See *Private Eye* for details." And what was wrong, asked Mr. Motion, "with mixing with like-minded friends and dis-cussing topics of mutual interest? Isn't that what we all do?"

He also divulged that good poems (by other people; he didn't speak for himself) were "the result of some sort of negotiation between that side of the mind which is all intelligent, well read and clever, and the side which is like a primeval swamp." For the force of that, you need to bear in mind the pejorative British connotation of "clever." Let the poet cherish his swamp.

Or *her* swamp. Here's a prepublication interview with a Motion discovery, Ms. Fiona Pitt-Kethley. If we're to believe the heading, she "Plays the Slut and Bawd." "I've got a cynical, jaded mind," she tells the interviewer. "Loads of messed-up relationships, being poor, going to a snobbish school; these are all things that make you cynical." Yup. "I've applied for six Gregory Awards and been turned down six times. . . . Over the 25 years the awards have been made, only 18 have gone to women out of a total of 134." You see what she keeps score on, and here's the whinge of her muse:

> . . . The world still sees me as a nasty kid
> usurping maleness. A foul brat to be
> smacked down by figures of authority.
> All things most natural in men, in me
> are vice—having no urge to cook or clean,
> lacking maternal instincts. . . .

The deputy literary editor of the paper into which all that got dumped was co-editor, with Andrew Motion, of a major anthology. On another page of the same issue we find four excerpts from a forthcoming book about the late manager of The Who, a rock group remembered for its brio in smashing up guitars. The book's author? Andrew Motion. A good book, perhaps? Still, observe the interlocking; sigh, perhaps, for a British Flaubert.

* * *

* "Martian" is from a book title of Craig Raine's: *A Martian Sends a Postcard Home*.

On 19 April 1985 *The Times* published its obituary of Basil Bunting (b. 1900), mentioning but not stressing his stint after the war as Persian Correspondent for *The Times*. During the war, in Intelligence, he'd been Wing-Commander Bunting, with a chit entitling him to wear any uniform of any service. It was all so secret, apparently, that it limited his pension rights. His stories were fabulous, especially with children present: gunfire ripping the canvas from a descending plane, its passengers clutching at spars to hold it together—*bizarrerie* of that order. Later Mosaddeq kicked him out of Persia: a country on which, we'll remember, his expertise had begun out of a need to understand a book in Persian though Matthew Arnold never finished reading the translation. In Teheran (1951) he once stood outside his own door, unrecognized, in the midst of a hired mob, shouting "DEATH TO MR. BUNTING" with the best of them.

> Man's life so little worth,
> do we fear to take or lose it?
> No ill companion on a journey, Death
> lays his purse on the table and opens the wine . . .

—from *The Spoils* (1951): what he chose to put on record about the war. ("Remember, imbeciles and wits.") "One of Ezra's more savage disciples," as Yeats remembered him, he held that "the sense is mainly in the sound," meaning not whiffle boom plonk but a difference such as between

> Man's life so little worth

and

> Life being cheap

—which no more have the same meaning than have "Out, out, brief candle" and "Snuff the light."

If you weren't prepared to understand what he meant by the primacy of sound, then you likely didn't value poetry much at all, unless as a species of elegance. One time Bunting was careful with his emphasis: "I have never said that music is the only thing in poetry. I have said it is the only *indispensable* thing." Once sound was in place, it could carry little meaning or much. The Yeats of

> "I am of Ireland
> And the holy land of Ireland
> And time runs on," cried she . . .

was "saying" next to nothing; one end of a scale from the other end of which the *Divina Commedia* beckons. A 1914 phrase of Robert Frost's is helpful: "the sound of sense." He meant what comes over of a conversation heard "from behind a door that cuts off the words." Frost had the priorities right when he added, "A sentence is a sound in itself on which other sounds, called words, may be strung." Memory for verse may be chiefly a kinetic memory, obscure muscles re-enacting surges of utterance. Poetry has often outlasted understanding; Hesiod's contemporaries recited verses of Homer's from which the meaning of numerous words had vanished, and one remembers undergraduate Tom Eliot on the train from Cambridge to St. Louis, repeating over and over verses of Dante he couldn't then construe.

> A strong song tows
> us, long earsick.
> Blind, we follow
> rain slant, spray flick
> to fields we do not know. . . .

"Tow" . . . "follow" . . . "know": that's the governing contour, with "sick" and "flick" interposing. The rhyming "strong song" anticipates further spondees. "Blind" affirms ear taking primacy from eye. Are we perhaps Homer's crewmen, drawn by Sirens? That's a likely afterthought, sense ensuing on sound; yet no, this rain feels more northern than Mediterranean. Then "fields"—its sound a newcomer, also its image. After rain-blinded toil, fields?—a landfall as unforeseen in the reading as in the voyaging. The music firm, the semantics kept open by spareness: such is the texture of late Bunting.

Late Bunting went unpestered as well as unaided by any Raine or Motion of the 1960's. The *Times* obituary chided "his taste for out-of-the-way American publishers," hinting that he'd gone out of his way to make his writings "difficult to lay hold of in England."* But a little press in England, Fulcrum (a man named Stuart Montgomery), published *Briggflatts* in 1966. Twenty years later *The Times* would

---

* "By now I've had a long life. I've seen very many odd situations and I have never at any time seen people as wholly without experience of life as journalists."—Bunting, 1968.

be citing a pundit: "This autobiographical testament, hailed by Cyril Connolly as 'the finest long poem to have been published in English since *Four Quartets*', elegiacally celebrates the poet's own life in lines stripped to a lyric intensity that achieves maximum effectiveness where a certain Northumbrian roughness or looseness of speech-texture is allowed to poke through as the writer expresses and rejects what he has learned about his nature over the years." You can make what you want of that, even diagram its syntax, in time you'd be better spending on *Briggflatts*.

> Brag, sweet tenor bull,
> descant on Rawthey's madrigal,
> each pebble its part
> for the fells' late spring.
> Dance tiptoe, bull,
> black against may.
> Ridiculous and lovely
> chase hurdling shadows
> morning into noon.
> May on the bull's hide
> and through the dale
> furrows fill with may,
> paving the slowworm's way. . . .

"Brag, sweet tenor bull": the strongest opening line since "And then went down to the ship." "May" is the white blossom on the hawthorn, of course, not the month; "Rawthey" a stream,* the "madrigal" its purl and chirple. And the "slowworm"? "A small harmless scincoid lizard, *Anguis fragilis*, native to most parts of Europe; the blindworm" (*OED*). Bunting does assume our knowledge of names, not, if you think about it, an arrogant assumption.

His more important assumption is that we'll share his trust in the world's variousness. The bull is not "tenor" because fancy wants a musical bull. Bunting as a boy heard that bull on a farm near Throckley, bellowing "in the most melodious tenor, a beautiful tenor voice. In spring, the bull does in fact, if he's with the cows, dance, on the tip of his toes, part of the business of showing off, showing that he's

---

* Though *An Introduction to Fifty Modern British Poets* (Pan Literature Guides, 1979), prepares us to "meet the lively bull, Rawthey." Its author's excuse will have to be his education: Harvard with an Oxford chaser.

protecting them. . . . It is delightful, and it bears such a strong resemblance to the behavior of young men in general and . . . well all
creatures." Word after word, the stanza simply *records*. Nothing's in
it so as to signify something else.

Briggflatts is a long poem about lost ("murdered") love, about "now"
caught up in "then" (my now and then, the nows and thens of history),
about the viability of bardic idiom, about music. So to speak; the
trouble with that sentence is a trouble with "about," unavoidable but
unavoidably periphrastic. Take a "bardic" passage that includes the
death of Eric Bloodaxe at Stainmore:

> Loaded with mail of linked lies,
> what weapon can the king lift to fight
> when chance-met enemies employ sly
> sword and shoulder-piercing pike,
> pressed into the mire,
> trampled and hewn till a knife
> —in whose hand?—severs tight
> neck cords? Axe rusts. Spine
> picked bare by ravens, agile
> maggots devour the slack side
> and inert brain, never wise. . . .

That's sweaty with the chaos of combat and murder, near-primitively
alliterative, dense with small words enjambed, yet paying so detached
an attention to pattern that it ends every line with an open "i." (I've
cut it short; there are thirteen more such lines.) The more you settle
into it, and the rest of the poem it collects and refracts, the less tempted
you are by such a word as "about." Elsewhere a gray rat can "thread,
lithe and alert, Schoenberg's maze." Yet just before the poem's voice
brings itself to say

> Where rats go go I,
> accustomed to penury,
> filth, disgust and fury . . .

it has found itself at ease in saying this:

> As the player's breath warms the fipple the tone clears.
> It is time to consider how Domenico Scarlatti
> condensed so much music into so few bars

with never a crabbed turn or congested cadence,
never a boast or a see-here; and stars and lakes
echo him and the copse drums out his measure,
snow peaks are lifted up in moonlight and twilight
and the sun rises on an acknowledged land.

It's all far from London, and it ends on the open sea:

Great strings next the post of the harp
clang, the horn has majesty,
flutes flicker in the draft and flare.
Orion strides over Farne.
Seals shuffle and bark,
terns shift on their ledges,
watching Capella steer for the zenith,
and Procyon starts his climb.

Furthest, fairest things, stars, free of our humbug,
each his own, the longer known the more alone,
wrapt in emphatic fire roaring out to a black flue.
Each spark trills on a tone beyond chronological compass,
yet in a sextant's bubble present and firm
places a surveyor's stone or steadies a tiller.
Then is Now. The star you steer by is gone,
its tremulous thread spun in the hurricane
spider floss on my cheek; light from the zenith
spun when the slowworm lay in her lap
fifty years ago. . . .

. . . Finger tips touched and were still
fifty years ago.

Sirius is too young to remember.

Sirius glows in the wind. Sparks on ripples
mark his line, lures for spent fish.

Fifty years a letter unanswered;
a visit postponed for fifty years.

She has been with me fifty years.

Starlight quivers. I had day enough.
For love uninterrupted night.

Nox est perpetua una dormienda: a poem so English, so shot through
with Northumbrian dialect, can yet close in marrying itself with un-

cited Latin. And the dialect matters: matters, most of all, for the sounds of many words, which (Bunting said) "Southrons would maul." His own recording is available. He used to say that Wordsworth composed his poems "by shouting them aloud," and shouting, he stipulated, northern sounds close to his own; his evidence was Wordsworthian rhymes that don't work in BBC English. Though Wordsworth left no recordings, Basil Bunting once read his "Michael" and "The Brothers" for the BBC.

This triumphant poem—vital as bull and slowworm—thrives on its disregard of Wells and Bennett and Bloomsbury, of the news and the isms and *The Yellow Book* and *The Times*, of everything save unsleeping northern speech and what draws on the poet's tactile authority: rubbing stones, sailing boats. "I've rubbed down gravestones and that's how I know how it feels to rub down a gravestone. And how your fingers ache on the damn job." That's an honest, and desperate, rejection of much communality gone facile; Shakespeare could feel safe in being without the experience of watching sheep, of killing, of wearing a crown. "A reply to Greek and Latin with the bare hands," wrote William Carlos Williams in a like plight. He and Bunting even ignored much that readers had come to expect, and to taste their pleasures we must relearn our reading skills. During the long and prolific career of Williams, he and thousands of readers did come to terms: an advantage denied Bunting, whose output was part-time and sparse, his major work very late. Such was the cost of *Briggflatts*, for the poet and for us. How much must authenticity jettison now, in a Rank Xerox world of trendy trivial motion!

Prodded into taking the *Collected Poems* over from Fulcrum, Oxford next let them go out of print, literature being what Philip Beaufoy knew it was, a commodity. London, in centralizing, had long since standardized: idiom and sound and decorum, also what one might permissibly expect.

> Aneurin and Taliesin, cruel owls
> for whom it is never altogether dark, crying
> before the rules made poetry a pedant's game. . . .
> . . . Follow the clue patiently and you will understand nothing.

A "clue"—a thread—led Theseus away from the tenor bull he'd slain.

Most rooted and regional of poems, *Briggflatts*—it draws on Northumbria with more concentration even than Carlos Williams brought to Jersey—was work done on the margins of the system by a man who'd spent most of his life away from his region, as far away as Italy, the Canaries, Persia, getting a living one way or another. A helter-skelter, hole-in-corner life, and what *was* he? But *The Times*, in a posture of respect, did manage to close its obituary on a note of climax:

Bunting was an Hon DLitt of the University of Newcastle of which he was also made an Hon Life Visiting Professor. He was President of the Poetry Society, 1972–76, and of Northern Arts, 1973–76.
He was twice married.

Ah. "Mr. Chaucer was deputy forester in the King's Forest at Petherton." "In 1813 Mr. Wordsworth was appointed Stamp Distributor for Westmoreland." No, the jest is too easy. Yet, with poetry editors paid to keep house lists refreshed by developing new talent—remorselessly, every season, another new talent—it's striking how it's not to their system that you look for anything vital; striking too how there's no authority, no Arnold, to say where the main currents run, who the real writers are. (There are people who can accurately tell you, but they haven't "authority.") Honors fall at whim; Empson, late in life, became Sir William; Cecil Day-Lewis, ex-red, became Poet Laureate. Later Larkin was backed for that office, but wasn't named. The *TLS* does its best, it really does. And any month now, we may look for another book about Virginia Woolf. Underneath, a deep doubt runs: has anything made any sense, Everyman will ask, since the time of Conrad and Wells and the rattling good stories?

NOTES

A FIRST SCAN

Page 5 Auberon Waugh: "Putting the Literary Clock Back," *Times Literary Supplement*, 21 Feb. 1986, 184.

 7 "effects that might be found ironical": F. R. Leavis, *New Bearings in English Poetry*, 1932, 3.

I : THE BEST OF TIMES

Page 9 Sarawak, etc.: sampled from the huge list in *Encyclopedia Britannica*, ed. 14, s.v. "British Empire."

 10 For Victorian titles cited, see Richard Altick, *The English Common Reader*, 1957, chh. 13, 15.

 11 For the tax debate: Altick, 348–54. *Times* a penny: R. C. K. Ensor, *England, 1870–1914*, 1936, 534, dates this event March 1914.

 12 "recoup initial investments . . .": Elizabeth L. Eisenstein, *The Printing Revolution in Early Modern Europe*, 1983, 28.

Ensor, 160.

Sales of *East Lynne*, etc.: Altick, 385.

 13 Marie Corelli's sales: Q. D. Leavis, *Fiction and the Reading Public*, 1939, 167. See also *Dictionary of National Biography*, 1922–30, s.v. "Mackay, Mary"; this interesting article is by Michael Sadleir.

Can-can paragraph abridged from Marie Corelli, *Wormwood*, N.Y., 1890, 244. Englishman on the steamer: ibid., Introductory Note, 7.

Corelli on the French: *Wormwood*, 5.

 14 Corelli "the prose Shakespeare": Q. D. Leavis, 289. Wilde on Corelli: J. Sutherland, ed., *Oxford Book of Literary Anecdotes*, 1975, 302. Corelli's friend: *DNB*, loc. cit. Corelli with James: Stanley Weintraub, *Aubrey Beardsley: Imp of the Perverse*, 1976, 117.

Protest from *The Quarterly*: see Q. D. Leavis, 160.

Gladstone on cheap paper: quoted by Reginald Pound, *The Strand Magazine*, 1966, 12.

 15 Altick, 364.

Bennett on London aspirants: *The Truth About an Author*, 1911, 38. "How to train

a Cook," etc.: from a magazine called *Woman*, as gleaned by Margaret Drabble in
Arnold Bennett, 1974, 56. Eight hundred copies: Frank Swinnerton, *Background
with Chorus*, 1956, 110.

16   Richard Garnett's judgment: rendered in the hearing of Ford Madox Hueffer, then
22. Ford's accounts (*Memories and Impressions*, 1911, 169, and *Return to Yesterday*,
1932, 52) differ in detail but not at all in import.
Virginia Stephen at Animatographe: Quentin Bell, *Virginia Woolf*, repr. 1976, 48.
She also saw a demonstration of "Roentgen's rays."
Keynes's bicycle: Robert Skidelsky, *John Maynard Keynes*, 1986, 52.

2 : THREE PUBLICS

Page 18   Copies of *The Master Christian*: Richard Altick, *The English Common Reader*, 1957,
313. Rationale of *Tit-Bits*: R. C. K. Ensor, *England 1870–1914*, 1936, 145.
The historic Manchester paragraph is reproduced in Reginald Pound, *The Strand
Magazine*, 1966, facing p. 24.
"a quick-witted child": quoted by Ensor, 312, from Hamilton Fyfe, *Northcliffe: An
Intimate Biography*, 1930. *Tit-Bits* items not otherwise identified are from the 3 April
1897 number.

19   Captain Ames and "Washington": *Tit-Bits*, 24 April 1897, 73. ". . . WHITE
CATS . . .": ibid., 5 June 1897, 182.

20   For Conrad and *Tit-Bits*: Jocelyn Baines, *Joseph Conrad: A Critical Biography*, 1960,
84; in May 1886 *Tit-Bits* had offered 20 guineas "for the best article entitled 'My
Experiences as a Sailor.' " For Joyce: Stanislaus Joyce, *My Brother's Keeper*, 1958,
91–92; he'd have tried his hand a decade or so after Conrad, aged 14 or 15. My
own guess, for reasons that will appear, is mid-1897. Miss Stephen: Quentin Bell,
Virginia Woolf, vol. 1, 1972, ch. ii. Bennett: Margaret Drabble, *Arnold Bennett*,
1974, 54–55. Beardsley: Stanley Weintraub, *Aubrey Beardsley: Imp of the Perverse*,
1976, 16–17.
A Dublin jakes: see James Joyce, *Ulysses*, end of the "Calypso" episode.

28   *Secret Agent* reviews: Norman Sherry, ed., *Conrad: The Critical Heritage*, 1973, 188,
202. Though such reviews weren't typical—the *TLS*, which had condescended to
Nostromo, called *The Secret Agent* "marvellously managed" (Sherry, 185)—
Jocelyn Baines (Baines, 346) says the book's sales were "mediocre." (And so were
Nostromo's.)
"Baffled, baffled . . .": from "Tragedy of Error," in *Tales of Henry James*, ed. Leon
Edel, vol. i, 1962, 44.

29   Frenzy of meetings: Ernest Rhys, *Everyman Remembers*, 1931, 233. Pound and
Everyman: see Rhys's Introduction to No. 381, *Everyman and Other Interludes*, xx,
dated 1909. In what Pound's help consisted is unknown.

30–1 Dent on Johnson: J. M. Dent, *My Memoirs*, 1921, 20. On spelling: ibid., 9. Dent
weeping, cold water, preventing wars: Rhys, 234, 240. Dent screaming, Rhys's pay:
Frank Swinnerton, *Background with Chorus*, 1956, 31, 32.

31–2 Dent on copyrights and on his readership: *Memoirs*, 97–98.

35   Leslie Stephen: Bell, vol. 1, ch. iii.

36   The *Yellow Book* prospectus: Weintraub, 102.
Denunciations: for these and many more, see Katherine Lyon Mix, *A Study in Yellow*,
1960, 87–93.
James on Harland and on *The Yellow Book*: Mix, 60, 91. The letter to Mr. and Mrs.

William James (28 May 1894, from the Grand Hotel, Rome) is in *Henry James Letters*, ed. Leon Edel, vol. III, 1980, 478–83.

37 Kate Greenaway on Beardsley: Mix, 274.
Dent's Chaucer and the *bons mots*: Weintraub, 31–35, 45, 47; Dent, *Memoirs*, 45–47.

38 Max Beerbohm on the drawing: Weintraub, 107. He was writing to his pal Reggie Turner.

41 Garnett's prediction: Ford Madox Ford, *Return to Yesterday*, 1932, 52; whether Ford reported the words or invented them, their point remains.
C. H. Sisson remarks: in his *English Poetry 1900–1950*, repr. 1981, 17.

41–2 Arthur Waugh in *The Yellow Book*: his essay on "Reticence in Art" was in the first volume. Waugh on Eliot et al.: see Forrest Read, ed., *Pound/Joyce*, 1967, 87. Waugh was proud enough of the review to reprint it in his 1919 *Tradition and Change*, which he dedicated to Evelyn Arthur St. John Waugh, then 16.

3 : A NARRATIVE INHERITANCE

Page 43–4 Conventions of naming: For a book-length treatment, see K. C. Phillipps, *Language & Class in Victorian England*, 1984, where I found most of these examples. Phillipps stresses that usage was in constant flux throughout the nineteenth century and still is. The distinction between U and non-U is a semi-comic simplification, first proposed in 1954.

44 Shaw's Cockney: from *Major Barbara*, quoted in Raymond Chapman, *The Treatment of Sounds in Language and Literature*, 1984, 69. And as Chapman notes, even Shaw could not arrange twenty-six letters into anything like a full phonetic rendition.
"Class": Charles Tomlinson, *Collected Poems*, 1985, 248.
"How many thousands a year . . .": Margaret Drabble, *Arnold Bennett*, 1974, 198.

45 Wells composing *The Time Machine*: There were seven versions at least, and what he did in 1894 was prepare the fifth for serial publication. The familiar book text (May 1895) is the sixth. Wells never took that much trouble with a book again. See Bernard Bergonzi, "The Publication of *The Time Machine*, 1894–5," *Review of English Studies*, vol. xi, no. 41, 1960, 42–51.

46 Wells and Swift: Peter Kemp, *H. G. Wells and the Culminating Ape*, 1983, 201.

49 Verne on Wells: Frank D. O'Connell, ed., *"The Time Machine" and "The War of the Worlds,"* 1977, 303.
Standard of eating among the poor: Lovat Dickson, *H. G. Wells: His Turbulent Life and Times*, 1969, 24.

49–50 Wells underground: Kemp, 119, and see the whole of his ch. 3. Latin, height, accent, mustache: Dickson, 24, 35, 34, 45. Science lighting a match: "The Rediscovery of the Unique," *Fortnightly Review*, July 1891, quoted by Dickson, 48, and reprinted in full in O'Connell.

50 Resemblance of "Heart of Darkness" to *The Time Machine*: This page was in typescript when Professor Patrick A. McCarthy sent me a draft of his article for the *Journal of Modern Literature*, vol. xiii, no. 1, 37–60. I am glad of his confirmation.

52 ". . . densely distressed": "The Secret Sharer," pt. 2, para. 9.

52–3 Wells letter: to a Dr. Collins, quoted by Dickson, 39.

55 "It is not thus that men speak": Norman Sherry, ed., *Conrad: The Critical Heritage*, 1973, 117. Sherry guesses that the anonymous reviewer (*Academy*, 10 November 1900) "could well be Edward Garnett."

56 "impossible in style . . .": Sherry, 118. Montague on carelessness: ibid., 273.

56   Max Beerbohm's parody: from "The Feast," in *A Christmas Garland*, 1912. The feast, needless to say, is what natives make of the protagonist.
"The ever-ready suspicion of evil . . .": Conrad, "The Lagoon." I owe the collocation of Max and "The Lagoon" to Marvin Mudrick, *Conrad: A Collection of Critical Essays*, 1966, 5–6. And let me here light a candle for my late old friend, our time's Johnsonian critic.

57   "Gazing down into the black shaft . . .": Though I've used this example before (in *Gnomon*, 1958) I repeat it out of inability to find another as brief. Mudrick (38 ff.) surveys more extended instances, from "Heart of Darkness," of "details intensely present, evocatively characteristic of the situations in which they happen, and prefiguring from moment to moment an unevadable moral reality."
Mudrick on *Heart of Darkness*: Mudrick, 44. Masefield on ditto: Sherry, 141–42.

58   Robert Lynd on *Chance*: Sherry, 271–73. Conrad's rejoinder is in his preface to the 1920 reprint. Montague on *Chance*: Sherry, 273–76.
James on Conrad: Sherry, 263–70. The entire essay is reprinted in Leon Edel and Gordon Ray, eds., *Henry James and H. G. Wells*, 1958, 178–215, and in James's *Notes on Novelists*, 1931, 271–80.

59   Reviews of *Chance*: Sherry, 284, 281–82.

4 : THE TONE OF THINGS

Page 65   The Boy whose name was Jim is of course in Hilaire Belloc's *Cautionary Tales* (1907). At the Zoo he ran away from his Nurse and was eaten by a Lion, and "When Nurse informed his Parents, they / Were more concerned than I can say."

67   ". . . Venetian lamp . . . ," ". . . velvet brocade": Henry James, *The Spoils of Poynton*, New York Edition, 1908, ch. vii, 70, 71.
". . . relics of Waterbath . . ." and "old brandy-flasks . . .": ibid., chh. ii, xiii, 19, 145.

68   Deficient "life" in someone else's book: e.g., in two letters of 1900 and 1902 to H. G. Wells, in Leon Edel & Gordon N. Ray, eds., *Henry James and H. G. Wells*, 1958, 67, 76.
A reviewer of 1895: He was H. G. Wells, as we'll see. The excerpt is from "The Altar of the Dead." See Patrick Parrinder & Robert Philmus, eds., *H. G. Wells's Literary Criticism*, 1980, 91.

69   Fear of self-parody: Leon Edel, *Henry James*, vol. v, 387.
"He conveyed in every phrase . . .": Chatman, *The Later Style of Henry James*, 1972, 110.
"phenomena": ibid., 47, 81.
Arthur Mizener: in his Introduction to S. Gorley Putt, *The Fiction of Henry James*, 1966. "What was dreadful . . .": *The Spoils of Poynton*, ch. 1. Ezra Pound: in Washington, 1952. See my *The Pound Era*, 1971, 10–12.
The twenty-eight-word sentence: Chatman, 91.

70   New York Edition royalty: Edel, vol. v, 434.
Wells on *Almayer's Folly*: Sherry, 1973, 53. On *An Outcast of the Islands*, ibid., 73–76; also in Parrinder & Philmus, 88–92.
". . . Christian virgin": Edel, vol. iv, 65. Edel also thumbnails the three critics, 65–72. Wells's fourth play: See Edel & Ray, 43. He'd seen just two before taking on the job, after which *Guy Domville* was the second he reviewed; the first was Wilde's *An Ideal Husband*.

71 Shaw and Bennett on *Guy Domville*: Edel, vol. iv, 86–87. Edel & Ray, 48–52, reprint the Wells review entire.

"I bothered him": Edel & Ray, 17. James on a bicycle: Edel, vol. v, 22. Northcliffe: Reginald Pound & Geoffrey Harmsworth, *Northcliffe*, 1959, 55 ff.; see esp. 56–57 for the cyclists' dangerous life.

James and Gosse: Edel & Ray, 52. Eight writing-tables: Edel, vol. v, 126. James on *The Time Machine*: Edel & Ray, 63.

72 The proposed collaboration: Edel & Ray, 80–82.

A scenario: the only interpretation the letters will bear. Wells next asked to see sample scenarios for James's own novels, but James was unable or reluctant to produce them.

73 *Anticipations* and *1984*: Lovat Dickson, *H. G. Wells*, 1969, 89. James on *Anticipations*: Edel & Ray, 76. Bloom's fantasies: *Ulysses*, Gabler ed., 1986, 15: 1685–94.

". . . huge flat foot of the public": James's 1895 notebook entry for "The Next Time" in Matthiessen & Murdock, ed., *The Notebooks of Henry James*, 1947, 180.

"The Younger Generation": Edel & Ray, 178–215; for the quoted sentence, see 190.

74 "The Distinguished Thing": Years later Edith Wharton reported these famous words as having been recalled by James to Howard Sturgis. Edel, vol. v, 542.

The never-forgotten sentences are in *Boon*, 1915, 106–8.

75 James on *Ann Veronica*: Edel & Ray, 122. Wells on discursiveness: ibid., 136. H.G.'s public response (11 April) followed H.J.'s private challenge (October 1909) by about eighteen months.

5 : AN EDUCATION

Page 76 "He Bids His Beloved Be at Peace" (from *The Wind Among the Reeds*, 1899) is Poem #53 in Richard J. Finneran, ed., *W. B. Yeats: The Poems*, 1983. Yeats at 18 Woburn Buildings: Joseph Hone, *W. B. Yeats*, 1942, end of ch. 5.

77 Makin on Yeats: see Peter Makin, *Pound's Cantos*, 1985, 5.

". . . bitter black wind . . .": "Red Hanrahan's Song About Ireland," 1904 (Finneran, #84). ". . . Come near . . .": "To the Rose Upon the Rood of Time," 1893 (Finneran, #17).

78 "Dream-heavy": Yeats, "The Song of the Happy Shepherd" (Finneran, #1).

79 *Evening Standard* review: quoted in Noel Stock, *The Life of Ezra Pound*, 1982, 55. For the split-up of Lane and Mathews, see Stanley Weintraub, *Aubrey Beardsley: Imp of the Perverse*, 1976, 104–5, 118. "Two peaks of Parnassus": Stock, 55.

79–80 Reviews of *Personae* and *Exultations* excerpted from Eric Homberger, ed., *Ezra Pound: The Critical Heritage*, 1972, 44, 56, 66. "white breast of the dim sea": from Yeats's "Who Goes with Fergus" (Finneran, #32); it dates from 1892, when it was a song in *The Countess Cathleen*.

80 "O sweet everlasting Voices": Yeats, "The Everlasting Voices" (Finneran, #41). For the "Laudantes" sequence, which Pound later chose not to preserve, see *Collected Early Poems of Ezra Pound*, ed. Michael John King, 1976, 117–20; Mary de Rachewiltz receives credit (ibid., xvi) for her brilliant explanation of the title. Yeats's story in *The Savoy* (November 1897) was "The Tables of the Law," greatly admired by James Joyce.

81 The route to Yeats: for details, see Stock, 59–60, 66. J. J. Wilhelm (*The American Roots of Ezra Pound*, 1985, 206) traces a slightly different chain. The date, April

1909, appears in Omar Pound & A. Walton Litz, eds., *Ezra Pound and Dorothy Shakespear: Their Letters, 1909–1914*, 1984, 360.

81   "an alien figure . . .": Pound & Litz, viii.

82   Yeats in 1909: for more on this, see my *A Colder Eye*, especially the chapter called "A Dwindling Gyre."
"out of a mouthful of air": Yeats, "He Thinks of Those Who Have Spoken Evil of His Beloved" (Finneran, #65). "Adam's Curse": Finneran, #83.

83   ". . . great dim figure . . .": D. D. Paige, ed., *The Letters of Ezra Pound*, No. 21. The date is 13 August 1913.
". . . deep in Ben Jonson": Allan Wade, ed., *The Letters of W. B. Yeats*, 1955, 478.

84   "Impetuous heart . . .": from a song in *The Countess Cathleen* (Finneran, #A37).
"What need you . . . ": "September 1913" (Finneran, #115).

85   Praise of Coole: "Upon a House Shaken by the Land Agitation" (Finneran, #105). "Men Improve with the Years" (Finneran, #146).

86   Fishmonger's shop, gilt plaque: Stock, 68. Suspended carcasses: Douglas Goldring, *South Lodge*, 1943, 16. Ford's fiscal ineptitude: Arthur Mizener, *The Saddest Story: A Biography of Ford Madox Ford*, 1971, ch. 14. Goldring, 30, records the half-crown price for the 192-page first issue.

87   Glance at an opening paragraph: Mizener, 168. The three generations: when he talked about Ford, which was often, Pound always stressed this "zoning" of generations.
"Altaforte": in *Personae of Ezra Pound* (the final collection of 1926, not the book of 1909), 28–29. "To break the pentameter . . .": *The Cantos of Ezra Pound*, 518. Written in the Reading Room: Stock, 68. ". . . could never be very important": ibid. Stock's source is Pound's "How I Began," *T.P.'s Weekly*, 6 June 1913.

87–8   "who introduced him . . .": Wilhelm, 205.

88   Yeats vs. Ford: Pound in conversation, 1948. "and for all that . . .": *Cantos*, 525. "I cannot read poetry . . .": Ford, *Collected Poems*, 1936, Appendix, 334, 336; the essay had been written in 1911 to preface his *Collected Poems* of that year.
"Under the lindens . . .": in Ford's 1936 *Collected Poems*, 163; previously published in his *Poems for Pictures* (1900) and *From Inland* (1907), two books unlikely to reach Philadelphia, Pa., or Crawfordsville, Ind. The Middle High German words are from George F. Jones, *Walther von der Vogelweide*, 1968, 46.

89   "Sith no thing . . .": from "Planh for the Young English King," in Pound's 1926 *Personae*, 36–37; first published in *Exultations*, 1909. The original is by Bertrans de Born.
"That roll . . .": see my *The Pound Era*, 1971, 80. ". . . Of Audiart . . .": from "Dompna Pois de me no us cal," in the 1926 *Personae*, 105, as first published in *Poetry and Drama*, London, March 1914.

90   "subnauseating sissiness . . ." and "What is the sense . . .": Ford, *The March of Literature*, 1938, 698. This huge book is a perpetual delight to dip into if you're careful not to trust its information. I shall always honor the memory of the librarian who shoved it toward me when I was 16.
Ford on "Lotos Eaters" and "To the Queen": *The March of Literature*, 699, 700.

91   "On Heaven": Ford's 1936 *Collected Poems*, 3–17. "it is absolutely the devil . . .": Pound in "The Prose Tradition in Verse," *Literary Essays*, 1954, 371–77.

93   "If you are *good*, Fordie . . .": Basil Bunting, *viva voce*, 1980. I can vouch for nothing about the story save that I heard it.

93–4   "Style" in England: Ford, *Return to Yesterday*, 1932, 215.

94   "She informed George Cannon . . .": Arnold Bennett, *Hilda Lessways*, 1911, I.xiii.3.
"The sky . . .": *Howards End*, Penguin ed., ch. xiv, 92.

"Dear girl . . .": ibid., ch. xxxviii, 227.

95 Malory and Caxton: examples from N. F. Blake, *Non-Standard Language in English Literature*, 1981, 52.

96 "foreword": For its date see *OED*; it was a fetish of F. J. Furnivall, co-founder of the Early English Text Society. For more on the crankery, see Austin Warren's contribution to *Gerard Manley Hopkins, by The Kenyon Critics*, 1945, 82–84. Trench's lecture is ch. 2 of his *English Past and Present*; yes, that's in Everyman's Library. "The Seafarer" (*Personae*, 64–66) was written in 1912.

97 Pound on Ford: from his 1939 obituary essay (*Nineteenth Century and After*, Aug. 1939, reprinted in Richard A. Cassell, ed., *Ford Madox Ford*, 1972, 33–36.

98 ". . . Once engrossing bridge of Lodi . . .": from *Poems of the Past and the Present*, 1901, and dated "1887." It's still worse when we obey Hardy's note and say "Loddy."

99 Storer on "pictures": "Poetry Narrative and Drama," an essay appended to *Mirrors of Illusion*; see p. 102.

". . . 'School of Images' . . .": *Personae*, 251. Hulme's tiny poem was salvaged by Alun R. Jones, in *The Life and Opinions of T. E. Hulme*, 1960, 180. "In a Station of the Metro" (*Personae*, 109) was first published in April 1913.

101 "Happiness, too . . .": from "Old Earth," in Samuel Beckett, *For to End Yet Again*, 1976, 53. "all dishevelled wandering stars": from "Who Goes with Fergus?" (Finneran, #32).

Pound on verbs: e.g., in the letter to Iris Barry that hails "Fenollosa's big essay on verbs, mostly on verbs" (*Letters*, 82).

102 Donne's apocalyptic sonnet: "At the round earth's imagin'd corners . . ."

102–3 "esthetic of the glimpse": in *The Pound Era*. Kouwenhoven points out: see his *Half a Truth Is Better than None*, 1982, 147–204; the quoted phrase is on p. 166. "Like a skein of loose silk . . .": Pound, *Personae*, 83.

103 *"La lune blanche"*: Verlaine, *La Bonne Chanson*, vi.

104 "if lineation . . .": Charles O. Hartman, *Free Verse*, 1980, 52.

Flint and Hulme: quoted by Stock, 64–65.

"Which shall I first bewail . . .": *Samson Agonistes*, lines 151–58.

"I will make the poems . . .": "Starting from Paumanok," 6.

105 "unmetrical sprawling lengths . . .": Rupert Brooke in *Cambridge Review*, 1909; see Eric Homberger, 58–59.

106 "And pass on the tradition . . .": *Cantos*, 506.

6 : THE LAWRENCE BUSINESS

Page 107 Ford on "The Odour of Chrysanthemums": from *Portraits from Life*, 1936; pp. 97–98 of the 1960 paperback reprint; also excerpted in Edward Nehls, ed., *D. H. Lawrence: A Composite Biography*, 1957, vol. I, 108–9.

108 Wells on public education: Nehls, 152; and see 558, n. 124. French and German: Harry T. Moore, *The Intelligent Heart: The Story of D. H. Lawrence*, Penguin, rev. ed. 1960, 58. ". . . scandalous tags of Latin . . .": related by Helen Corke in Nehls, 143.

Boys writing stories for sale: Moore, 115. Ranking thirteenth in English: ibid., 48.

109 "stallion," class poems, pictures: ibid., 101, 114–16.

110–11 Q. D. Leavis on best-selling vitality: *Fiction and the Reading Public*, 1939, 62, 64.

111 1,011 copies: Warren Roberts, *A Bibliography of D. H. Lawrence*, ed. 2, 1982, 21.

111   "almost wept before the magistrate . . .": Lawrence, in a 1924 essay excerpted in
Nehls, 328. Sir John chided Sir George: Moore, 258.
Lynd and Shorter on *The Rainbow*: Moore, 254. Leonard Woolf on Lynd: quoted
in *The Oxford Companion to English Literature*, ed. 5, 1985, s.v. "Lynd, Robert
Wilson." *DNB* on Lynd: *DNB, 1941–1950*, 543.

112   "The world, he seemed to say . . .": Arthur Waugh, *Tradition and Change: Studies
in Contemporary Literature*, 1919, 250. He is reviewing *Henry James* by Rebecca
West.
Some six thousand books: according to David Lodge, *Working with Structuralism*,
1981, 128.

112–13   *TLS* excerpts: gleaned from *The Egoist*, 1 June, 15 June, 1 July, 1914; May
1918. The *sottisiers* were probably compiled by Ezra Pound.

113   Gerald Gould and Yeats: Gould's son, the late Michael Ayrton, painter and wit,
told me the story. Gould's poem: D. B. Wyndham Lewis & Charles Lee, eds., *The
Stuffed Owl* (1930), 250. "Let us enjoy the fun . . .": Desmond McCarthy, bookman,
as quoted on the cover of the 1962 American reprint. Wyndham Lewis (whom do
not confuse with D. B. ditto) on laughter: *Monstre Gai* (1955), 1965 repr., 17.

114   Gerald Gould on *The Rainbow*: Moore, 254.
"They felt the rush of the sap . . .": *The Rainbow*, Penguin ed., 1949, 8.
Public hangman: Roberts, 20, where Methuen's act of contrition is also recorded
(21).

115   *The Egoist* and the printer: Jane Lidderdale & Mary Nicholson, *Dear Miss Weaver*,
1970, 147; for much illustrative material about struggles with printers, see chs.
5–9, *passim*. F. R. Leavis and *Ulysses*: Ronald Hayman, *Leavis*, 1976, 8.
"A loathsome study . . .": Moore, 348. "England of the peace . . .": ibid., 321.

116   "A large bony vine . . ." and "The pit-bank . . .": both from "The Odour of
Chrysanthemums," in *D. H. Lawrence: The Complete Short Stories*, Penguin ed.,
vol. 2, 283.
"The wages of work . . .": *The Complete Poems of D. H. Lawrence*, ed. V. de Sola
Pinto & Warren Roberts, 1967, 521.

117   "She turned away . . .": *Short Stories*, 296.
"Elizabeth sank down . . .": ibid., 300–301.

118   An historical novel: Roger Sale, *Modern Heroism*, 1973, 51. "red, crude
houses . . .": *The Rainbow*, 12. "pastoral": Sale, 53. "I came up to ask if you'd marry
me": *The Rainbow*, 45.

119   "What did he want . . .?": ibid., 448.
"She was caught up . . .": ibid., 456.
Sale on reading *The Rainbow*: Sale, 56–57.

120   "visionary authors . . .": ibid., 57.

121   "The poles of will . . .": *Studies in Classic American Literature*, 1923, Penguin ed.,
1977, 126.
"Smack the whimpering child . . .": "Education of the People," c. 1918, in *Phoenix*,
1936, 640. "ten hard, keen stinging strokes . . .": *Phoenix*, 621.
"to establish himself . . .": Moore, 312.

123   Whether "life" possessed any special quality: *The Rainbow*, 445. The speaker is a
lady physicist.
"You've no more use . . .": *Complete Poems*, 549.

7 : A POCKET APOCALYPSE

Page 124   Virginia Woolf on 1910: "Mr. Bennett and Mrs. Brown," in *Collected Essays*, vol. 1, 1967, 319–37. She wrote it in 1924.

125   "I can't tell you . . .": James T. Boulton & Andrew Robertson, eds., *The Letters of D. H. Lawrence*, vol. iii, 252. The letter is to Mary (Mrs. Gilbert) Cannan.

126   "his own wonderful sagacity": Virginia Woolf, *Roger Fry*, 1940, 130; and consult 128–45 for vignettes of Fry as the Met's European art-expert. "There they stood . . .": ibid., 152.

127   "pink" and "blue" periods: Richard Cork, *Vorticism and Abstract Art in the First Machine Age*, 1976, 20. Nearly a generation old: Cork, 17, quotes R. H. Wilenski: "examples of the art produced in Paris a quarter of a century before."
Woolf on Fry: Woolf, *Fry*, 159. Cork on Fry: Cork, 17.
Responses to the Post-Impressionist show: Woolf, *Fry*, 153–58.

128   Career of Tonks: *DNB, 1931–1940*, 866–67. Wyndham Lewis on Tonks: *Rude Assignment*, 1950, 119. "I shall resign . . .": Cork, 72.
Caricatures, Mussolini: Woolf, *Fry*, 156, 158.

130   "L'Art, 1910": *Personae*, 113.
Eliot on art and the event: "Tradition and the Individual Talent," 1919.

131   "Lo! sweetened with the summer light . . .": Tennyson, "The Lotos Eaters."
"The Coming of War: Actaeon": *Personae*, 107.

132   "Sombre and rich, the skies . . .": Lionel Johnson, "By the Statue of King Charles at Charing Cross."

133   Municipal goats: E. R. & J. Pennell, *The Life of James McNeill Whistler*, ed. 5, 1911, 222–23.

134   "all the magic of a slogan": Leon Edel, *Bloomsbury: A House of Lions*, 1979, 193. The phrases quoted from Bell are scattered through the first chapter of *Art*.

134–5   Bell on the Renaissance: *Art*, III.iii; on the connoisseur, ibid., I.i.

135   "A Minoan undulation . . .": Pound, *Personae*, 202.
"This alone . . .": *Art*, III.i.
"As late as 1958": Letter to H.K. from Robert Hughes, who adds, "I swear this is true."

136   "a fat, round body . . .": from Woolf's novel *The Wise Virgins*, where, Leon Edel assures us (Edel, 194), Clive Bell was intended.

136–7   "The man with the leaping mind": Ezra Pound, *viva voce*. "CHAOS OF ENOCH ARDENS": *Blast* #1, 19. "anything less essential than a noun or a verb . . .": W. K. Rose, ed., *The Letters of Wyndham Lewis*, 1963, 552–53. This letter of 1953 pertains to *Tarr*, but is still more applicable to *Blast*.

137   "But life is invisible . . .": Lewis, "Inferior Religions," in R. Rosenthal, ed., *Wyndham Lewis: A Soldier of Humor and Selected Writings*, 1966, 72–73.

138   "BLESS ALL PORTS": *Blast* #1, 23.
The Manifesto, with eleven signatures including Pound's and Lewis's, is in *Blast* #1, 30–43. Quoted phrases: 35, 39, 36.

8 : ARMAGEDDON

Page 141   "The rain drives on . . .": from Paul Nash, *Outlines*, 1949, quoted in Paul Thompson, *The Edwardians*, 1975, 277.

141–2   "Charm, smiling . . .": Pound, *Personae*, 191. "What passing-bells . . .": Owen, "Anthem for Doomed Youth." "The wheels lurched . . ." Rosenberg, "Dead Man's Dump." Sixty thousand casualties: Paul Fussell, *The Great War and Modern Memory*, 1975, 13. "the largest engagement . . .": Fussell, 12. Younger than 19: Fussell, 18.

142   "How calm those days were . . .": W. K. Rose, ed., *The Letters of Wyndham Lewis*, 1963, 291–93.

143   "Let us have no more nonsense . . .": Shaw, *What I Really Wrote About the War*, 1932, 25. "Enormous overdoses": ibid., 97.

Laurence on Shaw's courage: Bernard Shaw, *Collected Letters, 1911–1925*, ed. Dan H. Laurence, 1985, 239–40.

144   "In the right key . . .": ibid., 315.

Shaw on Ervine's leg: ibid., 551.

144–5   Shaw to Wells, to the journalist: ibid., 439, 562.

145   Shaw on Oedipus: ibid., 16.

"the brains of a ram . . .": ibid., 14.

146   Shaw as sewing-machine: Yeats, *Autobiography*, 1958, 188.

To Lawrence, Molly Tompkins, Dolmetsch, Hamon: *Letters 1911–1925*, 884, 792, 385, 120.

147   ". . . like Mr. Jellyby . . ." and "an amusing humbug": ibid., 357–58.

"Beethoven was modern . . .": ibid., 373.

"My deliberate rhetoric": ibid., 374.

149   North of the Thames: R. C. K. Ensor, *England, 1870–1914*, 1936, 509. He adds that provincial cities (Liverpool, Manchester) had been electrified while London still lingered in a former age. Quarter-million horses: Paul Thompson, *The Edwardians*, 1975, 44.

150   "Ting a ling ling": *Sweeney Agonistes*, of course; in Eliot's *Complete Poems and Plays*, 75.

151   Four hundred screens: Donald Spoto, *The Dark Side of Genius: The Life of Alfred Hitchcock*, 1984 paperback, 36. 266 cinemas: Margaret Drabble, *Arnold Bennett*, 1974, 268. Cinema held lowbrow: Spoto, 56. *East Lynne, Sorrows of Satan:* ibid., 57, 59. King and Queen see a film: ibid., 79.

152   ". . . in its thirteenth thousand . . .": John Lehmann, *The Strange Destiny of Rupert Brooke*, 1980, 70. "a record . . .": Christopher Hassall, *Edward Marsh: Patron of the Arts*, 1959, 533.

"harder to fall in love . . .": Hassall, 42. Brooke souvenirs: ibid., 13. Eliot on Georgians: *The Egoist*, vol. 5, March 1918, 43.

152–3   Marsh on Stravinsky: Hassall, 237. "When reciting . . .": ibid., 606. "it was difficult . . . ": ibid., 583.

153   Waugh on Georgian metrics: "The New Poetry," reprinted in his *Tradition and Change*, 1919, 17. Yes, the same essay that contained his "drunken helot" assault on non-Georgian Eliot.

"a violence . . .": Hassall, 684–86. ". . . a thick blaze of being . . .": ibid., 687.

154   Brooke on John: ibid., 148. Flecker on Brooke: ibid., 266. Waugh on Brooke: Waugh, 28–29.

155   Churchill's eulogy: Lehmann, 151. "He did his duty . . .": Lehmann, 154. James on Brooke: Hassall, 314.

bed at 10 Downing Street: Lehmann, 128. Dean of Saint Paul's: the celebrated ("gloomy") Dean Inge, on Easter 1915, in Lehmann, 144.

157   "inherent ugliness . . .": Waugh, 27.

"There were by then three centres . . .": Herbert Read, *The Cult of Sincerity*, 1969, 101–2.

158   *Wheels*: John Pearson, *The Sitwells*, 1978, 106. *Art and Letters*: ibid., 125–26. "their own alternative Bloomsbury": ibid., 127.

158–9   Cowley on Mansfield: Jeffrey Meyers, *Katherine Mansfield*, 1978, 227. Woolf on Mansfield: Antony Alpers, *The Life of Katherine Mansfield*, 1980, 259. McCullers and Mansfield: Meyers, 260.

159   "a soppy edition . . .": Meyers, 293. Orwell on Mansfield: ibid., 261. Lawrence to Murry: ibid., 258. Murry's dream: ibid., 257. "a little mole . . .": ibid., 76.

159–60   The Sitwells and *Lady Chatterley*: Pearson, 222–32. "gilded bolshevism": ibid., 126.

160   Waugh and Ford: In Jeffrey Heath, *The Picturesque Prison: Evelyn Waugh and His Writing*, 1982, 256, 318, the similarities are deftly outlined, though said to be "perhaps" unconscious.

9 : BLOOMSBURY

Page 161   "Duncan's androgynous affections . . . ": Leon Edel, *Bloomsbury: A House of Lions*, 1979, 213.
　　　　Keynes on Einstein: quoted by Edel, 49.

161–2   "ascetic and austere": quoted by Edel, 265. ". . . pleasures of human intercourse . . .": Moore, *Principia Ethica*, 1903, sect. 113. Clive, Virginia, Duncan: Quentin Bell, *Virginia Woolf, 1882–1912*, 1976 paperback, 139.

162   Keynes on Bentham and Marx: Robert Skidelsky, *John Maynard Keynes*, vol. I, 1986, 143.
　　　　Beatrice Webb on Moore: quoted by Colin Welch in *The American Spectator*, December 1986, 43.
　　　　Skidelsky on Moore: in his superb *John Maynard Keynes*, vol. I, ch. 5. Keynes on ugly working men: ibid., 195.

163   Robert Skidelsky on Cambridge: "The Science of Treason," *Sunday Times* (London), 22 June 1986, 51, reviewing Andrew Sinclair's *The Red and the Blue: Intelligence, Treason and the Universities*.

164   "satirist rather than poet": W. B. Yeats, ed., *The Oxford Book of Modern Verse*, 1936, xxii.
　　　　"the full tide of human existence": Boswell's *Life*, Oxford Standard Authors ed., 1953, 608.

165   ". . . Beside this thoroughfare . . .": Pound, *Personae*, 196.
　　　　Keynes's speculations and Grant: Edel, 146.
　　　　Soap opera: see Jill Johnston in *New York Times Book Review*, 24 Aug. 1986, 12–13, on the American appetite for Bloomsbury phenomena.
　　　　"marvellous Boy . . .": Wordsworth, "Resolution and Independence."

166   "Am I in love . . .": *The Diary of Virginia Woolf*, vol. III, 1980, 87.

167   Virginia's traumas: Edel, 85–86, and Bell, 42–43. "invulnerably dense": Bell, 96. Jean O. Love: in *Virginia Woolf: Sources of Madness and Art*, 1977, 16, 195–208. ". . . wisest decision . . .": Bell, 187.

168   Swinnerton on anonymity: Frank Swinnerton, *Background with Chorus*, 1956, 45. "It is the custom . . .": *TLS*, 12 Aug. 1909, repr. in Virginia Woolf, *Granite and Rainbow*, 1958, 167.

169   "It was only . . ." and "To feel anything . . .": *The Voyage Out*, Harcourt paperback, 9, 36. "She is completely aware . . .": Constance M. Rourke, *The New Republic*, 5 May 1920, quoted by Mitchell A. Leaska, *The Novels of Virginia Woolf from Beginning to End*, 1977, 12.

169–70   "Mr. Bennett and Mrs. Brown": Virginia Woolf, *Collected Essays*, vol. I, 1967, 319–37. "illiterate, underbred": *Diary*, vol. II, 1978, 189. Virginia Woolf on Harriet Weaver: quoted by Leonard Woolf, *Beginning Again*, 1964, 246.

170   "DEAREST,—This is my address . . .": *Clayhanger*, Penguin ed., 1954, ch. 21:i, 290.

171   "stupendous": Margaret Drabble, *Arnold Bennett*, 1974, 202. For the standard misreading see, e.g., Frank Swinnerton's Preface to the Penguin *Clayhanger*. Moments "of pure character": Drabble, 182.

172   "The Georgian novelist . . .": *Collected Essays*, vol. I, 333.

173   "to try this sentence and that . . .": ibid., 332.
      ". . . Mr. Joyce and Mr. Eliot . . .": ibid., 334.

174   "great beauty . . .": *Diary*, vol. II, 178. "a d——d good poem": ibid., 257. Pound's calendar: D. D. Paige, ed., *The Letters of Ezra Pound*, 1951, #185, undated letters from Pound to Margaret Anderson at the University of Wisconsin, Milwaukee, and *The Little Review*, Spring 1922, 2, 40.

175   "That is all . . .": *Mrs. Dalloway*, Harvest ed., 15.

176   "a queasy undergraduate . . .": *Diary*, vol. II, 189.
      "wonderful": ibid., vol. III, 9.

178   Mrs. Leavis on Dorothy Sayers: in *Scrutiny*, vol. VI, 1937–38, 338–40. "venomous . . .": James Brabazon, *Dorothy L. Sayers*, 1981, 153.
      "She had reached the park gates . . .": *Mrs. Dalloway*, 11.
      "a highly evasive kind of associational magic": Leaska, 111.

179   "the shadow play . . .": ibid., 85. Peter Conrad: private letter, 1976.
      "I see . . .": *The Waves*, repr. 1946, 6.
      "And time . . .": ibid., 131.

180   "a remote and misty isle . . .": David Daiches, *The Novel and the Modern World*, 1939, 160.
      "her mind": *To the Lighthouse*, 27–8.

181   Plate through the window: *To the Lighthouse*, 296. Square root of 1,253: ibid., 159.
      "What did it all mean . . .": *To the Lighthouse*, 159.

182   "Yet it would be hung . . .": *To the Lighthouse*, 267.
      Sales of *To the Lighthouse*: Leonard Woolf, *Downhill All the Way*, 143, 147.

10 : FRIGHTFUL TOIL

Page 183   "Honest criticism . . .": Eliot, *Selected Essays*, 7. "History can be servitude": "Little Gidding."
      ". . . a first-hand opinion of Shakespeare?": "Observations," *The Egoist*, May 1918, 69.
      "that inexhaustible nebula . . ." *Selected Essays*, 259.

184   Criticisms of *The Waste Land*: cited in Robert E. Knoll, ed., *Storm over the Waste Land*, 1964, 9–11. Squire cited in *Scrutiny*, vol. I, March 1933, 403.

185   "for a long time": Valerie Eliot, ed., *The Waste Land: A Facsimile of the Manuscripts*, 1971, xvii–xviii. Longing for time to think about it: ibid., xx. "partly on paper": ibid., xxi. For detailed evidence of the poem's chronology see my essay, "The Urban Apocalypse," in A. Walton Litz, ed., *Eliot in His Time*, 1973, 23–49, from which some of the present paragraphs are adapted.
      "With civil war just past . . .": Mark Van Doren, *The Poetry of John Dryden*, ed. 3, 1946, 9. Eliot's review, which appeared in the 9 June 1921 *TLS*, is reprinted in *Selected Essays* as "John Dryden."
      "London, the swarming life . . .": *Facsimile*, 31, 43.

186   "Unreal City . . .": ibid., 31. The final text alters one word and deletes five.
187   Seventeen more stanzas: ibid., 31–35, 43–47.
188   Johnson on verses: Boswell's *Life*, Oxford Standard Authors ed., 1953, 362. Lines supplied for Goldsmith: ibid., 355–56.
189   Were these *carbuncles?*: told me by Marshall McLuhan, who heard it from Wyndham Lewis about 1945.
190   "unprecedented heat and drought": asserted, and connected with *The Waste Land*, by Anthony Burgess, *Flame into Being*, 1985, 164. That's the same year we find Lawrence, in his pajamas, dealing with Italian snakes.
192   Pound on sonnet and canzone: Ezra Pound, *Literary Essays*, 1968, 168.

II : A KNOT OF CRITICS

Page 196   Fry on art and science: *Athenaeum*, 6 June 1919, 434–35. He's discussing two articles signed "S." in the issues of 11 April and 2 May.
Richards on art and science: *Athenaeum*, 27 June 1919, 534–35.
197   Leavis against "taste": F. R. Leavis, *Education and the University*, 1948, 38. "unappreciated, the poem isn't 'there' . . .": ibid., 68; "You cannot": ibid.
198   "cannot be inherited . . .": Eliot, "Tradition and the Individual Talent," in *Selected Essays*, 1932, 4.
199   "The Common Pursuit": Eliot, "The Function of Criticism," in *Selected Essays*, 14.
"network of tentacular roots . . .": Eliot, "Ben Jonson," in *Selected Essays*, 135. The date is 1919.
Comparison and Analysis: Eliot, "The Function of Criticism" (1923), in *Selected Essays*, 21. Sayers and Guinness: James Brabazon, *Dorothy L. Sayers*, 1981, 136.
200   "exclusion felt as a pressure . . .": F. R. Leavis, "The Literary Mind," in *Scrutiny*, vol. I, May 1932, 22.
". . . terrible nebula of emotion . . .": Eliot, "Andrew Marvell," in *Selected Essays*, 259.
201   Biographical details on Richards from Reuben A. Brower's interview: Brower, Vendler, & Hollander, eds., *I. A. Richards: Essays in His Honor*, 1973, 17–41.
Bentham's mummy: see Nigel Dennis, "A Treasury of Eccentrics," *Life*, 2 Dec. 1957. Stonehenge: I. A. Richards, "Recollections of C. K. Ogden," *Encounter*, Sept. 1957, 10–12.
202   The diagram: *Principles*, 116. John Holloway: in B. Ford, ed., *New Pelican Guide to English Literature*, vol. 7, 104. D. W. Harding: in *Scrutiny*, vol. I, 1933, 338. Harding's article (327–38) stands up well after half a century as a fair assessment of I.A.R.'s significance.
Getting data for *Practical Criticism*: described by Joan Bennett, "How It Strikes a Contemporary," in Brower, Vendler, & Hollander, 52.
203–4   "insincerity": *Practical Criticism*, 95.
204   "rhymes *must* be perfect . . .": ibid., 296. " 'Ah, this is a description . . .' ": ibid., 297.
205   ". . . most expensive kind of education . . .": ibid., 316.
206   Richards on Empson: *Furioso*, vol. I, no. 3, Spring 1940; quoted by James Jensen in *Modern Language Quarterly*, vol. 27, 1966, 245.
207   Empson on "Bare ruined choirs . . .": *Seven Types of Ambiguity*, rev. ed. 1947, 2–3.
"Whenever a receiver of poetry . . .": ibid., xv.
"the general assurance . . .": ibid., 256. "shocking amount of nonsense": ibid., xii.

207　"A Woman Homer Sung": *Collected Poems*, ed. Finneran, #92.

208　The Shakespearean "pitch" quotations are from *Richard II*, i.1; *I Henry VI*, ii.3; *II Henry VI*, ii.1; *Hamlet*, iii.1; and there are more. For "pitch that defiles," see *Much Ado*, iii.3; *Love's Labour's Lost*, iv.3; *I Henry IV*, ii.4.
"interpretive communities": Stanley Fish, *Is There a Text in This Class?*, 1980, 14–15.

209　Students "always know . . .": ibid., 347.
" 'Making up our minds . . .' ": *Practical Criticism*, 317.

210　The story about Leavis's imputing anti-Semitism was told me by Arthur Mizener; alas, I've forgotten his source. "a thwarted genius": Donald Davie, *viva voce*.
Leavis reprinted *Mass Civilization and Minority Culture* as Appendix III of *Education and the University* (1948), 141–71. Arnold: *Education*, 143. Edgar Rice Burroughs: ibid., 150. Advertising copy: ibid., 151.

211　On Wordsworth's cultivated reader: ibid., 157.
Eliot on difficulty and silliness: *The Use of Poetry and the Use of Criticism*, 1933, 150.

212　Biographical details on Leavis from John Harvey's memoir in *Encounter*, May 1979, 59–67.
Eliot the "American": Leavis, *The Living Principle*, 1975, 197.

213　"the wickedest thing . . .": Empson, *Milton's God*, 1961, 251.

12 : A DISHONEST DECADE

Page 214　He called it: in "September 1, 1939," long his best-known poem but suppressed by him in 1966.
"was well received . . ." and ". . . professor of poetry . . .": *Oxford Companion to English Literature*, ed. 5, 1985, 50.
Auden and Huxley: I've been anticipated here by Joseph Warren Beach; see *The Making of the Auden Canon*, 1957, 244–45.

214–15　"Your letter comes . . .": "The Letter" (1927), in Edward Mendelson, ed., *W. H. Auden: Collected Poems*, 1976, 39. (*Poems*, in these notes, always means this edition.) "He, the trained spy . . .": "The Secret Agent" (1928), *Poems*, 41.

215　"For now he was awake . . .": "Herman Melville" (1939), *Poems*, 200.
"Cajoling, scheming . . .": "Voltaire at Ferney" (1939), *Poems*, 199.
"The provinces . . .": "In Memory of W. B. Yeats" (1939), *Poems*, 197.
"Some beasts are dumb . . .": c. 1972, *Poems*, 665.
". . . but someone in the small hours . . .": "Nocturne" (c. 1972), *Poems*, 670.

216　"Sir, no man's enemy . . .": "XXX" in the 1930 *Poems*, later retitled "Petition," but absent from the Mendelson edition because omitted by Auden from collections after 1950.

217　". . . a rebellious wing . . .": from "The Song," *Poems*, 474.
"Seekers after happiness . . .": *Poems*, 62.
Charles Madge and Lenin: quoted by John Wain in Walford Davies, ed., *Dylan Thomas: New Critical Essays*, 1972, 2.
". . . revolution and privileged self-interest . . .": C. H. Sisson, *English Poetry: 1900–1950*, repr. 1981, 208.

218　"Faridun watched the road . . .": Basil Bunting, "From 'Faridun's Sons,' by Firdusi," *Criterion*, vol. XV, no. 60, April 1936, 421–23.

219　Arnold and Firdausi: see Park Honan, *Matthew Arnold: A Life*, 1981, 280 and note

35 on 465. Bunting learning Persian: C. F. Terrell, ed., *Basil Bunting: Man and Poet*, 1981, 50–51.

219   "... Remember, imbeciles ...": Basil Bunting, *Collected Poems*, 1978, 4. It's dated 1925.

221   "Victor": Auden, *Poems*, 138–41.
"According to his powers ...": ibid., 89.

222   "Every morning ...": Terrell, 28.
"Read *The New Yorker* ...": "Under Which Lyre," *Poems*, 259–63. This was a Phi Beta Kappa poem, read at Harvard.
"Isherwood noted ...": Joseph Warren Beach, *The Making of the Auden Canon*, 1957, 253.

224–5   Rossetti in the station: Robert Murray Davis, *Evelyn Waugh: Writer*, 1981, 8, shows us how Waugh retouched this careful account for inclusion in his *Rossetti* two years later. I've imported the "buns" from the revised version.

225   "He was a man of middle age ...": Waugh, *When the Going Was Good*, Penguin ed., 13. The paragraph dates from 1929.

229   Lord Dawson and George V: see, e.g., *Time*, 8 December 1986, 55.

13 : BARDS AND BARD-WATCHERS

Page 231   Cardboard coffins: Malcolm Muggeridge, *The Infernal Grove*, 1974, 74.

232   "Now as I was young and easy ...": "Fern Hill," in Dylan Thomas, *Selected Writings*, 1946, 79.

233   His own list: cited by John Fuller in Walford Davies, ed., *Dylan Thomas: New Critical Essays*, 1972, 206.

234   Roget's *Thesaurus*: See David Holbrook's account of the work-sheets of "Poem on His Birthday," in Davies, 182–89.

236   "a sack of meal ..." and "the beast most innocent ...": Poem XX in *The North Ship*.
"This empty street ...": "Triple Time," in *The Less Deceived*, 35.

238   Davie on Larkin: Donald Davie, *Thomas Hardy and British Poetry*, 1972, 64–65.
"The two young men ...": Ford Madox Ford, first page of *Some Do Not* (1924), later the opening of the *Parade's End* tetralogy.

239   "... First slum ...": "Going, Going," in *High Windows*, 1974, 22. "Man hands on misery ...": "This Be the Verse," ibid., 30.
"Books are a load of crap": "A Study of Reading Habits," in *The Whitsun Weddings*, 31.
"Who's ... Borges?": *Paris Review* interview, 1982, in Larkin, *Required Writing*, 1984, 60. (The book's indexer has omitted this embarrassment.) Parkman: ibid., 140. Reading: ibid., 70.

240   "... in good health ...": ibid., 66. Foreign languages: ibid., 69. Three P's: ibid., 72, 292–93.
"It seems to me undeniable ...": ibid., 72. Joyce: ibid., 297.

241   "... [the loaf] was one day old ...": Wyndham Lewis, "Time the Tiger," in *Rotting Hill*, repr. 1986, 162. The story is set in 1949.

242   "So we cracked into him ...": Anthony Burgess, *A Clockwork Orange*, second paragraph of ch. 2. "Litso" means "face."

244   The Corinthians' letter to Saint Paul: Ronald A. Knox, *Enthusiasm*, 1950, ch. ii.

246   Larkin on writing poems: *Required Writing*, 83, 71.
"that suffocation ...": Tomlinson, *Some Americans*, 1981, 18–19.

246   "Warm flute": Tomlinson, *Collected Poems*, 1985, 3.
       "If I had possessed . . .": *Some Americans*, 10.

246–7 First encounter with Pound: ibid., 1–2. "For three years . . .": "Hugh Selwyn
       Mauberley," in Pound, *Personae*, 187. ". . . is almost afraid that I . . .": "The Garden,"
       ibid., 83. ". . . light against heavy beat": *Some Americans*, 3–4.

248   "It happens . . .": Larkin, *Required Writing*, 71.
       "The Atlantic": *Collected Poems*, 17.

249   "Farewell to Van Gogh": ibid., 36.

250   "The Picture of J.T.": ibid., 74.

252   "Walking to Bells": ibid., 69.

253   "Flat-dwellers": ibid., 244.

254   ". . . In the dark . . .": from "Weatherman," ibid., 168.

255   Craig Raine: based on his own account, in *The Guardian* (Weekend Arts), 5 Oct.
       1985.
       Andrew Motion: based on "Poetry in Motion," in *The Guardian* (Weekend People),
       20 Oct. 1984, where a photo by Alan Titmuss does make him look shrewdly sensitive.

256   Pitt-Kethley interview: *Observer*, 13 Apr. 1986. The excerpt is from "Sky Ray
       Lolly," in her collection of the same name, Chatto & Windus, 1986.
       Deputy literary editor: Blake Morrison, b. 1950, sometime Poetry Editor of the
       TLS; poems published by Faber and by Chatto & Windus. The anthology he and
       Motion co-edited was the *Penguin Book of Contemporary British Poetry* (1982).

257   Bunting anecdotage: *viva voce* at various times. For the "DEATH TO MR. BUNTING"
       story, see Carroll F. Terrell, ed., *Basil Bunting: Man and Poet*, 1981, 60.
       "Man's life so little worth . . .": Bunting, *Collected Poems*, 1978, 25. "One of Ezra's
       more savage disciples" and ". . . mainly in the sound": *Scripsi* (Melbourne), vol. I,
       no. 3/4, 1982, 27, 28.

257–8 Music indispensable: Bunting to H.K., National Public Radio interview, 1980.
       The Yeats is #287 in Finneran's edition. Frost on "sound of sense": quoted by
       Donald Davie, *TLS*, 23 Nov. 1979.

258   "A strong song tows . . .": Bunting, Coda to *Briggflatts*, in *Collected Poems*, 59.
       Bunting on journalists' experience of life: he said it to Jonathan Williams; quoted
       in Terrell, 60.

259   "in the most melodious tenor . . .": Terrell, 33.

260   "Loaded with mail . . .": *Collected Poems*, 46.
       ". . . Schoenberg's maze": ibid., 47. "Where rats go . . .": ibid., 55.
       "As the player's breath . . .": ibid., 54.

261   "Great strings . . .": ibid., 58.

262   "I've rubbed down gravestones . . .": Terrell, 198. "A reply to Greek and Latin
       . . .": *Paterson*, epigraphs.
       "Aneurin and Taliesin": *Collected Poems*, 53.

INDEX